THE REVELS PLAYS
General Editor: Clifford Leech

THE SCOTTISH HISTORY OF
JAMES THE FOURTH

Mantegna: *Family and Court of Marchese Lodovico Gonzaga*, showing a dwarf attending on a court lady (*Mantua, Palazzo Ducale*)

The Scottish History of
James the Fourth

ROBERT GREENE

EDITED BY
NORMAN SANDERS

THE REVELS PLAYS

METHUEN & CO LTD
11 NEW FETTER LANE · LONDON EC4

This edition first published 1970

Introduction, Apparatus Criticus, etc.
© 1970 Norman Sanders
Printed in Great Britain by
The Broadwater Press Ltd, Welwyn Garden City, Herts.
Distributed in the U.S.A. by Barnes & Noble Inc.
SBN 416 15230 9

For
MARJORIE

General Editor's Preface

The Revels Plays began to appear in 1958, and in the General Editor's Preface included in the first few volumes the plan of the series was briefly sketched. All those concerned in the undertaking recognized that no rigid pattern could be proposed in advance: to some extent the collective experience of the editors would affect the series as it developed, and the textual situation was by no means uniform among the plays that we hoped to include. The need for flexibility is still recognized, and each editor indicates in his introduction the procedures that have seemed best in relation to his particular play.

Nevertheless, we were fairly convinced that in some matters our policy would remain constant, and no major change in any of these respects has been made. The introduction to each volume includes a discussion of the provenance of the text, the play's stage-history and reputation its significance as a contribution to dramatic literature, and its place within the work of its author. The text is based on a fresh examination of the early editions. Modern spelling is used, archaic forms being preserved only when rhyme or metre demands them or when a modernized form would not give the required sense or would obscure a play upon words. The procedure adopted in punctuation varies to some extent according to the degree of authority which an editor can attribute to the punctuation of the copy-text, but in every instance it is intended that the punctuation used in a Revels volume should not obscure a dramatic or rhetorical suggestiveness which may be discerned in the copy. Editorial stage-directions are enclosed in square brackets. The collation aims at making clear the grounds for an editor's choice wherever the original or a frequently accepted modern reading has been departed from. Annotations attempt to explain difficult passages and to provide such comments and illustrations of usage as the editor considers desirable.

When the series was planned, it was intended that each volume should include a glossary. At an early stage, however, it was realized that this would mean either an arbitrary distribution of material between the glossary and the annotations or a duplication of material. It has therefore become our practice to dispense with a glossary but to include an index to the annotations, which avoids duplication and facilitates reference.

Act-divisions are employed if they appear in the copy-text or if the structure of the play clearly points to a five-act division. In other instances, only scene-numbers are inserted. All act- and scene-indications which do not derive from the copy-text are given unobtrusively in square brackets. In no instance is an editorial indication of locality introduced into a scene-heading. When an editor finds it necessary to comment on the location of a scene, this is done in the annotations.

The series continues to use the innovation in line-numbering that was introduced in the first volume. Stage-directions which occur on lines separate from the text are given the number of the immediately preceding line followed by a decimal point and 1, 2, 3, etc. Thus 163.5 indicates the fifth line of a stage-direction following line 163 of the scene. At the beginning of a scene the lines of a stage-direction are numbered 0.1, 0.2, etc.

The present volume continues the recently established procedure in the handling of '-ed' verbal terminations. Previously we used '-ed' in past tenses and past participles when the termination was probably syllabic, and '-'d' elsewhere. Now we use '-ed' for non-syllabic terminations and '-èd' for syllabic. This seems in line with our attempt to give the reader an edition with modernized spelling while at the same time indicating the metrical pattern. It follows that in such a form as 'studied' we now imply a probably dissyllabic pronunciation, and have dropped the form 'study'd'. Moreover, in verbs and adjectives ending in '-e', the second person singular and the superlative are given as '-est', whether or not the termination appears to be syllabic. In prose passages only '-ed' and '-est' are used.

GENERAL EDITOR'S PREFACE

The Revels Plays have begun with the re-editing of a number of the best-known tragedies and comedies of the later Elizabethan and Jacobean years, and there are many such plays to which the techniques of modern editing need to be applied. It is hoped, however, that the series will be able to include certain lesser-known plays which remain in general neglect despite the lively interest that an acquaintance with them can arouse.

It has always been in the forefront of attention that the plays included should be such as deserve and indeed demand performance. The editors have therefore given a record (necessarily incomplete) of modern productions; in the annotations there is, moreover, occasional conjecture on the way in which a scene or a piece of stage-business was done on the original stage. Perhaps, too, the absence of indications of locality and of editorial scene-headings will suggest the advantage of achieving in a modern theatre some approach to the characteristic fluidity of scene and the neutrality of acting-space that Shakespeare's fellows knew.

CLIFFORD LEECH

Toronto, 1969

Contents

GENERAL EDITOR'S PREFACE	*page* vii
PREFACE	xiii
ABBREVIATIONS	xv
INTRODUCTION	xix
1. Robert Greene and his Connection with the Stage	xix
2. Date	xxv
3. Sources	xxix
4. The Play	xxxvi
5. The Text	lv
The Quarto of 1598	lv
Modern Editions	lx
This Edition	lxi
THE SCOTTISH HISTORY OF JAMES THE FOURTH	1
APPENDIX	
G. B. Giraldi Cinthio's *Hecatommithi*, Decade III, Novel I	133
INDEX TO ANNOTATIONS	143

Illustrations

Frontispiece: Mantegna: *Family and Court of Marchese Lodovico Gonzaga*

Page 2:   The title page of the *1598 Quarto*

ACKNOWLEDGEMENTS

I would like to express my thanks to Phaidon Press Ltd for permission to reproduce Mantegna's painting of the *Family and Court of Marchese Lodovico Gonzaga* from their book entitled *Paintings and Drawings of Mantegna* by E. Tietze-Conrat, and to the Trustees of the British Museum for permission to reproduce the title page of their edition, C.34.g.20, of *James the Fourth* by Greene.

Preface

It is a pleasant duty to acknowledge the help and support of various kinds I have received in connection with the preparation of this edition. To Allardyce Nicoll I record a gratitude for all it is possible for a student to owe a teacher and a friend. For general help in the study of Greene's works over a number of years I have benefited from the conversation and knowledge of I. A. Shapiro, J. Parr, J. R. Brown, B. A. Harris, A. J. Lavin, S. W. Wells, and the late C. J. Sisson. Many of my present colleagues gave assistance in solving specific problems, among whom I should like to mention E. W. Stockton, T. W. Wheeler, J. Gill, J. Hansen, N. Isaacs, A. Rapp, R. Marius, and R. Duncan. Miss E. Goehring and J. Dobson and the Library staff of the University of Tennessee gave their time and knowledge quite unselfishly; and I am grateful to K. L. Knickerbocker for arranging for me to be relieved of some of my academic duties for the purpose of working on this edition. J. G. McManaway, the Folger Library's bibliographer, answered all my queries concerning the copy-text with the expertise and helpfulness that have long been associated with him. The University of Virginia kindly allowed me to consult the work done on the play by G. W. Williams, who personally gave me much additional help. The General Editor of this series has extended to me assistance, advice, and patience far in excess of any demanded by his official rôle, and has used his wide scholarship to save me from many errors. Finally, the dedication inadequately acknowledges a gratitude for practical assistance at every stage of the work, and for the creation of an atmosphere in which it is pleasant to work—and to live.

NORMAN SANDERS

Knoxville, Tennessee
1968

Abbreviations

	EDITIONS OF *JAMES THE FOURTH*
Q	1598 quarto.
Q (BM)	British Museum copy (c.34.g.20).
Q (FO)	Folger Library copy (12308).
Q (HN)	Huntington Library copy (61133).
Q (VA)	Victoria and Albert Museum copy (4247.18.k.17).
Collins	J. C. Collins, ed., *Plays and Poems of Robert Greene* (1905), II.
Dickinson	T. H. Dickinson, ed., *Robert Greene* (Mermaid Series, 1909).
Dyce[1]	Alexander Dyce, ed., *The Dramatic Works of Robert Greene* (1831), II.
Dyce	Alexander Dyce, ed., *The Dramatic and Poetic Works of Robert Greene and George Peele* (1861).
Grosart	A. B. Grosart, ed., *Life and Complete Works of Robert Greene* (1881–6), XIII.
Lavin	J. A. Lavin, ed., *James the Fourth* (The New Mermaids, 1967).
Manly	J. M. Manly, ed., *Specimens of Pre-Shakespearean Drama* (Boston, 1897), II.
Thorndike	A. H. Thorndike, ed., *Minor Elizabethan Drama* (Everyman's Library, 1910), II.

Names not listed above which appear in the collations are acknowledgements made by Dyce, in his 1861 edition, for suggestions and emendations adopted from earlier notes and articles in various periodicals.

WORKS OF REFERENCE, ETC.

Abbott	E. A. Abbott, *A Shakespearian Grammar* (1869).
Arber	E. Arber, *A Transcript of the Registers of the Company of Stationers of London*, 5 vols. (1875–94).
Fitzherbert	John Fitzherbert, *Book of Husbandry* (1534), ed. W. W. Skeat (English Dialect Society, XXXVII, 1882).
Libr.	*The Library*.
Lyly	John Lyly, *Works*, ed. R. W. Bond, 3 vols. (1902).
M.L.N.	*Modern Language Notes*.
M.L.R.	*Modern Language Review*.
M.P.	*Modern Philology*.
M.S.R.	Malone Society Reprints.
N. & Q.	*Notes and Queries*.
Nashe	*The Works of Thomas Nashe*, ed. R. B. McKerrow, 5 vols. (1904–10); revised by F. P. Wilson (1958).
O.E.D.	*A New English Dictionary*, ed. J. A. Murray, H. Bradley, W. A. Craigie, and C. T. Onions, 13 vols. (1888–1933).
P.M.L.A.	*Publications of the Modern Language Association*.
P.Q.	*Philological Quarterly*
Scot.	Scottish word or Scotticism.
S.E.L.	*Studies in English Literature* (Texas).
S.P.	*Studies in Philology*.
sp. h.	speech heading.
Tilley	M. P. Tilley, *A Dictionary of Proverbs in England in the Sixteenth and Seventeenth Centuries* (Michigan, 1950).
T.L.S.	*Times Literary Supplement*.

For quotations and references the following editions have been used: for Shakespeare, P. Alexander's one-volume 'Tudor' edition (1951); for Greene's prose works, A. B. Grosart's fifteen-volume edition of the complete works (1881–6); for Greene's other plays, J. C. Collins's two-volume edition of the plays and poems (1905); for Greek and Latin authors, the Loeb editions. The titles of Shakespeare's plays are abbreviated in accordance with the practice of C. T. Onions in his *Shakespeare Glossary* (1911; rev. 1946).

Introduction

1. ROBERT GREENE AND HIS CONNECTION WITH THE STAGE

Robert Greene was one of the talented young men usually known as the 'University Wits' who some time in the mid-1580s made their separate ways from one of the two universities to London and there, during short lives, made a living from their pens.[1] The four or five plays known for certain to have been written by him constitute but a small part of his literary output, for he was also the author of some thirty-six very popular prose works in a variety of genres: euphuistic novels, arcadian romances, semi-autobiographical adventures, framework tales, literary repentance pieces, and fictionalized reportage of London's criminal underworld. His name has also been associated with many anonymous plays of the period and his hand detected in plays attributed to other playwrights,[2] most notably Shakespeare's Henry VI plays.

From the allusion to Greene in Thomas Lodge's *Euphues' Shadow* as 'Norfolciensis', which supports his own claim in *The Repentance of Robert Greene*, the playwright would seem to have originated in Norwich; and the baptismal entry for 11 June 1558 in the register of St George's, Tombland, referring to the second child of a saddler, Robert Greene, and his wife Jane, is generally accepted as recording his birth. He probably attended the Free Grammar School in Norwich from where he may have gone up to Corpus Christi, Cambridge, as a sizar in the Easter Term of 1573, and

---

[1] The fullest treatments of Greene's life are by Collins, I, 1–69, and by R. Pruvost in *Robert Greene et ses Romans* (Paris, 1938).

[2] e.g., *The Contention of York and Lancaster, Edward III, Fair Em, George a Greene, The Troublesome Reign of King John, A Knack to Know a Knave, The Thracian Wonder, King Leir, Locrine, Mucedorus, The Taming of a Shrew, Thomas Lord Cromwell.*

moved to St John's College in the Michaelmas Term of 1575.¹ It was as a member of the latter college that he received his B.A. on 22 January 1580; and between this date and 1583, when he received his M.A. at Clare College, he began to write his first euphuistic pamphlet, *Mamilia*, with an eye to the London market.²

The bare outline of Greene's subsequent literary career in London furnished by the publication dates of his numerous works can be filled out by reference to a group of semi-autobiographical pamphlets, *Greene's Mourning Garment* (1590), Part II of *Francesco's Fortunes* (1590), *Greene's Vision* (1592), and *Greene's Groatsworth of Wit* (1592), and to the avowedly autobiographical *Repentance of Robert Greene* (1592). From these works we gather that Greene travelled in Italy and Spain, perhaps immediately following the receipt of his initial degree; and that in 1585 he married a gentleman's daughter in his home town, whose name may have been Dorothea³ and by whom he had a child. His life in London, after deserting his family in 1586, was apparently spent in a bohemian and dissipated existence sustained by the money he earned by writing for the press, and after 1587–8 for the stage as well.

In *Greene's Groatsworth of Wit*⁴ there is a passage describing how the hero Roberto, whose life according to Greene agrees in most part with his own, at a low point in his fortunes is persuaded by a chance acquaintance to become a playwright:

> What is your profession, said *Roberto* ? Truly sir, saide hee, I am a player. A player, quoth *Roberto*, I tooke you rather for a Gentleman of great liuing, for if by outward habit men should be censured, I tell you, you would bee taken for a substantiall man. So am I where I dwell (quoth the player) reputed able at my proper cost to build a Windmill... why, I am as famous for Delphrigus,

[1] For possible interpretations of the Cambridge records, see K. Mildenberger, 'Robert Greene at Cambridge', *M.L.N.*, LXVI (1951), 546–9, and J. Parr, 'Robert Greene and his Classmates at Cambridge', *P.M.L.A.*, LXXVII (1962), 54.

[2] Part I of *Mamilia* was entered in the Stationers' Register on 3 October 1580, and Part II, entered on 6 September 1583, is signed 'from my Studie in Clare Hall the vij of Iulie'.

[3] In Gabriel Harvey's account of the letter which the dying Greene sent to his wife, she is addressed as 'Dol' (*Four Letters*, ed. G. B. Harrison (1923), p. 22).

[4] Grosart, XII, 131–2.

and the king of Fairies, as euer was any of my time. The twelue
labors of Hercules haue I terribly thundred on the Stage, and plaid
three Scenes of the Deuill in the High way to heauen. Haue ye so
(said *Roberto*?) . . . but how meane you to vse mee? Why sir, in
making Playes, said the other, for which you shall be well paid, if
you will take the paines.

Whether or not this is an accurate description of Greene's own
introduction to the profession of playwright is open to doubt,
though the fact that he tells almost the same story in *Francesco's
Fortunes* probably indicates that his entry into the theatre world
was a chance affair similar to this. The hero of the latter pamphlet
'getting him home to his chamber writ a Comedie, which so generally pleased all the audience, that happie were those Actors in short
time that could get any of his workes, he grewe so exquisite in that
facultie'.[1] It was apparently otherwise with Greene's own initial
dramatic efforts. For, strongly under the spell of the outstanding
success of Marlowe's *Tamburlaine* (1587-8), Greene penned a
feeble imitation of that play in *Alphonsus, King of Aragon* (?1588),
and was for his pains pilloried on the public stage. As he complains
himself of the incident,[2]

> I keepe my old course, to palter vp some thing in Prose, vsing mine
> old poesie still, *Omne tulit punctum*, although latelye two Gentle-
> men Poets, made two mad men of Rome beate it out of their paper
> bucklers; and had it in derision, for that I could not make my verses
> iet vpon the stage in tragicall buskins, euerie worde filling the
> mouth like the faburden of Bo-Bell, daring God out of heauen with
> that Atheist *Tamburlan*.

The jibe here at Marlowe was to be the start of a series of similar
attacks in *Menaphon* (1589), *Francesco's Fortunes*, *Farewell to Folly*
(1591), *Greene's Vision*, and finally in *Greene's Groatsworth of Wit*.
This animosity towards Marlowe, however it was occasioned, was
to prove ultimately beneficial to Greene as a dramatist. For, where
he had initially imitated, he now turned to burlesque and parody of
the Marlovian vein; and this release from so influential a model
enabled him to compose plays from those materials which were far
more congenial to his proper talents.

---

[1] Grosart, VIII, 128-9.   [2] Preface to *Perymedes* (1588), VII, 7-8.

Within the next two or three years Greene completed at least his four known extant plays and probably had a hand in others which now either are lost or cannot be positively identified as his.[1] Although their order of writing is disputable, those plays we know to be by him must have been composed in rapid succession at the same time as his repentance and coney-catching pamphlets and the sundry other pieces he was producing during the last two or three years of his life. This is easily believed because Greene's great verbal facility is one of the aspects of his character most stressed by his contemporaries. His friend, Thomas Nashe, for example, refers to it often, and claimed that 'in a night & a day would he haue yarkt vp a Pamphlet as well as in seauen yeare, and glad was that Printer that might bee so blest to pay him deare for the very dregs of his wit'.[2]

Whether it was *Friar Bacon and Friar Bungay* or *Orlando Furioso* that followed close on *Alphonsus* is not known for certain; but either play's marked superiority in dramatic technique and in the quality of the writing supports the claim of one critic[3] that Greene's early mastering of the elements of his craft and the sudden emergence of a distinctive kind of comedy in *Friar Bacon and Friar Bungay* 'resembles those sudden changes in the biological world that have received the name of mutation rather than evolution'.

There is a good deal of evidence to suggest that, during the late 1580s and early 1590s, Greene was indeed considered to be the 'famozed Arch-plaimaking poet' he claimed he was.[4] From his own testimony and that of contemporaries like Nashe, Gabriel Harvey, and Henry Chettle[5] there emerges the picture of Greene as the raffish littérateur, notorious alike for his public breastbeating, his long hair and 'jolly long red peake, like the spire of a steeple', his unsavoury connections with the cut-purse Cutting Ball and his

---

[1] The Greene canon comprises *Alphonsus, Orlando Furioso, Friar Bacon, James the Fourth,* and *A Looking Glass for London and England* (with Thomas Lodge). The two anonymous plays most frequently thought to have been written by him are *Selimus* and *George a Greene.*
[2] Nashe, *Strange News*, I, 287.
[3] T. M. Parrott, *Shakespearean Comedy* (New York, 1949), p. 88.
[4] *Greene's Groatsworth of Wit*, XII, 134.
[5] Nashe in his *Anatomy of Absurdity* and *Strange News*, Harvey in his *Four Letters*, and Chettle in his *Kind-Hart's Dream*.

sister, his drunkenness, blasphemies, libels, whoring, and his ready tongue and pen. Apparently a familiar figure on the London scene, Greene was as likely to be found lavishly emptying his purse in a literary alehouse as frequenting the brothels of Southwark, while writing plays for the acting companies whose theatres were located in the same district. *Friar Bacon and Friar Bungay* was acted by the Queen's Men, Lord Strange's Men, and Lord Sussex's Men, and was Philip Henslowe's property; *Orlando Furioso*, with its fine part for the celebrated actor Edward Alleyn, Greene sold to the Queen's Men first and later a second time to the Admiral's Men while the royal company 'were in the country'[1]; *A Looking Glass for London and England* (written in collaboration with Thomas Lodge) was played by the Queen's Men and revived by Strange's Men; and *James the Fourth* may have been written to be played at court.[2]

Owing principally to his literary quarrel with the Harvey brothers, which Greene initiated in 1592 with the publication of *A Quip for an Upstart Courtier*, there can be pieced together a detailed knowledge of Greene's final days. According to Gabriel Harvey's *Four Letters and Certain Sonnets, especially touching Robert Greene* (1592) and Thomas Nashe's *Strange News of the Intercepting of Certain Letters* (1592), some time in August 1592 it would appear that, while dining with Nashe, Will Moxon, and others, Greene over-indulged in Rhenish wine and pickled herrings, which excess brought on the serious illness from which he died on 2 or 3 September. In his sordid lodgings in the Dowgate home of a shoemaker, one Isham, Greene spent the last days of his life, plagued by his intermittently felt but very strong puritanical conscience, moved to write a letter to his wife repenting his ill-treatment of her and begging her to pay his debts, and sustained by his self-pitying anger at what he considered to be the ingratitude of the acting profession.

Also occupying Greene's time during these August days was the composition of two prose works, *Greene's Groatsworth of Wit* and his *Repentance*, both of which were published after his death by Henry Chettle. It is these, together with Harvey's attack on Greene

[1] *The Defence of Coney-Catching*, XI, 75–6.
[2] See p. xxix below.

in the *Four Letters* and Nashe's defence of his friend in *Strange News*, which make the playwright's death, along with Marlowe's, the best documented of the whole period. It was also by means of one passage in the first of these works that Greene was to ensure for himself a notoriety which has lasted far longer than that based on his numerous petty vices which so impressed his contemporaries. In an epistle addressed to 'those Gentlemen his Quondam acquaintance, that spend their wits in making Plaies' Greene exhorts them not to trust the players:

> for there is an vpstart Crow, beautified with our feathers, that with his *Tygers hart wrapt in a Players hyde*, supposes he is as well able to bombast out a blanke verse as the best of you: and beeing an absolute *Iohannes factotum*, is in his owne conceit the onely Shakes-scene in the countrey.[1]

It is generally agreed that the reference here is to Shakespeare and that the italicized words are a parody of the Duke of York's line to Queen Margaret in *3 Henry VI*: 'O tiger's heart wrapp'd in a woman's hide' (I. iv. 137); but exactly what set of circumstances lay behind the attack is still a matter for debate. It has been suggested variously[2] that Greene is levelling a general accusation against the acting profession as a whole by singling out one of their number who has already begun to emerge as a playwright to challenge the supremacy of the university-trained writers; or that he is accusing Shakespeare of plagiarizing his work in the Henry VI plays; or that Greene had collaborated in the writing of these plays with Shakespeare whose greater talents had dominated the partnership; or that the Henry VI plays represent a Shakespearian rewriting or pulling together of works originally produced by Greene and others.

Unless fresh evidence is forthcoming, the meaning of the allusion will never be clear, for while on the one hand Henry Chettle in *Kind-Hart's Dream* (1592) makes a special point of defending

---

[1] *Greene's Groatsworth of Wit*, XII, 144.

[2] For the many theories concerning the authorship of the Henry VI plays and the interpretations placed on Greene's attack in *Greene's Groatsworth of Wit* see the most recent discussion in the introductions to A. S. Cairncross's editions of the plays in the (new) Arden Shakespeare, published in 1957 (Pt 2), 1962 (Pt 1), 1964 (Pt 3).

INTRODUCTION

Shakespeare against Greene's attack in *Greene's Groatsworth of Wit*, one 'R.B.' in *Greene's Funerals* (1594) is equally certain that 'men that so Eclipst his fame: / Purloynde his Plumes'.[1] But no one who knows Greene's works well can avoid the suspicion that his literary presence lurks somewhere in the background of certain scenes and speeches in the Shakespeare trilogy. Further, it may be said that, while the distance between Shakespeare's and Greene's achievements could hardly be greater, there are tantalizing similarities between their comedies which suggest a definite kinship in their art.

For, if Polonius' castigation of that vile word 'beautified' perhaps indicates that Greene's attack still mildly rankled as late as 1601, then Shakespeare's transformation in 1614 of Greene's best romance, *Pandosto*, into *The Winter's Tale* may be seen as a testimony of possible forgiveness, and does imply a degree of admiration for a writer who first used so many of the situations, character types, and dramatic structures which were to be the groundwork of Shakespeare's comic art.

2. DATE

Despite the claim on the title-page of the 1598 Quarto that *James the Fourth* 'hath bene sundrie times publikely plaide', there is no contemporary record concerning the play's performance, or, indeed, of its existence prior to the Stationers' Register entry of 14 May 1594.[2] Efforts to date the play's composition more accurately than simply '1588–92' have produced a little factual evidence and a good deal of speculation based on literary judgments.

F. G. Fleay[3] was the first to suggest that the Latin title-page 'poesie' or motto *Omne tulit punctum* can help in dating the play. We know that Greene chose his own mottos,[4] and further that this Horatian tag had become associated with him in the public's mind.[5]

---

[1] See E. K. Chambers, *William Shakespeare* (1930), II, 188–90.
[2] See p. lv below.
[3] *A Biographical Chronicle of the English Drama, 1559–1642* (1891), I, 250–66.
[4] Greene refers to the motto himself in *Perymedes*, VII, 7; and makes a point of his having changed it in *Greene's Vision*, XII, to 'sero sed serio'.
[5] It is associated with Greene by Thomas Nashe in his *Anatomy of*

Fleay was wrong, however, in limiting Greene's use of the tag to between August 1589 and October 1590, for eight of Greene's prose works carried it between 1584 and 1590.[1] This means that no great weight as a factor for limiting the period of composition can be placed on the motto's presence, for which, in any case, Creede the printer may have been responsible in 1598 after Greene's death. If Greene did prepare the title-page himself, however, then the play was written before November 1590, when *Greene's Mourning Garment*, which first bears his newly adopted motto 'sero sed serio', was entered in the Stationers' Register.[2]

A number of scholars have attempted to support Fleay's 1590 date by connecting some lines in the play with particular contemporary events. For example, C. M. Gayley[3] has taken Dorothea's reference to the difficulty of survival in the Irish Wars (III. iii. 121) to be a reflection of the news of the uprising in Fermanagh in 1590, coming as it did after a period of comparative quiet which had lasted since the suppression of Desmond's revolt in 1583.[4] He points also to Dorothea's lines when confronting Jaques in IV. iv. 48–9:

> Shall never Frenchman say an English maid
> Of threats of foreign force will be afraid,

and suggests that they may well have been intended as a compliment to the still-maiden Elizabeth, who had been aiding the Huguenot cause with money and troops in France ever since Henri IV's request for aid in September 1589.[5] While it is true that Greene's patriotic emotions may have been stimulated by such

---

Absurdity, I, 10; by Gabriel Harvey in his *Four Letters*, ed. G. B. Harrison (1923), p. 40; and in *The Return from Parnassus*, ed. J. B. Leishman (1949), ll. 209–10.

[1] *Arbasto* (1584), *Penelope's Web* (1587), *Pandosto* (1588), *Ciceronis Amor* (1589), *Menaphon* (1590), *Never Too Late* (1590), *Opharion* (entered 1590).

[2] *Francesco's Fortunes* (1590), which also bears the motto 'sero sed serio', may have been written before the *Mourning Garment* but it was not entered in the Stationers' Register.

[3] *Representative English Comedies: From the Beginnings to Shakespeare* (1903), I, 415–17.

[4] See J. B. Black, *The Reign of Elizabeth* (2nd ed., 1959), pp. 473–83.

[5] See J. F. Neale, *Queen Elizabeth* (1934), ch. 19.

events as these, the Irish wars and English defiance of the French were topics to which allusions might well be expected at almost any point during Elizabeth's reign, even as Greene in this play could allude to the Spanish Armada at IV. iii. 65-8 some time after the event.

Ruth Hudson's[1] evidence that there are allusions in the play to contemporary events in the Scotland of James VI (discussed in the section on the sources below, pp. xxxiv-xxxv) can certainly be questioned in some of its details; but there can be no doubt, from Bohan's claim in the Induction (ll. 106-9) that the King of Scots' susceptibility to flattery and the influence of parasites make his court similar to that of James VI, that Greene had in mind some dramatic commentary on real happenings in Scotland. Further, it is clear that much of the talk and rumours about Scotland circulating in London during the summer and autumn of 1590 do have some relevance to aspects of the play.

The various strands of literary evidence brought forward to help date the play are slight and subjective in themselves, but do tend to support a late-1590 dating. Gayley notes that the archaic prefix 'alder-' ('aldertruest' at V. vi. 192) occurs only once elsewhere in Greene's works, namely in *Greene's Mourning Garment* (1590) where a shepherd is described as 'The Alderleefest Swain of all'[2]; and that the episode in the same pamphlet where Philador comforts the passionate young man is very similar to the exchange between Nano and Dorothea in II. ii. 104-5.[3] The moral atmosphere of the play is also seen to be similar in its pietism to that of the pamphlets Greene was writing during his repentance period, which began in 1590; and the scenes of roguery in the play do have a general resemblance to and some underworld vocabulary in common with his series of coney-catching pamphlets which the publication of *A Notable Discovery of Cosenage* incepted in 1591.

Gayley also places great emphasis on a complicated argument based on the resemblance between Ida's lines at I. i. 120-1:

> And weel I wot, I heard a shepherd sing
> That, like a bee, Love hath a little sting:

[1] See p. xxxiv, note 1 below.   [2] Grosart, IX, 143.
[3] Grosart, IX, 196-9.

and a passage in George Peele's *The Hunting of Cupid*, the date of which is highly conjectural:

> What thing is love? for (well I wot) love is a thing
> It is a prickle, it is a sting,
> It is a prettie, prettie thing.

Gayley claims that Greene was the debtor here and, dating Peele's play early in 1590, suggests that *James the Fourth* was written midway in the same year. Resemblances of this kind, however, cannot be given much weight, as any influence they point to can work either way; and both the sentiment and the rhyme are so common in the lyric poetry of the period and in Greene's other works that little can be proved by them.[1]

Another type of literary argument which has a bearing on the date of the play's composition is its relationship to the other plays in the Greene canon. There is almost unanimous agreement among scholars that *James the Fourth* was the last play Greene wrote. The qualities supporting this impression are: the wider imaginative scope displayed in the author's handling of his customary materials; the greater flexibility of the blank verse; the functional variety in the deployment of prose, blank verse, and rhymed couplets; and the noticeable absence of the dense and merely decorative allusions to classical myth and history, which are so typical of *Alphonsus King of Aragon*, *Orlando Furioso*, and *Friar Bacon and Friar Bungay*. Most readers of the plays would probably agree with these observations, but it is always dangerous to assume that the less good writing of any author must perforce have been written before the better. However, there is one stylistic argument concerning the order of Greene's plays which is more convincing than any of those already mentioned. U. M. Ellis-Fermor[2] has sensitively traced the way in which, after initially writing under the strong influence of Marlowe's successful dramas, Greene gradually worked this alien presence out of his plays, beginning with slavish imitation, passing through animosity and satire, until

---

[1] See Dickinson's discussion of the argument in his edition, pp. xlvii–xlix.
[2] U. M. Ellis-Fermor, 'Marlowe and Greene: A Note on their Relations as Dramatic Artists', *Studies in Honor of T. W. Baldwin*, ed. D. C. Allen (Urbana, 1958), pp. 136–49.

INTRODUCTION   xxix

finally in *James the Fourth* Greene's 'genius had by then prevailed over an influence that, noble in itself, might yet have proved fatal to it'.[1] *Friar Bacon and Friar Bungay* can be dated 1589–90,[2] which would again place *James the Fourth* in 1590 at the earliest.

In conclusion, we may say that while no clear documentary proof exists to date the play with any certainty, most of the pointers tend to support a date in the summer or autumn of 1590. It is not possible to connect the play with any particular company, as Greene's plays were performed at various times by the Queen's Men, Lord Sussex's Men, the Admiral's Men, and Lord Strange's Men. But if there is anything to be said for the suggestion that the Quarto's stage direction on K1^v (v. vi. 57.1), '*Enter* Adam, *and Antiques*', may indicate that John Adams was the actor intended to play the part of Oberon,[3] then Greene had in mind the Queen's Men when writing the play. If this was the company which bought the play, then it may well have been one of those performed at Court by them on 26 December 1590 or at one of their five performances at court during 1591.[4]

3. SOURCES

Greene's source for the plot of *James the Fourth* was discovered in G. B. Giraldi Cinthio's *Hecatommithi* by P. A. Daniel[5] and W. Creizenach,[6] apparently independently. Cinthio's book comprises one hundred stories told by ten ladies and gentlemen sailing to Marseilles after the sack of Rome in 1527. The story Greene used is that told by one of the men, Quinto, as the first novel of the third decade. No sixteenth-century English translation of Cinthio's work has survived, although the book was known in England,[7] and

---

[1] *Ibid.*, p. 146.
[2] For the most recent discussion of the date, see D. Seltzer's edition of the play in the Regents Renaissance Drama Series (Lincoln, Nebraska, 1963), pp. ix–x.
[3] See E. K. Chambers, *The Elizabethan Stage* (1923), III, 330.
[4] *Ibid.*, pp. 105–6.
[5] *Athenaeum*, 8 October 1881, p. 465.   [6] *Anglia*, VIII (1885), 419.
[7] Some of the stories were used by William Painter in his *Palace of Pleasure* (1566–7), and others formed the sources for *Othello*, *Measure for Measure*, and for Beaumont and Fletcher's *The Custom of the Country*, Shirley's *Love's Cruelty*, and Middleton's *The Witch*.

it has been suggested that there was such a translation now lost.¹ Greene may have read the Italian original, for he knew the language sufficiently well to translate the anonymous pamphlet *La Burza Reale* and publish it as *The Royal Exchange* in 1590; but I have been unable to find any verbal echoes to indicate that it was this version specifically that he used for the play, or that he used Cinthio's own dramatic adaptation of the story, the neo-classical *Arrenopia* (1583). A French translation of the *Hecatommithi* was made by Gabriel Chappuys and published in 1583–4. Greene could read French, for he had published in the same volume as his *Gwydonius* (1584) a translation of Louis Labé's *Débat de Folie et d'Amour*; and I think it possible that the characterization of Jaques in the play together with the quite extensive use of French may indicate that it was the French rather than the Italian version from which Greene worked.² One small factual detail supports this impression. In v. i and v, where Dorothea is disguised as a young man, the 1598 Quarto at certain points displays a confusion in the use of personal pronouns and possessive adjectives applied to her (e.g., at v. i. 66, 67, 68, 69; v. v. 51, 55); and this confusion is twice reflected in the appropriate sections of the French version (e.g., sig. 2N2ʳ: '[Arenopia] ayant prins à Reba vne maison à louage, il s'en partit de là'), but not in the Italian original (sig. R8ᵛ: '[Arenopia] presa in Reba vna casa a pigione, indi si dipartí').

Greene follows the order of the principal events of Cinthio's narrative with remarkable faithfulness and has his dramatic equivalents of all the main characters. Astatio, King of Ireland, like his counterpart in the play, the King of Scots, is married to a virtuous princess, Arenopia (Dorothea), daughter of the King of Scotland (King of England). On a journey to visit his father-in-law, he falls in love with Ida, the daughter of the Lady of Mona (Countess of Arran), whom he tries to seduce via the mother with the promise of material rewards. Realizing that he will be able to possess Ida only by offering her marriage, Astatio persuades one of his captains

---

¹ e.g., by M. R. Ridley, ed., *Othello* (New Arden Shakespeare, 1962), p. 238.

² A translation of Chappuys's French translation of the novel is printed in the Appendix.

(Jaques) to kill his queen. Arenopia, like Dorothea, discovers the plot against her life and flees from the court disguised as a young man, accompanied only by her page (Nano). She is overtaken by the Captain and is wounded during his attack on her, but is saved by the intervention of a knight of Reba (Sir Cuthbert Anderson), who takes her to his house and grows jealous of his wife's (Lady Anderson's) attentions to his guest. Astatio finds that his murder plot has been fruitless because Ida has married a young nobleman of Mona (Lord Eustace), and is forced to take up arms against his father-in-law, who has invaded Ireland in order to avenge his daughter's death. Arenopia persuades the Knight of Reba to take her to her husband's court, where the revelation of her identity brings about a reconciliation between herself and her husband and a cessation of the war between Ireland and Scotland.

In dramatizing the narrative Greene selected those parts of it which were most susceptible of stage treatment, and all his changes are made with an eye to greater theatrical effectiveness. In the opening scene he does not follow his source's stress on the years of happy marriage or Astatio's encountering Ida and her mother while parted from his wife; instead we see the immediate aftermath of Dorothea's wedding and the sudden revelation of the King of Scots' passion for Ida, who is already present at court. In the King of Scots' illicit suit, Greene allows Ida herself to reject the proposal rather than have her mother make the refusal on her behalf as happens in the source. Dorothea at first cannot believe in her husband's guilt: her realization of it is a gradual one as she is informed of the plot by the Scottish nobles, in contrast with Arenopia's fortuitous acquisition of Astatio's letter to the Captain detailing the plans for the murder. Dorothea's resolve to disguise herself in order to escape is almost forced upon her by her friends, and her behaviour in disguise is both more natural and dramatically moving, and shows none of the Amazonian qualities and martial efforts displayed by the soldierly and self-sufficient Arenopia. Greene also sharpens the impact of events during Dorothea's sojourn with the Andersons by giving Sir Cuthbert's jealousy some grounds in his wife's strong sexual attraction to the disguised queen, as well as by showing Lady Anderson's sudden revulsion against herself on discovering Dorothea's true identity. Neither of these incidents has any counterpart in the source.

More significant than Greene's selection of episodes is his lifting of Cinthio's tale from the level of personal history to something much broader in scope. For, without losing sight of the emotional centre of the story, he gives it a wider context in national, moral, and human terms. The King of Scots' passion for Ida is seen as merely the outstanding symptom of an unkingly incapacity to rule his country effectively. By creating the character of Ateukin, who has no model in Cinthio, Greene is able to suggest how the King of Scots' weakness spreads outwards and downwards in his realm. The effect of the parasite's influence is charted in scenes like II. ii, where the King of Scots, confronted by his disgusted nobles, dismisses their advice and turns his back on the Church in the person of the Bishop of St Andrews; or in I. iii, as Sir Bartram indicates his scarcely veiled discontent to the visiting Lord Eustace; or in a scene of choric comment supplied by the Divine, the Lawyer, and the Merchant in V. iv. In the comic scenes, too, devoted to the subparasites, Slipper, Andrew, and Jaques, we see Ateukin's corruption seeping into the lower levels of society as the King's Purveyor is braved by Andrew and Jaques in III. ii, or Slipper lords it pretentiously in IV. iii, or Andrew plots the path of his self-interest in IV. v.

A moral contrast with the King of Scots' and Ateukin's machinations is created by Greene's development of the leading female parts. By making Dorothea much less self-sufficient than Arenopia, the playwright is able to portray a loyalty preserved in fear and distress which can be moving in action and believable in its moral triumph at the end. A further contrast with the corrupt court is also provided by Greene's expansion of the rôles of the Countess of Arran, Ida, and Lord Eustace. Around these three characters he constructs an idyllic picture of provincial country life with the two women aware of the shallowness of the court life and its temptations, content with their lot, and respected by their neighbours. When a suitable husband for Ida appears in the person of Eustace, then his suit can be received favourably by the mother with a proper show of prudence, and delightedly by the daughter with a decorous display of modest coquetry.

Each of the scenes dealing with this group is juxtaposed by Greene with the sordid courtly intriguing. Ateukin, with his first proposal to Ida in II. i, breaks into the lyrical exchanges between Eustace and Ida; then, later, his appearance with Jaques, in the hunting scene in IV. i, bearing the news of Dorothea's supposed death, is immediately followed by the hunters' celebration of Ida's betrothal to Eustace; and later still the two villains make their appearance at the young couple's wedding which appropriately signals their downfall and flight.

As will be obvious from the above discussion, Greene derived little from his source so far as characterization is concerned. The King of Scots shares Astatio's fundamental weaknesses which lead to ruthless egoism, the Lady of Mona has a moment of wisdom and piety comparable with the Countess of Arran's, and Arenopia has a long speech of forgiveness for her husband similar to Dorothea's in v. vi. But, for the rest, the characters are Greene's own creations based on little more than hints in Cinthio's story: Ida, Eustace, Nano, and Lady Anderson are all developed from a line or two in the source. The Scottish nobles, Andrew, and the comic characters have no part at all in the original narrative.

But the most important change is the character of Ateukin, who is absent from the source. In his use of this combination of parasite, flatterer, and Machiavellian villain, Greene would need no literary model, as the type was to haunt the London stage from the building of the theatres in the 1570s to their closure in 1642. However, W. F. McNeir,[1] taking note of the fact that Greene did name the play *James the Fourth*, has suggested that an original for the character may have been an Italian adventurer named John Damien, who ingratiated himself with the historical James IV by his pretensions to skill as a surgeon and apothecary, and continued to abuse the King's confidence by practising alchemy and astrology in order to pander to his master's weakness for the occult. The account of Damien's influence could have been found by Greene either in Holinshed's *Chronicle* or in the source Holinshed used, John Leslie's *History of Scotland* (1571).

[1] 'The Original of Ateukin in Greene's *James IV*', *M.L.N.*, LXII (1947), 376–81.

A strong case has also been made for the play's connection with the later history of Scotland. Ruth Hudson[1] tests against the news of Scotland and James VI, current in London during the summer and autumn of 1590, Bohan's words to Oberon in the Induction:

> In the year 1520 was in Scotland a king, overruled with parasites, misled by lust, and many circumstances too long to trattle on now, much like our court of Scotland this day. (ll. 106–9)

Miss Hudson lists the following major topics of conversation in London at this time: (1) rumours of James VI's troubles with his powerful nobility after his return from his marriage trip to Denmark, where he had come under the influence of Chancellor Maitland; (2) Burghley's reception of a letter from the English Ambassador at the Scottish court, Sir Robert Bowes, reporting discontent among the Scottish nobles; (3) reports from Scotland that James VI's main weakness was his susceptibility to flattery.

Building on this general resemblance between the play's King of Scots and James VI, Miss Hudson points to some moments in the play which imply the influence of current events. She suggests that the Bishop of St Andrews' words to the King of Scots in II. ii reflect the tone of Elizabeth's letters to James; that Oberon's prevention of Bohan's drawing his sword is an allusion to James's notorious fear of weapons; that Sir Bartram's report to Eustace in I. iii that the Queen is 'so-so' is a reference to Anne of Denmark's rumoured pregnancy during the summer of 1590; and that the sentiments lauding the unity of England and Scotland in V. vi are a comment on the question of James's possible succession to the English throne and the subsequent uniting of the two kingdoms.

While some of Miss Hudson's speculations about details of the play may be questioned, there is, nevertheless, sufficient evidence to indicate that Greene did have in mind some such parallel between the play and events in Scotland in 1590, and further that Greene's play may have been one of those which occasioned the complaint from Scotland that 'comedians of London... scorn the king and the

---

[1] 'Greene's *James IV* and Contemporary Allusions to Scotland', *P.M.L.A.*, XLVII (1932), 652–67.

people of this land in their play'.[1] Such speculation on the play's topical relevance is also strengthened by the references to the Spanish Armada (IV. iii. 66–7), the Irish wars (III. iii. 121), and the French threat (IV. iv. 48–9).

Greene's most important structural innovation, so far as his treatment of the source is concerned, was his placing the main plot within the framework material. There had been many 'framed' plays previous to 1590, nine of which are extant[2]; and Greene's own first attempt at play-writing, *Alphonsus King of Aragon*, had taken just this form. Of course, Cinthio's tale is itself a framework story growing out of a debate, as were so many of Greene's own earlier prose pamphlets.[3] For the material for his framework, Greene drew on the tradition of the malcontent or melancholy man—a type which was to achieve special prominence in the drama of the late 1590s—and on the body of fairy lore familiar to most Englishmen of the time.

At specific points in the play Greene used his miscellaneous knowledge and reading, even as he had in the composition of his numerous prose works. No one familiar with Greene's methods of composition can be surprised at the allusions to Ovid, Aristotle, and Lucretius; or the common proverbs expanded into blank-verse lines; or the passages based on North's *Plutarch* and Fitzherbert's *Book of Husbandry*; or the sometimes marked similarities to situations and characters in his own earlier pamphlets.[4]

---

[1] Quoted in E. Rickert's 'Political Propaganda in *A Midsummer Night's Dream*', *M.P.*, xxi (1923), 53–87, 133–54.

[2] I take this calculation from R. Hosley's 'Was There a "Dramatic Epilogue" to *The Taming of the Shrew*?', *S.E.L.*, I, 2 (1961), 32–4.

[3] *Planetomachia* (1585), *Penelope's Web* (1587), *Euphues his Censure to Philautus* (1587), *Perymedes* (1588), *Alcida* (1588), *Ciceronis Amor* (1589), *Opharion* (1590), *Greene's Mourning Garment* (1590).

[4] For example, Dorothea's situation and fortunes follow in a general way the story of Barmenissa in *Penelope's Web* (1587); the story of Ida is similar to Fawnia's in *Pandosto* (1588), and Argentina's in *Opharion* (1590); and the final scene of the play resembles several such scenes in many of the pamphlets (see A. H. Maclain, 'Greene's Borrowings from his own Prose Fiction in *Bacon and Bungay* and *James the Fourth*', *P.Q.*, XXX (1951), 22–9).

4. THE PLAY

One of the interests of Greene's best works, both in prose and drama, lies in the way they provide an accurate mirror for the age's dramatic and literary preoccupations. They are historically valuable in the broadest sense of the term: that is, they allow us to see in action the basic materials, ideas, thought-patterns, structures, attitudes, fashions, and assumptions on which the greatest masterpieces of the period are built. The key to the whole corpus of his work perhaps can be found in the way it was apparently written: as Greene himself puts it, in *Greene's Groatsworth of Wit*, 'to mitigate the extremities of his want'. With 'present necessity' ever at his back, Greene in his prose pamphlets was always nearly abreast or slightly ahead of the fashionable trends; and it is to be expected that when he turned to writing for the theatre the same habits would prevail. Thus, in view of the success of Marlowe's *Tamburlaine*, it was natural that he should attempt an imitation in *Alphonsus King of Aragon*. It was equally natural that, when it became obvious to him that he could not make his blank verse 'jet upon the stage in tragical buskins', it was to the more congenial materials of narrative or romantic comedy that he turned and with which he found theatrical success.

Despite the title of *James the Fourth*, the play is in fact what Irving Ribner[1] has called it: 'a quasi-historical will-o'-the-wisp': and one can sympathize with the sometime owner of the British Museum copy, who scored out the title-page words 'of Iames the fourth, slaine at *Flodden*' and replaced them with 'or rather fiction of English & Scotish matters comicall'.[2] In so titling his play,[3] Greene was characteristically attempting to appeal to the London theatre-public's taste for dramatic history which, in view of the increasing number of English history plays being written at the

---

[1] I. Ribner, *The English History Play in the Age of Shakespeare*, 1965 ed., p. 11.

[2] See the reproduction on p. 2.

[3] As the play is almost certainly printed from Greene's holograph (see pp. lvii–lx), one may assume that the head-title was the author's rather than the printer's; although the title-page may well have been of Creede's devising in 1598.

time, appears to have grown quite remarkably in the years 1587–99. However, the historical elements in the play are of minimal importance dramatically and are factually quite inaccurate. Indeed, what Greene does in placing a tale from Cinthio in the historical setting of the Scottish court is to establish the pattern for historical romance and provide an early attempt at that dramatic hybrid of which *Cymbeline* is probably the best example.[1]

The strengths and weaknesses of *James the Fourth* are due to this combination of genres, circumstances of composition, and the special habits of the author. As it will be argued on textual grounds, the 1598 Quarto was set up from Greene's 'foul papers'[2] and thus represents Greene in the act of composing a play with all the signs present of the rapidity which, according to Thomas Nashe, was typical of his method.[3] In it we also find the heterogeneous elements which go into the making of even the best examples of romantic comedy; sometimes they are wastefully used, and sometimes blended to achieve intellectual and dramatic coherence. At certain points, one can perceive a laboured crudity of execution; at others, a half-realization of the profundity such materials are capable of conveying.

The plotting is skilful, the exposition being, as Kenneth Muir[4] has claimed, 'particularly fine'. The opening scene is eminently stage-worthy, with the splendid entry from the royal wedding of kings, the bridal couple, courtiers, ladies, and attendants, and Ateukin lurking in the background. Then there quickly follows the symbolic enthronement of Dorothea, while the villain stands apart from the society he is to corrupt and bring to near ruin. The subsequent revelation of the King of Scots' infatuation with Ida is rapid; and his credibly presented impulse to make a first approach to her leads logically to both his receptiveness to Ateukin's suggestions and his employment of the parasite as go-between in the affair. The scene is also functionally dramatic, because the downfall of Ateukin

---

[1] See Ribner's remarks on the place of the play in the development of the English history play as a whole, *op. cit.*, pp. 89, 237, 252.
[2] See pp. lvii–lx below.   [3] See *Strange News*, I, 255–355, *passim*.
[4] Kenneth Muir, 'Robert Greene as Dramatist', *Essays on Shakespeare and Elizabethan Drama in Honor of Hardin Craig*, ed. R. Hosley (Columbia, Missouri, 1962), p. 50.

and the failure of the King's plots are to be conveyed in a parallel scene (v. ii) where the elaborately staged wedding of Lord Eustace and Ida is to constitute, and provide a background to, the news which signals the end of the flatterer's influence. It is as though Greene wishes us to see by structural means the villain's power growing out of the weakness of one marriage (Dorothea's and the King's) into a short reign of triumph only to be defeated by the ideal marriage of Ida and Eustace.

Between these two scenes of symbol and spectacle, this design is kept before the audience by constant juxtaposition of the progress of the two affairs, one aspect of each being balanced against the other throughout. For example, Ida's witty fending off of the King of Scots (I. i. 100 ff.) is counterbalanced by Ateukin's confident assertions of success and his belief in his own powers of persuasion in the same scene (ll. 201 ff.). Similarly, the moral stance of Ida and the Countess of Arran on the subjects of court life and love in II. i. 1–30 is quickly followed by Ateukin's first approach to Ida that we see in the play in ll. 109 ff. The success of Eustace's suit for Ida's hand (IV. ii) is flanked, on the one hand, by Dorothea's plan to escape the death planned for her and, on the other, by Andrew's murderous arrangements with Jaques (IV. iii). The moment of Ateukin's apparent triumph in the announcement of Dorothea's death and his hoped-for success with Ida (IV. v) is preceded by the scene showing Dorothea safe with the Andersons (IV. iv), and succeeded by one illustrating her recovery from her wounds (V. i). At one point, the parallel between scenes takes on an added symbolic dimension when Ateukin comes to inform the King of Scots of his plans for the queen's death while the monarch has taken a stand to kill a hunted deer (IV. i). This is a circumstance which reflects Jaques' hunting down of Dorothea in the forest (IV. iv), and which is contrasted with the healthy erotic connotation given to the stricken hart brought by the Huntsmen to Eustace and Ida in IV. ii.

Yet, while such evidences of basic plotting skills are clearly present, none of the possible subtleties of conception or execution they offer are well developed. The contrasts and parallels such scenes project in stage terms are not taken up verbally as would have been the case with a better poet. Almost all the episodes remain a testimony to Greene's powers of dramatic invention and instinctive sense of comic design; but, at the same time, they are a witness to his hurried execution and lack of profundity of mind.

The comic scenes display a similar skill in their internal arrangement and a knowledge of the necessity for dramatic function in their distribution. At the most obvious level they display Greene's realization of the need for variety, and they are intrinsically entertaining. Their deployment also illustrates a sense of theatre. I. ii follows the serious presentation of Ateukin's intrigues and the King of Scots' weakness, showing the parasite's preening himself and laying the ground for Nano's accompaniment of Dorothea on her flight from the court. Slipper's appearance in II. i lightens the melodrama of Ateukin's attempted seduction of Ida; and his humorous quibbling with the Countess of Arran effectively covers the whispered conversation. It thus permits the build-up of a mild suspense until Ateukin's expression of discouragement indicates to the audience that Ida has remained uncorrupted. In III. i, Slipper is again used in various ways: to show how Ateukin is regarded below-stairs, and to out-Machiavel his master in stealing the lease of the manor for Sir Bartram, which enables him to light upon the King's warrant and thus be the agent by which Dorothea's life is saved and the happy ending ensured. His function is, in this respect, a plot device similar to the one involving that other shallow fool, Dogberry in *Much Ado about Nothing*, who likewise inadvertently brings the truth to light. Elsewhere in the play, the Clown also projects in comic terms the broad corruption of Scottish society, illustrating, for example, how every parasite has a sub-parasite, as he betrays Ateukin and is himself betrayed by Andrew. Nano, who is the witty Fool to Slipper's Clown, is similarly functional in that it is he who originates the plan to disguise Dorothea in III. iii, and is the means of revealing the queen's true identity to Lady Anderson in V. v. Greene uses the dwarf also to control tone, when his conversation prevents the scene with Dorothea in the forest (IV. iv) from becoming mawkish, and when his presence later allows the play to finish on a note of some lightness.

Rather less successful as part of a coherent dramatic design are those scenes in which Greene attempts to convey the wider implications of the personal moral issue at the centre of the play. Quite clearly he intended the audience to perceive that the King of Scots' weakness as an individual seeps downwards to poison society at every level by virtue of the fact that he is a ruler. The idea was a commonplace during the Elizabethan period, and is one that Ateukin perverts to persuade the King of the necessity for Dorothea's murder:

> Why, prince, it is no murder in a king
> To end another's life to save his own;
> For you are not as common people be,
> Who die and perish with a few men's tears;
> But if you fail, the state doth whole default,
> The realm is rent in twain in such a loss.
> And Aristotle holdeth this for true,
> Of evils needs we must choose the least:
> Then better were it that a woman died
> Than all the help of Scotland should be blent.
> 'Tis policy, my liege, in every state,
> To cut off members that disturb the head,
> And by corruption generation grows,
> And contraries maintain the world and state.
> (IV. v. 35–48)

Purely in political terms the King of Scots' personal actions will have international repercussions for the country he rules; and it is appropriately the Bishop of St Andrews, the representative of the Lords Spiritual, that voices them:

> Thou well mayst see, although thou wilt not see,
> That every eye and ear both sees and hears
> The certain signs of thine incontinence.
> Thou art allied unto the English king
> By marriage: a happy friend indeed
> If usèd well; if not, a mighty foe.
> Thinketh your grace he can endure and brook
> To have a partner in his daughter's love?
> Thinketh your grace the grudge of privy wrongs
> Will not procure him change his smiles to threats?
> (II. ii. 127–36)

Yet, apart from this scene and some well-managed dialogue in the scene (I. iii) where Sir Bartram conveys to Eustace the impact of the King of Scots' behaviour on the secular nobility, none of Greene's attempts to illustrate the implications of these ideas come off. Thereafter, the Scottish nobles sink into muttering and personal intrigue, the display of corruption at the lower levels being left to Slipper's antics, Jaques' braving the King's Purveyor (III. ii), Andrew's scheming to win favour from the English King as Ateukin's fall approaches, and the odd line by a moralizing Huntsman (IV. i. 6). The scenes depicting the King of England's devastation of Scotland fail lamentably, owing to Greene's lack of those poetic and conceptual talents that had enabled Marlowe to succeed so conspicuously in *Tamburlaine*. The result is that V. iii and V. vi are composed of hollow rant and empty bombast, devoid alike of verbal and theatrical grandeur.

The most ambitious attempt to universalize the theme of galloping corruption is the conversation between the Divine, the Merchant, and the Lawyer (V. iv). Greene's authorship of this scene has been questioned by F. G. Fleay[1] and others, who have remarked that it is similar in manner to those scenes usually attributed to Thomas Lodge in *A Looking Glass for London and England*. However, there are no strong arguments on the grounds of either style or content for doubting Greene's authorship, and the scene remains an obvious attempt to convey the effects on Scotland of the King of Scots' behaviour. It may certainly be seen, as Lavin claims,[2] as an example of an obsolescent dramatic method in which 'generalised types generically named' are employed for a homiletic purpose. Nevertheless, as it stands in the play, it is quite well written but curiously peripheral and unintegrated: it is 'never once brought into focus',[3] and remains an example of the Elizabethan fondness for the analysis of type-crimes in the tradition of 'character' writing.

So far as the structuring of the individual scenes is concerned, the conception of most is good, and several are very well executed. For example, Ateukin's approach to the King of Scots in I. i is finely paced from his impertinent interruption of the King's meditation, to the King's initial reaction of incredulity and then a blow, and on to the parasite's gradual manipulation of the King's desires

---

[1] *A Biographical Chronicle of the English Drama, 1559–1642* (1881), I, 265.
[2] Lavin, p. xviii. [3] Muir, *op. cit.*, p. 50.

for his own ends. In a similar way, Ateukin's introduction of the topic of the necessity of Dorothea's death and his quieting of the King's conscience with spurious argument in IV. v are well managed.

Some other scenes are successful in a rather different manner. For example, II. i brings together in a working harmony the main materials with which Greene is dealing throughout the play: Ateukin's intrigue and the King's illicit passion, the growing and contrasted love affair of Ida and Eustace, and the low comedy represented by Slipper. Here too Greene, now free of Marlowe's influence, realizes the value of functional stylistic variety. The scene opens with the leisurely paced blank verse of the Countess of Arran, appropriate to the chat of two women who know each other well, as they sit over their needlework:

> Fair Ida, might you choose the greatest good,
> Midst all the world in blessings that abound,
> Wherein, my daughter, should your liking be?
> (ll. 1–3)

Ida's reply to this sets up the first of the rhymed couplets which endow her subsequent remarks with an air of sententious moralizing on the state of affairs at the Scottish court, and enables her to move easily into her allegorical artifice (ll. 17–30) which slows down the tempo in preparation for Eustace's entry. The young man's interruption effectively breaks the rhyme and the complete iambic line, and then the conversation between him and the Countess is carried on in blank verse. The rhyme reappears with a lyric note as Eustace carries on his flirtation with Ida, which is again broken and the mood shattered by the appearance of Ateukin and Slipper. The verse becomes stilted in Ateukin's opening address, to which the Countess replies in jingling rhymes suitable for the expression of the childhood precepts she followed in Ida's upbringing. Slipper intervenes, and Ateukin falls into prose to deal with the Clown in his own idiom; he then turns to Ida to make his initial proposals on the King's behalf in blank verse varied with rhyming stychomythia as Ida verbally routs the parasite. A long section of prose humour, involving the Countess and Slipper, is used to cover Ida's talk with Ateukin, which breaks out aloud again at l. 194 in a series of couplets which convey Ida's obduracy and Ateukin's defeat and discouragement.

In purely poetic terms IV. ii is perhaps the most attractive in the play and, as the climax of Eustace's wooing of Ida, is clearly designed to provide an idyllic counterbalance to the intrigue of the King of Scots and Ateukin. Metrically it takes its cue from the initial meeting of Eustace and Ida in II. i, and the discussion of dowers and rents between Eustace and the Countess (ll. 1-12) proceeds in regular decasyllabic rhyming couplets, changing to half-line questions and replies as the young man seeks to obtain from Ida an avowal of her affection for him (ll. 13-14). This she makes, after seeking her mother's permission, again in decasyllabic couplets. The celebration of the union is immediately effected by the entrance of the Huntsmen and the Ladies (l. 25) who perform a kind of pastoral masque couched in octosyllabic stanzas which praise the beauty and wisdom of Ida, present her with an image of love, and pay tribute to the Countess's great worth. As the lovers are left alone, Ida's final assertion of her love for Eustace, again in rhymed decasyllables, grows directly out of the Huntsmen's gift and its symbolic meanings.

Not all the scenes are so successful as these two in realizing the poetic possibilities of the materials and situations. The two scenes involving the disguised Dorothea and Lady Anderson (v. i and v) are adequate from the narrative point of view in showing Dorothea's recovery and her decision to intervene between her father and husband by using the good offices of Sir Cuthbert Anderson, but little more is achieved in them. However, this use of a woman disguised as a man does constitute, together with Lyly's in *Gallatea* (*circa* 1588), one of the earliest dramatic attempts by dramatists writing for London audiences to exploit what Clifford Leech called 'the piquancy of a situation in which a boy-player, acting the part of a young woman, had to wear the dramatic disguise of a boy'.[1] Greene's handling of the device in *James the Fourth* has none of the slight prurience which is associated with its use in Lyly's play and is certainly quite free from the morbid sexual perversity by which

[1] Clifford Leech, '*Twelfth Night*' *and Shakespearian Comedy* (Toronto, 1965), pp. 47-8.

it is surrounded much later in the plays of Beaumont and Fletcher. His use is more akin to Shakespeare's in *Twelfth Night* and *As You Like It* in that he does seem to be dimly aware that the situation could allow an implicit and deepening comment on the central action. For having the disguised Dorothea become the object of what Lady Anderson herself calls her 'insatiate lust', we do have a female version, as it were, of the King of Scots' own adulterous passion for Ida. Dorothea is thus innocently a threat to the Andersons' marriage, even as Ida was, equally innocently, a threat to Dorothea's own.

However, while Greene's use of the device in the play opens the door to that kind of tragi-comic tension which attains its perfection in the scenes in *Twelfth Night* involving Viola, Olivia, and Orsino, the opportunity is bungled by the half-development of the situation and the rushing over the implications of it. Dorothea's disguise like Viola's may certainly be 'a wickedness / Wherein the pregnant enemy does much' (*Twelfth Night*, II. ii. 28–9), but Greene makes little theatrical capital of it. In v. i. Sir Cuthbert's jealousy and agony of mind at his wife's behaviour are conveyed baldly in two empty couplets quite devoid of emotional conviction:

> In ripping up their wounds, I see their wit;
> But if these wounds be cured, I sorrow it. . . .
> I'll break off their dispute, lest love proceed
> From covert smiles to perfect love indeed.
> (ll. 15–16, 29–30)

And only slightly more skilful are Lady Anderson's temptation and repentance as she passes from guilt to shame to becoming Dorothea's willing helper in a space of five lines which have not been led up to in any dramatic or poetic sense:

> Blush, grieve, and die in thine insatiate lust! . . .
> I joy, my lord, more than my tongue can tell,
> Although not as I desired, I love you well;
> But modesty that never blushed before
> Discover my false heart. I say no more.
> (v. v. 53, 56–9)

In being based on Cinthio's *novella*, the play is an obvious example of that expansion of the subject-matter of English drama which characterized the playwriting of the period. And it was to Italy also that Greene turned in the creation of the one serious character he added to his source. Ateukin is Italianized vice, located at a Scottish court; and his characterization shares with most other aspects of the play the curious combination of imaginative conception and weak execution. He is effectively presented initially as an astrologer, and it is his apparent skill in prognostication that gains him his hold upon the King of Scots. Yet, after this moment, when Greene was able to use his relatively expert knowledge of stellar conjunctions, the whole subject is allowed to drop without further note. Instead, Ateukin emerges as the conventional parasite and flatterer with Machiavellian overtones. He has, we are told by Andrew (III. ii. 53), made notes on 'Machiavel' and he can use his tongue effectively to lead the King of Scots' mind from orthodox Tudor theory of monarchy, through absolutism, and on to the necessity for murder to strengthen his throne and country[1]; but it is mainly on his capacities as a flatterer that the play concentrates after the first act. Most of the characters define him as this kind of caterpillar in the commonwealth: a flattering Gnatho pranking it by the King's side, an ambitious man of whom the nobility are afraid and who brings the world to a wise pass, and the soother in whom the King puts too much trust. The Bishop of St Andrews, Douglas, Sir Bartram, the Purveyor—all stress this aspect of the villain, presumably so that the King of Scots may emerge as a young man misled instead of the self-driven lustful and tyrannical Astatio that Greene found in Cinthio's tale. And it is Ateukin himself who condemns his rôle, at his last appearance, and takes his flattering influence with him, leaving the King to be forgiven:

> O, cursèd race of men that traffic guile,
> And in the end themselves and kings beguile!
> Ashamed to look upon my prince again,
> Ashamed of my suggestions and advice,
> Ashamed of life, ashamed that I have erred,
> I'll hide myself, expecting for my shame.
> Thus God doth work with those that purchase fame
> By flattery, and make their prince their gain.
> (v. ii. 33–40)

[1] See p. xl above.

Andrew, Ateukin's lieutenant, is a variant of his master in being part-Machiavellian and part-Tudor-Vice as he revels in his skill of manœuvre and shares with the audience his knowledge of plots laid and to be laid. However, in some respects he also prefigures that kind of villain of which Bosola in John Webster's *The Duchess of Malfi* is the most complex version. For while Andrew takes part in his master's corruption, he is also one of the means by which moral comment is passed on it. In his penultimate appearance at the end of IV. v, he not only defines the world where 'sinners seem to dance within a net' (l. 80) and 'The flatterer and the murderer . . . grow big' (l. 81), but also attempts, like Bosola, to align himself on the side of good—albeit from motives of self-interest.

The King of Scots on whom Ateukin works is, in a similar way to his parasite, not totally coherent as a piece of characterization. Lustful and inconstant in his marriage without any convincing spiritual struggle, he quickly becomes susceptible to flattery and policy, and evolves into a version of the stage tyrant with all the conventional trappings associated with the rôle since Herod raged 'in the pagond and in the strete'.[1] Ateukin applies to him all the flattering terms and titles conventionally offered to the theatrical descendants of Herod:

> My dear, my gracious, and belovèd prince,
> The essence of my suit, my god on earth,
> Sit down and rest yourself; appease your wrath,
> Lest with a frown ye wound me to the death.
> O, that I were included in my grave,
> That either now, to save my prince's life,
> Must counsel cruelty or lose my king. . . .
> How kind a word, how courteous is his grace!
> Who would not die to succour such a king?
> (II. ii. 164–70, 177–8)

Under his minion's sway, the King of Scots dismisses his Lords Temporal and Spiritual, turns his back on the practices of his father's reign, and bolsters his dismissal of his nobles with the threat of physical violence:

---

[1] *Two Coventry Corpus Christi Plays*, ed. H. Craig (Early English Text Society, 1957), p. 27.

> On pain of death, proud bishop, get you gone,
> Unless you headless mean to hop away!
> (II. ii. 143–4)

His single moment of doubt in his course of action and his final repentance are neither sufficiently strong, dramatically or poetically, to make his place in the happy ending altogether acceptable.

As some critics have pointed out,[1] behind the figures of the King of Scots and Ateukin there stand ultimately the Everyman character and the Vice of the Morality plays. E. W. Talbert has seen in the action of *James the Fourth* merely the filling out of what is basically the Morality pattern: the Vice (Ateukin) gains sway over Everyman (the King); Good Counsel (the Bishop of St Andrews) is turned out of the court and Everyman becomes Tyranny; Virtue (Dorothea) departs from Everyman; the Vice flourishes assisted by his lieutenants (Slipper and Andrew); and policy within the court and the downfall of the Everyman character prefigure the national strife between England and Scotland in which the commons are afraid and the land spoiled by an invader.[2] As in many Moralities, the Vice is ultimately rejected and the Virtue figure reasserts control over Everyman, who restores law and order to his land and is reconciled to his good counsellors. When the play is viewed in this way, then the scene between the Divine, the Merchant, and the Lawyer emerges as merely an extreme example of the abstracted moral comment, which typified early Tudor plays, here unmixed with the influences of Italian romance. Many of the other central characters can also be fitted into this Morality scheme. Ida may be viewed as Chastity tested by a corrupted Everyman under the influence of Lust, the Countess of Arran as Wisdom or Content, and Eustace as Constancy. However, it is in the scenes concerned with these characters that the schematic abstraction seems irrelevant as criticism in that such a rigid schematization strikes one as being totally unrelated to the kind of impact they make as part of the play.

Dorothea has been the recipient of much critical praise both as

---

[1] e.g., E. W. Talbert, *Elizabethan Drama and Shakespeare's Early Plays* (Chapel Hill, North Carolina, 1963), pp. 92–5; and Lavin, pp. xvi–xx.

[2] Talbert, *loc. cit.*

forecast of 'the noblest type of womanhood in Shakespeare'[1] and as 'the best drawn woman figure in sixteenth-century drama outside Shakespeare's comedies',[2] though she too can be worked into the Morality pattern as Virtue on both the personal and national levels. But functionally she does not work in this way; apart from her final action in stepping between her warring father and husband and effecting a general reconciliation, she endures and waits for circumstances to favour her, instead of bringing about conditions in which her influence can work. The archetype which lies behind Dorothea is more obviously that on which all the good women in Greene's plays and prose works are based: namely, the figure of Patient Griselda, the lovely, constant, and finally redemptive woman. Clearly the type attracted Greene psychologically and its frequent use by him is one aspect of the complex of attitudes which made public self-castigation and flaunted repentance so attractive a literary stance to him. It is also hard not to believe that in the case of Dorothea there was involved Greene's memory of his treatment of his wife 'Dol' and his own succumbing, like the King of Scots, to what he calls 'the loathsome scourge of Lust'.[3]

Basic to the Griselda story (which apparently was already firmly developed in the folk-lore of many European cultures long before it was given definitive literary shape in the works of Petrarch, Chaucer, and Boccaccio) is an action comprising the testing of the heroine by her husband.[4] The woman responds to the disloyal behaviour of her lord with meek acceptance, and endures the conditions he creates for her with a constancy nothing short of the miraculous. It is, therefore, irrelevant to discuss the heroine in terms of 'character' in its usual sense of true psychological motivation and convincing behaviour patterns; rather, the figure is exemplary or emblematic. Her 'character' *is* how she responds to the treatment meted out to her, and the moral and human significance of her story lies in the plot and not in the personages.

The 'testing' of Dorothea's constancy follows the Griselda story

[1] J. M. Robertson, *Elizabethan Literature* (1914), p. 105.
[2] Allardyce Nicoll, *British Drama* (1925), p. 90.
[3] *Greene's Groatsworth of Wit*, XII, 136.
[4] W. Cate, 'The Problem of the Origin of the Griselda Story', *S.P.*, XXIX (1932), 389–405.

closely, and is rather more severe than that experienced by Greene's other dramatic treatment of the type, Margaret of Fressingfield in *Friar Bacon and Friar Bungay*.[1] Dorothea refuses point-blank to believe what the Scottish nobles tell her about her husband; she excuses his vices on the grounds of erring youthfulness; and she teaches them a lesson about their duty as royal counsellors. She then verbally places herself in the Griselda position, as she interprets her husband's intentions with regard to Ida and herself in terms of her model:

> Ah, Douglas, thou misconstrest his intent.
> He doth but tempt his wife, he tries my love:
> This injury pertains to me, not to you.
> The king is young; and, if he step awry,
> He may amend, and I will love him still. . . .
>   My friends and Scottish peers,
> If that an English princess may prevail,
> Stay, stay with him; lo, how my zealous prayer
> Is pled with tears!
>   (II. ii. 84–8, 93–6)

Later she clearly defines in herself the central qualities of the Griselda heroine:

> All these are means sufficient to persuade,
> But love, the faithful link of loyal hearts,
> That hath possession of my constant mind,
> Exiles all dread, subdueth vain suspect.
>   (III. iii. 3–6)

And towards the end of her trial she adds to these virtues obedience, when she describes her moral stance to Lady Anderson:

> Ah, lady, so would worldly counsel work,
> But constancy, obedience, and my love,
> In that my husband is my lord and chief,
> These call me to compassion of his estate;
> Dissuade me not, for virtue will not change.
>   (V. v. 67–71)

---

[1] See D. Seltzer's discussion of the topic in his edition of *Friar Bacon and Friar Bungay* (Regents Renaissance Drama Series, Lincoln, Nebraska, 1963), pp. xvii–xix.

Lady Anderson's response to this is at once an expression of admiration for Dorothea's virtues and the human reaction to the Griselda story itself:

> What wondrous constancy is this I hear!
> If English dames their husbands love so dear,
> I fear me in the world they have no peer.
>
> (ll. 72–4)

However, although Greene follows his model so closely, counting on his audience's recognition of the type, he also departs from it by introducing the element of the threat of death into the conventional testing situation. Fundamentally it is this change that prevents Dorothea from remaining the straightforward 'emblem' that Lavin claims her to be[1]; and also saves her from speaking by the book throughout the play. There are some signs that Greene was conscious of the literary pose he was striking, in that he relaxes it slightly at some points, and does so in a way that gestures in the direction of true psychology and humanity. For example, in her speech to the discontented nobles (II. ii), it is clear that, even when faced with the King's warrant for her death, Dorothea simply refuses to believe it. In her Griselda rôle she claims it for a test, but she also plots to escape, and she seizes upon the excuse of youthful recklessness—one which she can take up gratefully in the final scene when her husband's repentance proves she was right after all:

> Shame me not, prince, companion in thy bed;
> Youth hath misled—tut, but a little fault:
> 'Tis kingly to amend what is amiss.
> Might I with twice as many pains as these
> Unite our hearts, then should my wedded lord
> See how incessant labours I would take.
>
> (v. vi. 159–64)

She can also later step out of her Griselda rôle and lament her lot:

> Ah, Nano, I am weary of these weeds,
> Weary to wield this weapon that I bear,
> Weary of love from whom my woe proceeds,
> Weary of toil, since I have lost my dear.
> O weary life, where wanteth no distress,
> But every thought is paid with heaviness.
>
> (IV. iv. 1–6)

---

[1] Lavin, p. xx.

Perhaps the best way of illustrating the manner in which Dorothea moves out of her emblematic mould is to compare her with Margaret in *Friar Bacon and Friar Bungay*, whose diction, as W. W. Greg[1] puts it, persuades one that she spent her girlhood reading Greene's own courtly romances. Dorothea can certainly match her on occasion in this respect, but sometimes a note of directness and pertinent generalization of her lot creeps into her verse which is absent from that of the earlier heroine:

> What should I do? Ah, poor unhappy queen,
> Born to endure what fortune can contain!
> Alas, the deed is too apparent now.
> But O, mine eyes, were you as bent to hide
> As my poor heart is forward to forgive!
> Ah, cruel king, my love would thee acquit.
> O, what avails to be allied and matched
> With high estates that marry but in show?
> Were I baser born, my mean estate
> Could warrant me from this impendent harm;
> But to be great and happy—these are twain.
> (III. iii. 68–78)

In standard histories of the drama much is made of the way in which the framework material of the play anticipates both Shakespeare's characters and his employment of the same device. But Greene's management of it has not been overpraised. Among recent critics, Kenneth Muir[2] claims that 'the induction and choric interludes between the acts are tedious and unnecessary', and Lavin[3] sees them as 'an excuse for the introduction of inter-act jigs, hornpipes, and rounds, which are extraneous to the play'. Such observations are true enough, but Greene's employment of the device is also one example of an interest in the actor–audience relationship, which shows itself in all of his plays. In *Alphonsus King of Aragon*, his first play, the framework is provided by Venus and the nine Muses; and the play itself is of vital concern to these characters in that it is an attempt by Calliope to prove that her special area of literary composition is not dead to the world. In *A Looking Glass for London and England*, the prophet Oseas is seated on a throne high

---

[1] As cited by Seltzer, *op. cit.*, p. xviii.   [2] Muir, *op. cit.*, p. 50.
[3] Lavin, p. xv.

above the stage where he can see over the two worlds, of the play and of the audience; and so that, after witnessing the corruption of the people of Nineveh, he can turn to the theatre audience as belonging to 'lands unknowne', and draw the necessary moral lesson. In *Friar Bacon and Friar Bungay* the same kind of reflective dramatic situation is found within the action of the play, where, by means of Bacon's perspective glass, Greene can set up a play within the play at which the magician and Prince Edward are an unknown audience of the attempted marriage of Margaret and Lacy, or at which the sons of Serlsbie and Lambert can witness their fathers' quarrel and duel which cause their own deaths.[1]

In her discussion of *A Looking Glass for London and England*, Anne Righter[2] makes an interesting comment on the historical background to this use of the framework device:

> In those fifteenth and early sixteenth-century moralities from which *A Looking Glass for London and England* ultimately derives, there had been no need for figures like Oseas. Jonas could have addressed both Nineveh and London, the actors in one moment, the spectators in the next. For Lodge and Greene, however, in the last decade of the sixteenth century, such an attitude was no longer possible. The increasing naturalism of their theatre forced them to seek out some compromise between the rival claims of didacticism and dramatic illusion.

This is precisely what is being attempted in *James the Fourth*. Bohan and Oberon stand between the world of the play and that of the audience; for, as actors playing the rôle of an audience, they partake of both.

Bohan is a misanthrope, a malcontent, not naturally but made so by his experience and observation of life. As such he is an early stage example of that mental attitude which in the real life of the period could be either a psychological condition or an affected social pose—one that Greene himself adopted on his return from the continent[3]—and which in plays, particularly of the late-1590s

---

[1] For a discussion of this see N. Sanders, 'The Comedy of Greene and Shakespeare', *Early Shakespeare* (Stratford-upon-Avon Studies III, ed. J. R. Brown and B. A. Harris, 1961), pp. 35–53.
[2] *Shakespeare and the Idea of the Play* (1962), p. 76.
[3] See *The Repentance of Robert Greene*, XII, 172.

and early 1600s, was an essential ingredient of many celebrated characters, among whom Jaques in *As You Like It* is one example, and Hamlet, and Altofronto (in John Marston's *The Malcontent*), are the most successful major dramatic explorations. The play proper in *James the Fourth* is Bohan's illustrative example of why he is as he is, and is therefore a moral demonstration. By means of the framework the audience–actor division within the play is effectively blurred so that characters like Oberon, Slipper, and Nano can move across it with ease. The Scot's two sons, unlike their father, do not opt out of life (i.e., the play world) but take part in it at opposite ends of the moral spectrum: Slipper as lieutenant to the Vice, and Nano as the companion to Virtue.

One result of this blurring of the audience–actor barrier within the play is that, although Bohan's disillusionment with his own life (i.e., the present of the Induction and consequently of the theatre audience) is illustrated by a story which took place in 1520, time also is telescoped, so that Bohan's illustration becomes the court of his own day. Thus, his sons try out this world on their own behalf, and Ateukin can identify Nano as 'the old stoic's son, that dwells in his tomb' (I. ii. 118–19). In dramatic terms what is happening here is that Bohan is giving the world he has quitted a second chance for the real-life audience, who, by Greene's use of contemporary allusions to the age of Elizabeth and James VI, are also part of the play's world. As the action progresses, we see that, in this second-time-round, Virtue triumphs and the end is happy, with Nano, Bohan's representative, taking part in the finale of reconciliation and feasting. However, while the aims of Greene are clearly signposted in his use of the framework, again the execution of the idea is sadly lacking in coherence. There is no build-up to the climax where Bohan is lulled to sleep in his tomb, and the inter-act choruses go for little more than, as Hamlet puts it, 'inexplicable dumb shows and noise'.[1]

Yet despite all the limitations of Greene's play—the ideas he uses

---

[1] For interesting comment on the uniqueness of Greene's manipulation of time in the light of other literary treatments see C. Leech, 'The Shaping of Time: *Nostromo* and *Under the Volcano*', *Imagined Worlds*, ed. M. Mack and I. Gregor (1968), pp. 324–5.

so wastefully, the underdevelopment of situations and themes, and the frequent crudities of execution—there is a certain unity of tone which derives from what perhaps can be called the literary personality of the author. The sharp contrast between public and private life with their distinctive qualities comes over well, the stress falling naturally for Greene on the virtues of country rhythm and natural harmony; and there is the warning of the necessity for proper social and personal order. Certainly, there is no great profundity in the articulation of this vision, such as is found in later tragi-comedies or in Shakespeare's final romances, to all of which *James the Fourth* is a forerunner; but there is a spirit of generosity, an acceptance of traditional values, the awareness of evil combined with a belief that it is good which ultimately triumphs, and a general movement away from misanthropy and towards celebration and peace. The play's flavour comes from that mixture of the sweet and the sour, so characteristic of Greene, such as one finds in the lyric:

> Weep not wanton, smile vpon my knee;
> When thou art olde, ther's grief inough for thee;[1]

one part of which is the wistful perception of a possible peace and content amid the evil and general sordidness of life, which Greene himself could find only in the best of his writings.

With the knowledge of Greene's popularity as a dramatist in mind, one can readily accept the assertion of the title-page of the 1598 Quarto that *James the Fourth* was 'sundrie times publikely plaide' in sixteenth-century London. And while there is no concrete evidence as to which company performed the play originally, it has been suggested that it was the property of the Queen's Men and that it may have been performed at court.[2] I have been unable to find any record of subsequent performance until 1959, when the Drama Department of the University of Bristol, under the direction of Professor Glynne Wickham, staged the play in the open air during the months of July and August at Dartington Hall, Totnes, Devon, at Goldney House, Bristol, at Cirencester Park, and in the

---

[1] *Menaphon*, VI, 43.   [2] See p. xxix above.

Shakespeare Memorial Theatre Gardens at Stratford-upon-Avon.

The director rearranged the sections of the text concerning Oberon and Bohan to give a much firmer framework to the inset story in the manner of Andrea's Ghost and Revenge in *The Spanish Tragedy*; and also omitted the dumb show of Cyrus (Chorus VII of the present edition), replacing it with the scripted masque from Dekker's *Old Fortunatus*. The performance was well received and provided the undergraduate actors with some rich comic opportunities, and some scope for romantic playing. The garden settings offered the chance for some spectacular effects, including a game of golf in its original form, a scene on horseback, and a serenade from a barge.[1]

5. THE TEXT

The Quarto of 1598

The earliest extant edition of *James the Fourth* was published in quarto in 1598 by Thomas Creede. The printer had entered the title in the Stationers' Register, along with *The Famous Victories of Henry the Fifth*, on 14 May 1594, under the authority of Warden Cawood. The entry concerning it reads:[2]

> Thomas Creede Entred vnto him by the like warrant a booke intituled *the Scottishe story of JAMES the FFOURTHE slayne at Fflodden intermixed with a plesant Comedie* presented by OBORON kinge of ffayres.   vj^d

From this one might assume that there was an earlier edition of the play now lost. However, the fact that the earliest known edition of *The Famous Victories* is also dated 1598 suggests that the publication of both plays was delayed for some reason.

The Quarto comprises forty unnumbered leaves, collating A–K^4, of which A1 was presumably blank and A2^r is the title-page which reads:

> THE / SCOTTISH / Historie of Iames the / fourth, slaine at *Flodden*. / Entermixed with a pleasant Comedie, presented by / *Oboram* King of *Fayeries:* / *As it hath bene sundrie times publikely* /

---

[1] The information on which this paragraph is based was generously supplied to me by Professor Wickham.
[2] Arber, II, 648.

plaide. / Written by *Robert Greene*, Maister of Arts. / *Omne tulit punctum.* / [Device: McKerrow 299] / LONDON / Printed by Thomas Creede. 1598.

The text, which is divided into five acts with an Induction and interact 'choruses', begins on A3^r following the head-title 'THE SCOTTISH / Hystorie of Iames the / fourth, slaine at *Flodden.*' and ends on K4^r; and each opening has the running title 'The Scottish Historie / of Iames the fourth.' There are four extant copies of the Quarto located in the British Museum, the Victoria and Albert Museum, the Huntington, and the Folger Libraries respectively.[1]

Creede printed a large number of plays during the period, including two others by Greene: *A Looking Glass for London and England* in 1594, 1598, and 1602, and *Alphonsus King of Aragon* in 1599; and his output of plays has been subjected to detailed bibliographical scrutiny by George W. Williams,[2] whose study of the printing practices and the compositors of Creede's shop has been the starting-point for the present textual analysis.

The 1598 Quarto was set by two compositors with fairly distinct habits of spelling and type-setting.[3] Compositor A, who was almost certainly the more experienced workman, set sheets A, B, C, signature D1^r, and signatures H1^r-2^v; Compositor B, who may have

---

[1] The British Museum copy (c.34.g.20) has a facsimile leaf A4 which is full of errors; the copy in the Victoria and Albert Museum (4247.18.k.17), which was Dyce's copy, has an inaccurate facsimile corner of leaf H1 and sheet K wrongly imposed; the Huntington copy (61133) was formerly at Bridgewater House; and the Folger copy (12308) was once part of the Huth Collection.

[2] 'The Good Quarto of *Romeo and Juliet*', a Ph.D. dissertation presented at the University of Virginia in 1957.

[3] The main distinguishing features are: Compositor A sets proper names in roman type within italic stage directions; and when the catchword is keyed to the beginning of a new speech, he sets only the speech prefix; his preferred spellings are *here, bene, coin,* adverbs ending in *-ly,* the single *-e* form of words like *me, ye, we, he, she, be*; and French sections of the text occurring in his stint are set in roman type; Compositor B makes no typographical differentiation in stage directions; he sets as a catchword keyed to a new speech both the speech prefix and the first word of the line; and his spelling preferences are *heere, beene, quoine,* adverbs ending in *-lie, -our* rather than *-or* forms in words such as *favour*; and he regularly varies the single *-e* with the double *-ee* form, preferring the latter; he sets the French-language sections of his stints in italic type.

been an apprentice, set signatures D1^v–4^v, sheets E, F, G, signatures H3^r–4^v, and sheets I and K. However, it should be noted that, while such appears to have been the main division of the work, some of the evidence seems to indicate that there was some collaboration between the two men in the composition of the signatures A4^r, G4^r, H1^r, I4^r, I4^v, K1^r, and K4^v. Twelve running titles were employed in the printing and were imposed in no perceptible pattern, and certainly quite differently from other systems used in Creede's shop previous to the printing of this play.[1] This fact, taken together with the compositorial stints and the quality of the type-setting in them, may indicate, first, that the stints of the two men were not done simultaneously, and second, that the composition may have been related to the methods used in the instructing of an apprentice. A collation of the four extant copies of the Quarto shows little evidence of any regular or extensive proof-correction as the formes were going through the press. Only thirty-one press variants were noted, most of these being on the inner forme of sheet D and all being concerned with minor details of spelling and punctuation. In an uncorrected state of sheet K in the Victoria and Albert Museum copy the pages run K1^r, K3^v, K2^r, K4^v, K3^r, K1^v, K4^r, K2^v. This mix-up is the result of an incorrect imposing of the verso pages, which were exchanged diagonally in both the inner and outer formes, and may be additional pointers to the inexperience of Compositor B who set these pages.

The play as a whole is badly printed and littered with errors of every kind: misreadings, wrong spellings, mispunctuation, turned letters, mis-spacing, and some wild attempts to make sense of the French-language sections of the text. It is noticeable too that it is Compositor B who is the more prone to such errors, as he makes about twice as many mechanical mistakes as his fellow in a stretch of text of comparable length. However, even when allowance is made for the possibility that the bulk of the text is the result of inexpert setting, it is clear that both men were composing from copy which was almost certainly written in a difficult hand and also bore most of the signs of being an author's holograph rather than either a fair copy made for the printing house or a manuscript prepared

---

[1] See Williams, *op. cit.*, pp. 34–5.

for theatrical use. Indeed, it is reasonably certain that the copy for the Quarto was Greene's 'foul papers'[1] which were, according to Henry Chettle's testimony in *Kind-Hart's Dream* (1592), often ill written owing to the author's hand being none of the best.[2] The manuscript may well have been one of the 'many papers in sundry Booke sellers hands', which, again according to Chettle, Greene left at his death.[3]

The evidence pointing to this conclusion is of several kinds. Many of the stage directions are of a literary rather than a theatrical nature: for example, that at Induction, 0.1–4: '*Music playing within. Enter after* OBERON, *King of Fairies, an* Antic, *who dance about a tomb placed conveniently on the stage; out of the which suddenly starts up, as they dance,* BOHAN, *a Scot, attired like a Redesdale man, from whom the Antic flies.*' Others contain indications of personal appearance or attitude (e.g., I. i. 0.2–3: '... *and* ATEUKIN *with them aloof*'), of relationship (e.g., II. i. 0.1: '... *the* COUNTESS OF ARRAN *with* IDA *her daughter*'; I. i. 0.1–2: '*the* KING OF SCOTS, DOROTHEA *his Queen*'), of title rather than name (e.g., I. i. 154.1: '*Exeunt all saving the King and Ateukin*'; V. i. 0.1: '*Enter the Queen in a night-gown*'), of manner (e.g., II. ii. 3.1: '*They are all in a muse*'), of disguise (e.g., IV. iv. 0.1: '*Enter* NANO, DOROTHEA, *in man's apparel*'), of location (e.g., II. i. 0.1–2: '... *the* COUNTESS OF ARRAN *with* IDA *her daughter in their porch*'), of superfluous qualifications (e.g., II. i. 71.1: '... *with* SLIPPER, *the Clown*'; I. ii. 0.1–2: '... *with their bills, ready written, in their hands*'), and of alternative actions (e.g., V. vi. 57.2: '... *He makes pots, and sports, and scorns*'). More significantly, a number of stage directions are palpably authorial in their permissiveness and unspecific phrasing: for example, Induction, 94.1: '*The two dance a jig devised for the nonce*'; Chorus I. 0.1–2: '*Enter* BOHAN *and* OBERON, *the fairy king, after the first act; to them a round of* Fairies, *or some pretty dance*'; Chorus II. 13.1–2: '*Enter*

---

[1] In view of the evidence here presented, Collins's opinion that 'the text ... has evidently been printed ... from a stage copy' (II, 79), and Dickinson's view that 'the text shows indications that the play was either published from a stage copy or that type was set up by dictation' (p. 304) may both be discounted.
[2] H. Chettle, *Kind-Hart's Dream* (1592), ed. G. B. Harrison (1923), p. 5.
[3] *Ibid.*, p. 6.

SLIPPER *with a companion, boy or wench, dancing a hornpipe, and dance out again*'; IV. i. 0.1–2: '*After a noise of horns and shoutings, enter certain* Huntsmen, *if you please, singing, one way*'; Chorus IV. 12.1: '*Enter a round or some dance at pleasure*'; V. ii. 0.1–3: '*After a solemn service, enter from the Countess of Arran's house a service, musical songs of marriage, or a masque, or what pretty triumph you list*'. The entry direction for v. iii calls for the appearance of a 'ghost character' Samles in the train of the King of England, although he neither speaks nor is referred to during the scene, or indeed the whole play. At II. ii. 151.1 and III. ii. 49.1, Ateukin's entry is signalled by his Terentian type-name with '*Enter Gnatho*', and at v. ii. 0.3 the type-name is confused with the character-name: '... *to them Ateukin and Gnatho*'.

The forms of the speech prefixes show a variety which would be inconvenient if not unpractical in the theatre. Not only is there variation in the designation of all of the main characters (e.g., *Dorothea.* / *Doro.* / *Dor.* / *Do.*; *Ateu.* / *Ate.* / *At.*; *Oberon.* / *Ober.* / *Obir.*), but also differences in actual words, with Nano being denoted as *Nano.* / *Na.* / *N.* and as *Dwarf.* / *Dwar.* In addition, the King of England is inexplicably given the speech prefix *Arius.* / *Ari.* during his appearance in v. iii, and the King of Scots is identified by the same name in the stage direction at II. ii. 107.2. On one occasion, at I. ii. 36.2, Ateukin's name in the entry direction is made to serve also as the speech prefix; and there are omitted or erroneous speech prefixes in many scenes (e.g., at I. i. 184; I. ii. 8–9; I. iii. 62, 72; II. i. 75, 149, 163).

Within the text there are some abbreviations which would appear to have originated with the author as he composed rather than in the printing house. *S.* is used to indicate *Saint* at II. ii. 0.1 and *Sir* at IV. iv. 59.1; *Q.* is used for *Queen* at I. i. 31; *Ateukin* is abbreviated to *Ateu.* in two verse lines (I. i. 236, 277); *Aristotle* appears as *Arist.* at II. i. 180; and *Master* is abbreviated to *M.* at v. vi. 41. One abbreviation calls for the actor who is playing the part of Sir Bartram to improvise some words as he leaves the stage at the end of I. iii: 'Be Gad, she's blithe, fair, lewely, bonny, etc.'

There are some indications that the printer's copy, besides being crabbed, was also wrongly arranged at certain points. Under the heading '*After the first act*' and immediately following Chorus I. 15, there occur three choruses with dumb shows in them (printed in this edition at the end of the play and there called 'Additional Choruses'[1]) together with the fourteen lines which make up Chorus v of the present text.[2] It is quite clear that the lines of Chorus v were intended to end the play, and, further, that the three other choruses and dumb shows were written to be used after certain scenes of the play and not grouped together as they are in the Quarto. This confusion may have been due to some of the pages of the manuscript being misplaced before the compositors received it, or possibly due to the change of compositors at the point where these choruses and dumb shows occur in the Quarto (on signatures C4^v, D1^r, and D1^v). There is also the possibility that the confusion created by the misplacing of lines 30–45 of v. v in the Quarto may have been the result of a similar disordering of the manuscript, but it is more likely to be of printing-house origin, as the two compositors were probably working together on the pages concerned (signatures I4^r and I4^v).[3]

Modern Editions

There have been eight editions of the play published since 1598. The first was Alexander Dyce's in *The Dramatic Works of Robert Greene* (1831), which was later revised and included in *The Dramatic and Poetical Works of Robert Greene and George Peele* (1861). These were both modern-spelling texts based on a single copy of the Quarto now located in the Victoria and Albert Museum. The notes record most of the emendations made, which in general show Dyce's usually sound judgement. Alexander Grosart's old-spelling edition, included in his *Life and Complete Works of Robert Greene* (1881–6), was based on the Huth copy (now in the Folger Library) and contains some original emendations; in the main, however, Grosart follows Dyce's edition closely. J. M. Manly's old-spelling text in *Specimens of Pre-Shakespearean Drama* (Boston, 1897) was prepared from a handwritten copy of the British Museum's copy of the Quarto. It collates Dyce's and Grosart's

---

[1] See note on the 'Additional Choruses'.
[2] See note on Chorus v.   [3] See note on v. v. 30–59.

editions and introduces some emendations superior to theirs. For his old-spelling edition in *The Plays and Poems of Robert Greene* (1905), J. Churton Collins used handwritten copies of the British Museum and Victoria and Albert Museum exemplars as well as Dyce's and Grosart's works; and he provides the fullest commentary on the play up to this date. It should be noted that a number of emendations made by Grosart, Collins, and Manly are the result of their correcting or querying what were certainly scribal errors made by their copyists. T. H. Dickinson produced a modern-spelling text for inclusion in his *Robert Greene* for the Mermaid Series in 1909, largely based on the two London copies but also using Dyce's, Grosart's, and Collins's editions. Ashley Thorndike's edition of the play in the second volume of the Everyman Library's *Minor Elizabethan Drama* (1910) is heavily based on Dyce's edition. The two most recent editions of the play are that by A. E. H. Swaen, whose type-facsimile of the Quarto, based on the London copies, was prepared for the Malone Society in 1921, and that by J. A. Lavin for the New Mermaids Series (1967), which is a modern-spelling edition based on a collation of the four extant copies of the Quarto, and contains several new emendations and a fairly full commentary.

This Edition
This edition is based on the Folger Library's copy of the 1598 Quarto, which has been collated with the three other extant copies. The spelling is modernized in accordance with the general principles of the series, the Quarto's orthography being retained only where a rhyme is involved. As Greene in certain parts of the play used Scottish words or Scottish forms in the dialogue of some of the characters, the Quarto spellings have been allowed to stand wherever it is possible that Scottish pronunciation is being indicated. Those passages in bad sixteenth-century French in the Quarto have been corrected and put into modern French, with the Quarto's versions being recorded in the collations wherever more than simple modernization has been necessary to make sense of the original. Second person singular endings in -*est* have been elided where the metre seems to demand it (except with verbs ending in

-*e*), and past tense and past participles in -*ed* have been spelled thus, with a grave accent used to indicate where they seem to be syllabic.

Punctuation of this text is modern, although occasionally the Quarto's pointing has been retained where some special rhetorical effect appears to be aimed at and where no modern equivalent is appropriate.

The collations record all substantive departures from the Quarto and also substantive press variants between the four copies of it. Emendations made in previous modern editions, which have been adopted in this text, are signalled by the name of the first editor to propose them; unadopted but tenable readings and conjectures are also listed. The word 'so' before an editor's name indicates a rearrangement of the text first found in his edition. All quotations from the texts of previous editors are given in modern spelling, as the old-spelling texts of Grosart, Manly, and Collins contain inaccuracies due to some careless transcription.

The Quarto is divided into acts and choruses and these have been retained in this edition, with scene-divisions provided and placed in square brackets at the left-hand side of the page. Additions made to the Quarto's stage directions are placed in square brackets, and all changes made are recorded in the collations, except where they are expansions or additions in entry or exit directions where no confusion is possible.

Because of the bad state of the text and the evidence pointing to a difficult manuscript underlying it, the present editor has felt some degree of freedom in making emendations which clarify the meaning of the original: however, all have been defended in the notes on bibliographical or literary grounds. The major changes made are the moving of the choruses and dumb shows, which appear after the first act in the Quarto, to the end of the play where they are called 'Additional Choruses'; and the use of thirteen lines from the third of these as the final chorus of the play. The arguments for the latter change have been considered sufficiently strong to support the rearrangement and are given in the note on the text at that point. Likely points of insertion for the 'Additional Choruses' are given in the notes on them, but the arguments for these locations have been considered too speculative to warrant their being adopted. Two passages in v. v have been transposed to make sense of the Quarto's text and the literary and bibliographical reasons for the change have been set out at that point in the notes on the text.

All the glosses given in the notes have the support of *O.E.D.*, reference to which is given only where the meaning is unusual or where a quibble, pun, or new emendation is involved. All proverbs are identified by reference to Tilley, with the proverb being quoted only where Greene departs drastically from what according to Tilley was the usual sixteenth-century wording or where the saying is developed in the euphuistic fashion over several lines. Certain non-agreements of subject and verb were common in Elizabethan grammar; the various kinds are noted in the commentary on their first occurrence with the appropriate reference to Abbott and thereafter are ignored.

In his study of the stage Scotsman, J. O. Bartley[1] has demonstrated that the Scottish words, forms, and phrases which Greene uses in the speeches of some characters are generally accurate representations of the Scottish dialect and pronunciation. Bohan's speech in the Induction is heavily marked with dialect forms and words, but in his appearances thereafter Greene is content merely to tinge his lines with one or two Scottish forms. None of the other characters is consistently nationalized, though the speeches of some (e.g., Sir Bartram in I. iii) contain a few Scotticisms. In the notes of this edition the English equivalents of Scottish words and Scotticisms are given, and are signalled by the abbreviation 'Scot.'.

The speeches of Jaques are a mixture of English, French, and Italian words spelled in a way which indicates a Frenchified or Italianized pronunciation. English translations of the less elementary passages of French, and English equivalents of 'foreignized' words, are given in the notes to the text where they occur.

[1] *Teague, Shenkin and Sawney* (Cork, 1954), p. 85.

THE SCOTTISH HISTORY OF
JAMES THE FOURTH

THE SCOTTISH

Historie of Iames the fourth, slaine at Flodden.

Entermixed with a pleasant Comedie, presented by *Oboram* King of *Fayeries*:

As it hath bene sundrie times publikely plaide.

Written by *Robert Greene*, Maister of Arts.

Omne tulit punctum.

LONDON
Printed by Thomas Creede. 1598.

[DRAMATIS PERSONAE

OBERON, *King of the Fairies.*
BOHAN, *a misanthropic Scot.*
SLIPPER, *a Clown, Ateukin's servant,* ⎫ *Bohan's sons.*
NANO, *a Dwarf, Dorothea's servant,* ⎭
KING OF SCOTS.   5
ATEUKIN.
SIR BARTRAM, ⎫
DOUGLAS,
MORTON,
ROSS,   } *Scottish Lords.*   10
SIR CUTHBERT ANDERSON,
BISHOP OF ST ANDREWS, ⎭
ANDREW SNOORD, *Ateukin's servant.*
Purveyor *to the King of Scots.*
A Scout *of the Scottish Army.*   15
JAQUES, *a French Captain.*
KING OF ENGLAND, *Dorothea's father.*
EUSTACE, ⎫
PERCY,   } *English Lords.*
SAMLES, ⎭   20
Herald *of the English Army.*
A Tailor.
A Shoemaker.
A Cutler.
A Lawyer.   25
A Merchant.
A Divine.
DOROTHEA, *Queen of Scots.*
COUNTESS OF ARRAN.
IDA, *her daughter.*   30
LADY ANDERSON, *wife of Sir Cuthbert Anderson.*
Antics, Fairies, Lords, Ladies, Huntsmen, Revellers, Soldiers, and Servants.

SCENE: *Scotland.*]

Dramatis Personae] *first provided by Dyce; not in Q.*

The Scottish History of James the Fourth, slain at Flodden

[Induction]

Music playing within. Enter after OBERON, *King of Fairies, an Antic, who dance about a tomb placed conveniently on the stage; out of the which suddenly starts up, as they dance,* BOHAN, *a Scot, attired like a Redesdale man, from whom the Antic flies. Oberon manet.*

Boh. Ay say, what's thou?
Ober. Thy friend, Bohan.

0.1. *after*] *Manly;* Aster *Q.* *an*] *Q; and Dyce.* 0.1, 4. Antic] *Dickinson; Antique Q.;* Antics *Dyce;* Antiques *Grosart.* 0.4. *Redesdale*] *conj. Renwick; rid-stall Q;* Riddesdale *conj. Dyce¹; byrstall conj. Deighton; raskall conj. Bradley.* *flies*] *Q; fly Dyce.* 1. Ay] *Q;* Ah *Dickinson.*

Title] Q identifies James IV as the Scottish king slain at the battle of Flodden in 1513; but there is nothing in the play to support the connection between the hero, whose story according to Bohan at l. 106 takes place in 1520, and the historical figure. For possible relationships between the play and historical events, see Introduction, pp. xxxiii–xxxv.

0.1. *after*] Q's reading 'Aster' was probably due to a foul-case confusion between *f* and long *s*.

Oberon, King of Fairies] This is the commonest form of the name in Q, although it is spelt 'Oboram', 'Obiron', and 'Obiran' also. His size is that of a small man; see Chor. I. I.

an *Antic*] This was a technical term applied to the burlesque dance of an anti-masque; but here appears to indicate merely a group of dancers attired in grotesque costumes.

0.2. a tomb ... stage] As this tomb is not used elsewhere in the play (except possibly as Cyrus's tomb in Chorus VII) it would seem probable that 'conveniently' means away from the main acting area, perhaps to one side of the stage, as it would clearly be a nuisance to have it at the centre of the stage throughout the play. Glynne Wickham (*Early English Stages 1300–1660* (1959), II. i. 318) suggests that the Antics carried the tomb on to the stage with them from the tiring house, and that it may have been constructed, like the tomb in Farrington's Lord Mayor's Show of 1616, in the style of an arbour with a gallery or balustraded upper story to which

INDUCTION]   JAMES THE FOURTH   5

Boh. What wot I or reck I that? Whay, guid man, I reck no
   friend, nor ay reck no foe; al's ene to me. Git thee ganging,
   and trouble not may whayet, or ay's gar thee reckon me   5
   nene of thay friend, by the mary mass sall I.
Ober. Why, angry Scot, I visit thee for love. Then what moves
   thee to wrath?

Oberon and Bohan retire at ll. 110–14. However, the wording of the stage
direction suggests the presence of the tomb on the stage before Oberon and
the Antic enter; and further, the gallery to which Oberon and Bohan retire
would appear to have been separate from the tomb and is called elsewhere
'our harbour' (Chor. I. 14) and 'our cell' (Chor. II. 16). See also note to l. 110
below. Tombs were frequently demanded as stage properties, and Philip
Henslowe bought two for use by the Admiral's Men in 1598 (W. W. Greg,
ed., *Henslowe Papers* (1908), p. 116).

0.4. Redesdale man] W. L. Renwick (*M.L.R.*, XXIX (1934), 434) first suggested this emendation, noting that to a London audience of 1590 it would mean 'a Border reiver, one who belonged to the wild and lonely No-man's land on the edges of Scotland'. Renwick found later support from H. G. Wright (*M.L.R.*, XXX (1935), 347), who quoted William Bullein's *Dialogue both pleasaunt and pietifull . . . against the Feuer Pestilence* (1564–78), and also from J. C. Maxwell (*M.L.R.*, XLIV (1949), 88), who quoted from Thomas Wilson's *Arte of Rhetorique* (1585): 'his soyle (where he was borne) giueth him to bee an euill man: considering he was bredde and brought vp among a denne of Theeues, among the men of Tinsdale and Riddesdale, where pillage is good purchase, and murthering is coumpted manhood.' Thus Bohan would look wild and ferocious.

1. *Ay*] I. Greene is inconsistent in his use of the Scotticism 'ay' in Bohan's lines.
3. *wot*] know.
reck] care for.
Whay] why (Scot.).
guid] good (Scot.).
4. *al's ene*] all's one (Scot.).
Git thee ganging] be on your way (Scot.).
5. *may whayet*] my quiet. The pronunciation of 'wh' for 'qu' is Northern rather than Scottish.
ay's gar] I'll make (Scot.).
reckon] count (Scot.).
6. *nene*] none (Scot.).
thay] thy (Scot.).
mary mass] a mass in honour of the Virgin Mary. J. O. Bartley (*Teague, Shenkin and Sawney* (Cork, 1954), p. 82) suggests that this common Elizabethan oath was thought to be characteristic of Scottish speech in some plays of the period.
sall] shall (Scot.).

Boh. The deel a whit reck I thy love. For I know too well that
true love took her flight twenty winter sence to heaven, 10
whither till ay can, weel I wot, ay sall ne'er find love. An
thou lovest me, leave me to myself. But what were those
puppits that hopped and skipped about me year whayle?
Ober. My subjects.
Boh. Thay subjects! Whay, art thou a king? 15
Ober. I am.
Boh. The deel thou art! Whay, thou lookest not so big as the
King of Clubs, nor so sharp as the King of Spades, nor so
fain as the King a Daymonds; be the mass, ay take thee to
be the King of false Hearts. Therefore, I rid thee away, 20
or ay's so curry your kingdom that you's be glad to run to
save your life.
Ober. Why, stoical Scot, do what thou darest to me: here is my
breast, strike.

11. love.] loue: *Q corr.* (*BM, HN, VA*); loues *Q uncorr.* (*FO*).   19. a
Daymonds] *Manly;* Adaymonds *Q;* o' Daymonds *Dyce.*

---

9. *deel*] devil (Scot.).
a whit] a jot (Scot.).
10. *true . . . heaven*] Cf. Shakespeare's *Ven.*, 793–4: 'Call it not love,
for Love to heaven is fled, / Since sweating lust on earth usurp'd his name.'
The significance of 'twenty winter' is not clear, unless it means merely 'a
long time' as at l. 69.
sence] since (Scot.).
11. *ay can*] I can come (Scot.).
weel I wot] well I know (Scot.).
An] if.
13. *puppits*] a contemptuous term applied to a person (*O.E.D.*, 1); but
Bohan may be including the meaning 'an actor in a show' (*O.E.D.*, 3c) or
may be referring to the jerkiness of the fairies' movements in comparison
with his sons' jig.
year whayle] erewhile (Scot.).
19. *fain*] glad, well-disposed.
a Daymonds] of Diamonds (Scot.).
be the mass] See note to l. 6.   *be* = by.
20. *I rid*] I advise (Scot.).
21. *ay's*] I will (Scot.).
curry] beat, thrash.
you's] you will (Scot.).
23. *stoical*] austere.

Boh. Thou wilt not threap me; this whinyard has garred many 25
better men to lope than thou. [*Tries to draw his sword.*]
But how now? Gos sayds, what, will't not out? Whay,
thou witch, thou deel! Gad's fute, may whinyard!
Ober. Why, pull, man; but what an 'twere out, how then?
Boh. This, then: thou wert best be gone first; for ay'll so lop 30
thy limbs that thou's go with half a knave's carcass to the
deel.
Ober. Draw it out. [*Bohan draws his sword.*] Now strike, fool,
canst thou not?
Boh. Bread ay Gad, what deel is in me? Whay, tell me, thou 35
skipjack, what art thou?
Ober. Nay, first tell me what thou wast from thy birth, what
thou hast passed hitherto, why thou dwellest in a tomb
and leavest the world; and then I will release thee of these
bonds; before, not. 40
Boh. And not before? Then needs must, needs sall. I was
born a gentleman of the best bloud in all Scotland, except
the king. When time brought me to age and death took my

26. *Tries...sword.*] *Dyce; not in* Q.   33. *Bohan...sword.*] *Lavin; not in* Q.

---

25. *threap*] brave, outface (Scot.).
whinyard] a short sword which is often referred to as a typical Scottish weapon. J. O. Bartley, *op. cit.*, lists examples in *Club Law* (1595), v. ii, and *King Edward III* (1595), sig. B2.
garred] forced, compelled (Scot.).
26. *lope*] provincial form of 'leap'; or perhaps 'run'.
27. *Gos sayds*] Scottish euphemism for '(by) God's sides'.
28. *witch*] wizard, magician.
Gad's fute] Scottish euphemism for '(by) God's foot'.
31. *thou's*] thou wilt (Scot.).
32, 35. *deel*] See note to l. 9.
35. *Bread ay Gad*] (by) the bread of God; this was considered to be a typical Scottish oath. J. O. Bartley, *op. cit.*, lists examples in *Vowbreaker*, II. i, *Thierry and Theodoret*, v. i, and *Scots Figgaries*, I.
36. *skipjack*] whipper-snapper.
38. *passed*] endured.
39. *leavest*] abandonest.
41. *Then ... sall*] a variant of the proverb 'He must needs go that the devil drives' (Tilley D278).
42. *bloud*] blood (Scot.).
43. *time ... age*] I came of age.

parents, I became a courtier; where, though ay list not praise myself, ay engraved the memory of Bohan on the skin-coat of some of them, and revelled with the proudest.

Ober. But why, living in such reputation, didst thou leave to be a courtier?

Boh. Because my pride was vanity, my expense loss, my reward fair words and large promises, and my hopes spilt, for that after many years' service one outran me; and what the deel should I then do there? No, no; flattering knaves that can cog and prate fastest speed best in the court.

Ober. To what life didst thou then betake thee?

Boh. I then changed the court for the country, and the wars for a wife; but I found the craft of swains more vile than the knavery of courtiers, the charge of children more heavy than servants, and wives' tongues worse than the wars itself; and therefore I gave o'er that, and went to the city to dwell, and there I kept a great house with small cheer; but all was ne'er the near.

Ober. And why?

---

44. *ay list*] I desire.
45. *Bohan*] Q's spelling '*Boughon*' may be an attempt to convey Bohan's own pronunciation of the name.
46. *skin-coat*] skin, flesh.
47. *in such reputation*] so highly esteemed.
leave] cease.
49–54.] These attacks on life at court were commonplaces of the period; cf. *R3*, I. iii. 47–8: 'I cannot flatter and look fair, / Smile in men's faces, smooth, deceive and cog'; also Chapman's *Bussy D'Ambois* (ed. N. Brooke, 1964), I. i. 86–103.
51. *outran me*] got ahead of me (without merit).
53. *cog*] fawn, wheedle.
prate] talk idly.
speed] prosper.
57. *craft*] The pun is on the meanings 'skill' and 'deceit'.
swains] countrymen.
58. *charge*] expense.
60. *wars itself*] 'wars' is thought of here as a single activity and is treated thus grammatically.
61–2. *small cheer*] limited fare provided for entertainment.
62. *ne'er the near*] never the nearer (to my goal); a proverb (Tilley E27).

INDUCTION]   JAMES THE FOURTH   9

Boh. Because, in seeking friends, I found table-guests to eat
me and my meat, my wife's gossips to bewray the secrets   65
of my heart, kindred to betray the effect of my life; which
when I noted—the court ill, the country worse, and the
city worst of all—in good time my wife died—ay would
she had died twenty winter sooner, by the mass—leaving
my two sons to the world and shutting myself into this   70
tomb, where if I die, I am sure I am safe from wild beasts;
but whilst I live, cannot be free from ill company. Besides,
now I am sure, gif all my friends fail me, I sall have a
grave of mine own providing. This is all. Now, what art
thou?   75
Ober. Oberon, King of Fairies, that loves thee because thou
hatest the world; and to gratulate thee, I brought those
Antics to show thee some sport in dancing, which thou
hast loved well.
Boh. Ha, ha, ha! Thinkest thou those puppits can please me? 80
Whay, I have two sons that with one Scottish jig shall
break the neck of thy Antics.

70. and shutting] *Q;* I shut *Manly.*   77. those] *Q;* these *Dyce.*   82. neck] *Q;* necks *Collins.*

---

65. *gossips*] Technically these were women friends who assisted during a birth and acted as baptismal sponsors, but the word was often used to mean simply 'female cronies'.
bewray] betray, divulge.
66. *betray the effect*] destroy the efficacy.
68. *in good time*] opportunely.
70. *and shutting*] Dyce is perhaps correct in suggesting that some words are missing here. However, this kind of loose construction is typical of Greene in his prose works.
72. *cannot*] i.e., I cannot.
72–4. *Besides . . . providing*] Cf. Shakespeare's *Ado,* v. ii. 67–9: 'if a man do not erect in this age his own tomb ere he dies, he shall live no longer in monument than the bell rings and the widow weeps.'
73. *gif*] if (Scot.).
77. *gratulate*] please, gratify.
78, 82. *Antics*] See note to l. 0.1.
80. *puppits*] See note to l. 13.
82. *break the neck of*] destroy the effect of. This use antedates the first citation in *O.E.D.,* sb.[1] 5b.

Ober. That would I fain see.
Boh. Why, thou shalt. Ho, boys!

Enter SLIPPER *and* NANO.

Haud your clacks, lads; trattle not for thy life, but gather 85
up your legs and dance me forthwith a jig worth the sight.
Slip. Why, I must talk, an I die for 't; wherefore was my
tongue made?
Boh. Prattle, an thou darest, ene word more, and ay's dab this
whinyard in thy wemb. 90
Ober. Be quiet, Bohan. I'll strike him dumb, and his brother
too; their talk shall not hinder our jig. Fall to it; dance, I
say, man.
Boh. Dance, hummer, dance, ay rid thee.

The two dance a jig devised for the nonce.
Now get you to the wide world with more than my father 95

84. Ho] *Manly;* howe *Q.*   87. an I die for 't] *Dyce;* on Idy fort *Q.*
94. hummer] *This ed.;* Humer *Q.*   94.1. nonce] *Dyce;* nonst *Q.*

---

84. *Ho*] The Q spelling 'howe' was a common form of the exclamation.
84.1. *Slipper*] a type-name for a shifty or deceitful character; cf. *Oth.*,
II. i. 235–6: 'A slipper and subtle knave; a finder-out of occasion.'
Nano] from the Latin 'nanus' meaning 'dwarf'.
85. *Haud*] hold (Scot.).
clacks] a contemptuous term for 'tongues'.
trattle] chatter (Scot.).
for thy life] for (fear of) thy life.
89. *ene*] one (Scot.).
ay's dab] I'll thrust (Scot.).
90. *whinyard*] See note to l. 25.
wemb] sixteenth-century Scottish form of the word 'wame' (belly, abdomen).
91–2. *I'll . . . too*] Greene uses the same device in *Friar Bacon*, II. iii, where Bacon strikes Bungay dumb to prevent his marrying Lacy and Margaret.
94. *hummer*] a colloquial term for 'bouncer, thumper, one characterized by extreme activity'. This use antedates the first citation in *O.E.D.*, sb.[1] 3.
rid] See note to l. 20.
94.1. *jig*] This was a dance much used in the Elizabethan theatres, often after the performance of a play; see E. K. Chambers, *The Elizabethan Stage* (1923), I, 304: also C. R. Baskervill, *The Elizabethan Jig* (1929).
devised for the nonce] created for the occasion.

gave me: that's learning enough, both kinds—knavery
and honesty; and that I gave you, spend at pleasure.

Ober. Nay, for their sport I will give them this gift: to the
dwarf I give a quick wit, pretty of body, and awarrant his
preferment to a prince's service, where by his wisdom he 100
shall gain more love than common. And to loggerhead
your son I give a wandering life, and promise he shall
never lack; and avow that if in all distresses he call upon
me, to help him. Now let them go.

Exeunt [SLIPPER *and* NANO] *with curtsies.*

Boh. Now, king, if thou be a king, I will show thee whay I hate 105
the world by demonstration. In the year 1520 was in Scotland a king, overruled with parasites, misled by lust, and
many circumstances too long to trattle on now, much like
our court of Scotland this day. That story have I set
down. Gang with me to the gallery, and I'll show thee the 110

---

99. pretty] *Q;* prettiness *Grosart.*   awarrant] *Q;* a warrant *Manly.*
103. that] *Q; omitted Dyce.*

---

97. *that*] that which.
99. *pretty*] Previous editors postulate either an omitted substantive or an error for 'prettiness'. 'Pretty' as a substantive is not recorded in *O.E.D.*
awarrant] vouch for, guarantee.
101. *than common*] than is usual.
loggerhead] blockhead.
103–4. *that . . . help*] This kind of construction does occur in Greene's prose works and so may be allowed to stand here.
104.1 *curtsies*] usually applied to a feminine bow; but here the meaning is probably 'bows' ('courtesy', *O.E.D., sb.* 8).
106–7. *In the year . . . lust*] See note to the head-title.
108–9. *much . . . day*] See Introduction, pp. xxxiii–xxxv, for possible relationships between the play and contemporary events.
110. *Gang*] go, walk (Scot.).
gallery] That there was a gallery in most Elizabethan theatres is certain from contemporary pictorial evidence such as De Witt's drawing of the Swan Theatre and the illustrations on the title-pages of *Roxana* (1632) and F. Kirkman's *The Wits* (1672), and from the stage directions in dramatic texts of the period. To go much farther than this and attempt a description of its form and use is to indulge in speculation and controversy. However, so far as *James the Fourth* is concerned, a gallery similar to that shown in the De Witt drawing would be adequate for Bohan's and Oberon's retirement whether it was being used as a 'Lords' Room' for seating privileged mem-

same in action by guid fellows of our countrymen; and
then when thou seest that, judge if any wise man would
not leave the world if he could.

Ober. That will I see; lead and I'll follow thee. *Exeunt.*

---

bers of the audience or not. The various elaborate arrangements for staging aloft scenes suggested by some recent scholars (e.g., A. B. Weiner in *Theatre Survey*, II (1961), 15–34) are not necessary for this play. See also note to l. 0.2.

111. *guid*] good (Scot.).

Act I

[I. i] *Laus Deo detur in Aeternum*

Enter the KING OF ENGLAND, *the* KING OF SCOTS, DOROTHEA *his Queen, the* COUNTESS [OF ARRAN], *Lady* IDA, *with other Lords, and* ATEUKIN *with them aloof.*

K. *of Scot.* Brother of England, since our neighbouring land
    And near alliance doth invite our loves,
    The more I think upon our last accord,
    The more I grieve your sudden parting hence.
    First, laws of friendship did confirm our peace,   5
    Now both the seal of faith and marriage bed,
    The name of father, and the style of friend;
    These force in me affection full confirmed;
    So that I grieve—and this my hearty grief
    The heavens record, the world may witness well—   10
    To lose your presence, who are now to me
    A father, brother, and a vowèd friend.
K. *of Eng.* Link all these lovely styles, good king, in one;

---

1. i] *Attus primus. Scena prima.* Q, *after l.* 0.4.   1. land] Q; lands *Dyce.*

0.1. Laus . . . Aeternum] Let praise be given to God for evermore. This epigraph strikes one as coming straight from Greene's pen. His prose works of the period 1590–1 evidence a strong desire to repent of his earlier wicked ways.
  0.4. aloof] Ateukin stands apart from the main action, possibly to one side of the stage, until he approaches the King at l. 182.
  1. *our neighbouring land*] the fact that we have a common frontier.
  2. *invite*] encourage; this use antedates the first citation in *O.E.D.*, 2b.
  7. *style*] distinguishing name.
  12. *father*] i.e., father-in-law.
  brother] This was regarded as the traditional relationship between monarchs.
  13. *lovely*] affectionate.

13

And since thy grief exceeds in my depart,
I leave my Dorothea to enjoy   15
Thy whole compact, loves, and plighted vows.
Brother of Scotland, this is my joy, my life,
Her father's honour, and her country's hope,
Her mother's comfort, and her husband's bliss.
I tell thee, king, in loving of my Doll,   20
Thou bind'st her father's heart, and all his friends,
In bands of love that death cannot dissolve.

K. of Scot. Nor can her father love her like to me,
My life's light, and the comfort of my soul.
Fair Dorothea, that wast England's pride,   25
Welcome to Scotland; and, in sign of love,
Lo, I invest thee with the Scottish crown.
Nobles and Ladies, stoop unto your queen;
And trumpets sound, that heralds may proclaim
Fair Dorothea peerless Queen of Scots!   30

All. Long live and prosper our fair Queen of Scots!
                           [*They*] *install and crown her.*

Dor. Thanks to the King of Kings for my dignity;
Thanks to my father, that provides so carefully;
Thanks to my lord and husband for this honour;
And thanks to all that love their king and me.   35

15–16.] *so Dyce; divided in Q at* compact / Loues.   16. compact, loves] *This ed.;* compact / Loues *Q;* compact of loves *Dyce;* compacted loves *Grosart.*   17. this is my] *Q;* this my *conj. Walker.*   32. for my] *Q;* for this my *Dyce.*

---

14. *exceeds*] is out of the ordinary; this is an extension of the sense of the word, peculiar to Cambridge University, used by Greene in *Friar Bacon*, meaning to 'eat or celebrate more than usual'.

depart] departure.

15–31.] This passage is an ironical build-up against which the King of Scots' unfaithfulness is to be set at ll. 74 ff.

16. *Thy . . . loves*] The emendations of previous editors are made for the sake of metre, which is often irregular in the play.

compact] contract, covenant.

28. *stoop*] bow, curtsy.

31.1. install] Some kind of throne or elevated area, to which Dorothea is led by the King of Scots, is required on the stage.

SC. I] JAMES THE FOURTH 15

All. Long live fair Dorothea, our true queen!
K. of Eng. Long shine the sun of Scotland in her pride,
  Her father's comfort, and fair Scotland's bride!
  But Dorothea, since I must depart,
  And leave thee from thy tender mother's charge, 40
  Let me advise my lovely daughter first
  What best befits her in a foreign land.
  Live, Doll, for many eyes shall look on thee;
  Have care of honour and the present state;
  For she that steps to height of majesty 45
  Is even the mark whereat the enemy aims:
  Thy virtues shall be construèd to vice,
  Thine affable discourse to abject mind;
  If coy, detracting tongues will call thee proud.
  Be therefore wary in this slippery state; 50
  Honour thy husband, love him as thy life,
  Make choice of friends, as eagles of their young,
  Who soothe no vice, who flatter not for gain,
  But love such friends as do the truth maintain.
  Think on these lessons when thou art alone, 55
  And thou shalt live in health when I am gone.
Dor. I will engrave these precepts in my heart,
  And as the wind with calmness wooes you hence,
  Even so I wish the heavens in all mishaps
  May bless my father with continual grace. 60

44. Have] *Q;* With *Dyce.*

---

37. *in her pride*] in her most flourishing condition (*O.E.D.*, *sb.*¹ 9a).
40. *from*] away from.
44. *present state*] present high position.
46. *even the mark*] the very target.
47. *construèd to*] interpreted as.
49. *If coy . . . proud*] If you are quiet and retiring ('coy', *O.E.D.*, 2a), malicious gossip will interpret your behaviour as distant and disdainful ('coy', *O.E.D.*, 3). Cf. the use of 'coy' in the latter sense at l. 132.
50. *slippery*] requiring constant watchfulness, unstable.
52. *as . . . young*] I have been unable to trace the origin of this belief; presumably the reference is to some legend that the eagle separates its weak from its strong offspring.
56. *in health*] soundly, prosperously.

16   JAMES THE FOURTH   [ACT I

K. of Eng. Then, son, farewell;
   The favouring winds invites us to depart.
   Long circumstance in taking princely leaves
   Is more officious than convenient.
   Brother of Scotland, love me in my child;   65
   You greet me well, if so you will her good.
K. of Scot. Then, lovely Doll and all that favour me,
   Attend to see our English friends at sea;
   Let all their charge depend upon my purse:
   They are our neighbours, by whose kind accord   70
   We dare attempt the proudest potentate.
   Only, fair countess, and your daughter, stay;
   With you I have some other thing to say.
           *Exeunt all save the King [of Scots], the Countess
           [of Arran], Ida, Ateukin, in all royalty.*
   [*Aside*] So let them triumph that have cause to joy;
   But, wretched king, thy nuptial knot is death,   75
   Thy bride the breeder of thy country's ill.
   For thy false heart dissenting from thy hand,
   Misled by love, hast made another choice,
   Another choice, even when thou vowed'st thy soul
   To Dorothea, England's choicest pride;   80
   O, then thy wandering eyes bewitched thy heart.
   Even in the chapel did thy fancy change,

61–2.] *so Dyce; one line in Q.*   74. *Aside*] *Dyce; not in Q.*

---

62. *invites*] a common non-agreement in Elizabethan grammar; see Abbott, 333.
63. *circumstance*] ceremonious ado.
64. *officious*] (inconveniently) zealous.
66. *greet*] please.
will] desire.
67. *favour*] support.
68. *Attend*] be present.
69. *charge*] expense.
depend upon] be supplied by.
71. *attempt*] challenge, defy with force.
73.2. in all royalty] magnificently, with all pomp.
78. *hast*] The form is due to the thought that 'thy false heart' = 'thou'; for similar confusions see Abbott, 412, 415.

When, perjured man, though fair Doll had thy hand,
The Scottish Ida's beauty stale thy heart.
Yet fear and love hath tied thy ready tongue 85
From blabbing forth the passions of thy mind,
Lest fearful silence have in subtle looks
Bewrayed the treason of my new-vowed love.
Be fair and lovely, Doll, but here's the prize
That lodgeth here, and entered through mine eyes; 90
Yet, howsoe'er I love, I must be wise.
[*To the Countess*] Now, lovely countess, what reward or grace
May I employ on you for this your zeal,
And humble honours done us in our court,
In entertainment of the English king? 95
Count. It was of duty, prince, that I have done;
And what in favour may content me most
Is that it please your grace to give me leave
For to return unto my country home.
K. of Scot. But, lovely Ida, is your mind the same? 100
Ida. I count of court, my lord, as wise men do:
'Tis fit for those that knows what longs thereto;
Each person to his place: the wise to art,
The cobbler to his clout, the swain to cart.
K. of Scot. But, Ida, you are fair, and beauty shines 105
And seemeth best where pomp her pride refines.
Ida. If beauty (as I know there's none in me)
Were sworn my love, and I his life should be,

86. blabbing] *Q;* babbling *Collins.*   92. *To the Countess*] This ed.;
not in *Q.*

---

84. *stale*] stole; the word also had the meaning 'decoy', 'lure'.
88. *Bewrayed*] betrayed.
90. *here*] i.e., in the heart.
91. *wise*] skilful, clever.
93. *employ*] bestow.
96. *that*] See note to Ind. 97.
100. *mind*] purpose, intention.
102. *knows*] a common non-agreement in Elizabethan grammar; see Abbott, 333.
longs] is proper.
104. *clout*] a piece of leather used by a cobbler in mending shoes.

F

       The farther from the court I were removed,
       The more, I think, of heaven I were beloved.   110
K. of Scot. And why?
Ida. Because the court is counted Venus' net,
       Where gifts and vows for stales are often set;
       None, be she chaste as Vesta, but shall meet
       A curious tongue to charm her ears with sweet.   115
K. of Scot. Why, Ida, then I see you set at naught
       The force of love.
Ida.   In sooth, this is my thought,
       Most gracious king: that they that little prove
       Are mickle blest from bitter sweets of love.
       And weel I wot, I heard a shepherd sing   120
       That, like a bee, Love hath a little sting:
       He lurks in flowers, he percheth on the trees,
       He on kings' pillows bends his pretty knees;
       The boy is blind, but when he will not spy,
       He hath a leaden shot and wings to fly.   125

117–18.] *so Dyce; divided in Q at* king, / That.   125. shot] *Lavin;* foote *Q.*

---

112. *counted*] considered.
113. *stales*] traps, decoys; cf. l. 84 above.
114. *Vesta*] the Roman goddess of the hearth, whose sacred fire was tended by the Vestal Virgins.
115. *curious*] ingenious, clever.
sweet] pleasurable words.
117. *In sooth*] truly.
118. *little prove*] make small trial of it.
119. *mickle*] much, greatly.
120. *weel*] well (Scot.).
wot] know.
120–3. *I heard . . . knees*] These sentiments appear again and again in Greene's prose works, e.g., The Shepherd's Wife's Song in *Greene's Mourning Garment*, IX, 143a: 'Ah! what is loue! It is a pretty thing, / As sweet vnto a shepheard as a king.'
121. *Love . . . sting*] Cf. Peele's *Hunting of Cupid* (*c.* 1590): 'What thing is love for (well I wot) / Love is a thing. / It is a prick, it is a sting, / It is a pretty, pretty thing.'
124. *The boy*] i.e., Cupid.
will not spy] does not wish to discover (someone).
125. *leaden shot*] Lavin's emendation is demanded by the sense of the

SC. I]   JAMES THE FOURTH   19

  Beshrew me yet, for all these strange effects,
  If I would like the lad that so infects.
K. of Scot. [*Aside*] Rare wit, fair face, what heart could more
  desire?
  But Doll is fair and doth concern thee near.
  Let Doll be fair, she is won; but I must woo   130
  And win fair Ida; there's some choice in two.
  [*To Ida*] But, Ida, thou art coy.
Ida.   And why, dread king?
K. of Scot. In that you will dispraise so sweet a thing
  As love.
  Had I my wish—
Ida.   What then?
K. of Scot.   Then would I place   135
  His arrow here, his beauty in that face.
Ida. And were Apollo moved and ruled by me,
  His wisdom should be yours, and mine his tree.
K. of Scot. But here returns our train.

    Enters the train back [*led by* DOROTHEA].

      Welcome, fair Doll!

128. *Aside*] Dyce; not in Q.   129. near] Q; nigher *conj.* Manly.
132. *To Ida*] This ed.; not in Q.   133–6.] *so this ed.; divided in Q at* sweet / A thing ... wish. / What then? / Then ... here, / His.   139–40.] *so Dyce; divided in Q at* traine. / Welcome.   139.1. *Enters ... back*] *so Dyce; follows l. 140 in Q.*

---

lines; for it was Cupid's leaden arrow which produced aversion in the lover; see Ovid, *Metamorphoses*, i. 468.
 127. *infects*] Ida is viewing Love as a kind of disease.
 129. *near*] intimately, closely.
 131. *there's ... two*] i.e., Ida's presence ensures that he will not be bound forcibly to one woman.
 136. *here*] See note to l. 90.
 137. *Apollo*] the Greek god of sun, music, and poetry, but often alluded to, as here, as the god of wisdom by virtue of his knowing the future.
 138. *his tree*] The laurel was connected with Apollo by the legend in which Daphne was transformed into this tree while fleeing from the god. Ida alludes here to the laurel as a reward for giving the kind advice worthy of Apollo's praise, and perhaps also she hints that like Daphne she would flee from the attentions of an unwelcome suitor.

How fares our father? Is he shipped and gone? 140
Dor. My royal father is both shipped and gone;
    God and fair winds direct him to his home!
K. of Scot. Amen, say I. [*Aside*] Would thou wert with him too!
    Then might I have a fitter time to woo.
    [*To the Countess and Ida*] But, countess, you would be gone:
        therefore, farewell. 145
    Yet, Ida, if thou wilt, stay thou behind
    To accompany my queen;
    But if thou like the pleasures of the court—
    [*Aside*] Or if she liked me, though she left the court—
    What should I say?—I know not what to say— 150
    [*To them*] You may depart. And you, my courteous queen,
    Leave me a space; I have a weighty cause
    To think upon. [*Aside*] Ida, it nips me near;
    It came from thence, I feel it burning here.
            Exeunt all saving the King [*of Scots*] *and Ateukin.*
    Now am I free from sight of common eye, 155
    Where to myself I may disclose the grief
    That hath too great a part in mine affects.
Ateu. [*Aside*] And now is my time by wiles and words to rise,
    Greater than those that thinks themselves more wise.
K. of Scot. And first, fond king, thy honour doth engrave 160
    Upon thy brows the drift of thy disgrace;
    Thy new-vowed love in sight of God and men

---

143. *Aside*] Dyce; *not in* Q.   145. *To the Countess and Ida*] This ed.; *not in* Q.   148. thou like] Q; thou not like *Grosart*.   149. *Aside*] Grosart; *not in* Q.   151. *To them*] This ed.; *not in* Q.   152–3.] *so* Dyce; *divided in* Q *at* vpon: / Ida.   158. *Aside*] Dyce; *not in* Q.

---

    147. *accompany*] be a companion to, be a member of the train of.
    153. *it . . . near*] i.e., my passion affects me painfully.
    154. *It . . . thence*] i.e., the sting of love came from Ida. As Lavin notes, there is also a punning allusion to Mount Ida, a favourite haunt of Venus and Cupid.
    here] i.e., in the heart.
    157. *affects*] passions, desires.
    159. *thinks*] See note to l. 102.
    161. *drift*] course, progress; or perhaps 'scheme, plot'; cf. *Gent.*, II. vi. 43.

    Link thee to Dorothea during life;
    For who more fair and virtuous than thy wife?
    Deceitful murderer of a quiet mind,   165
    Fond love, vile lust, that thus misleads us men
    To vow our faiths, and fall to sin again!
    But kings stoop not to every common thought:
    Ida is fair and wise, fit for a king;
    And for fair Ida will I hazard life,   170
    Venture my kingdom, country, and my crown:
    Such fire hath love to burn a kingdom down.
    Say Doll dislikes that I estrange my love;
    Am I obedient to a woman's look?
    Nay, say her father frown when he shall hear   175
    That I do hold fair Ida's love so dear?
    Let father frown and fret, and fret and die,
    Nor earth nor heaven shall part my love and I.
    Yea, they shall part us, but we first must meet,
    And woo, and win, and yet the world not see 't.   180
    Yea, there's the wound, and wounded with that thought,
    So let me die, for all my drift is naught.
                  [*Ateukin approaches the King of Scots.*]
Ateu. Most gracious and imperial majesty—
    [*Aside*] A little flattery more were but too much.
K. of Scot. Villain, what art thou   185
    That thus darest interrupt a prince's secrets?
Ateu. Dread king, thy vassal is a man of art,

182.1.] *Dyce (subst.); not in Q.*   184. *Aside*] *Dyce; not in Q.*   184.] *so Dyce; assigned to K. of Scot. in Q.*   185–6.] *so Dyce; one line in Q.*

---

    163. *Link*] a common non-agreement in Elizabethan grammar; see Abbott, 412.
    172. *Such . . . down*] The allusion is probably to the love of Paris and Helen which caused the burning of Troy.
    173. *estrange*] remove from its proper place.
    182. *my drift*] the purport of my speech.
    184.] Q's assigning of this line to the King is clearly wrong, as its tone is out of keeping with his reaction to Ateukin's interruption. Greene wishes to emphasize here the calculation in Ateukin's approach.
    187. *man of art*] scholar.

22   JAMES THE FOURTH   [ACT I

     Who knows by constellation of the stars,
     By oppositions and by dire aspects,
     The things are past and those that are to come.   190
K. of Scot. But where's thy warrant to approach my presence?
Ateu. My zeal, and ruth to see your grace's wrong
     Makes me lament I did detract so long.
K. of Scot. If thou know'st thoughts, tell me what mean I now?
Ateu. I'll calculate the cause   195
     Of those your highness' smiles, and tell your thoughts.
K. of Scot. But lest thou spend thy time in idleness
     And miss the matter that my mind aims at,
     Tell me,
     What star was opposite when that was thought?   200
                           He strikes him on the ear.
Ateu. 'Tis inconvenient, mighty potentate,
     Whose looks resembles Jove in majesty,
     To scorn the sooth of science with contempt.
     I see in those imperial looks of yours

189. dire] Grosart; drie Q.   195–6.] *so Dyce; divided in Q at* smiles, /
And.   199–200.] *so Dyce; one line in Q.*   200.1.] *so Q (in roman);
follows l. 199 Lavin.*

---

   188. *constellation*] configuration or position (an astrological term).
   189. *oppositions*] an astrological term meaning 'the relative positions of any two heavenly bodies when exactly opposite each other when viewed from the earth's surface'.
   dire aspects] Grosart's emendation of Q's 'drie' is almost certainly correct. 'Dry' was a term used in medieval psychology to describe the complexion of people, and would not have been applied to 'aspects' which, like 'oppositions', was an astrological term and meant the way in which the planets, from their relative positions in the heavens, look upon or 'aspect' each other. With his expert astrological knowledge, evinced in his *Planetomachia* (1585), Greene is using the term accurately to mean 'positions of planets considered malign by astrologers'.
   192. *ruth*] pity, sorrow.
   193. *detract*] delay.
   194. *mean I now*] have I in mind at this moment.
   200. *opposite*] See note to l. 189.
   201. *inconvenient*] unreasonable.
   202. *resembles*] See note to l. 102.
   203. *sooth*] truth.

JAMES THE FOURTH

The whole discourse of love: Saturn combust, 205
With direful looks at your nativity,
Beheld fair Venus in her silver orb;
I know by certain axioms I have read,
Your grace's griefs, and further can express
Her name that holds you thus in fancy's bands. 210
K. of Scot. Thou talkest wonders.
Ateu.   Naught but truth, O king.
'Tis Ida is the mistress of your heart,
Whose youth must take impression of affects;
For tender twigs will bow, and milder minds
Will yield to fancy, be they followed well. 215
K. of Scot. What god art thou, composed in human shape,
Or bold Trophonius to decide our doubts?
How know'st thou this?

208. axioms] *Dyce;* exiomies *Q.*   209–10.] *so Dyce; divided in Q at* name, / That.

205–7. *Saturn ... orb*] J. Parr (*Tamburlaine's Malady* (1953), pp. 50–6) has demonstrated the astrological accuracy and appropriateness of Ateukin's diagnosis. Saturn's being combust means that it was within $8\frac{1}{2}$ degrees of the sun or that it and the sun were in platic, or inexact, conjunction. That Saturn 'beheld' Venus means that the two planets were 'aspecting' each other, and since the aspect is 'direful' then it must be 'quadrat' or 'opposite', the two malefic aspects in astrology. If Saturn in conjunction with Sol was in quadrat aspect with Venus, it follows that Sol and Venus were also in quadrat aspect. Ateukin leads the King to believe that this configuration reveals 'the whole discourse of love' and presages union with Ida. The aspect between Sol and Venus is vitally concerned with determining a man's marriage partner; however, the quadrat aspect means that James will not possess Ida. Parr also notes that these particular configurations between Sol and Venus at the King's nativity would endow him precisely with those qualities he exhibits throughout the play, including 'loss of good name, cheated by servants, full of heavy thoughts ... infamous by reason of woman, treacherous to women especially those of his own family'.

208. *axioms*] i.e., astrological propositions.
210. *fancy's bands*] the bonds of love.
215. *fancy*] amorous inclination.
followed well] persistently pursued.
217. *Trophonius*] the son of Erginus of Boeotia who with his brother, Agamedes, built a temple at Delphi in honour of Apollo. After his death he was consulted as an oracle in a cave at Lebadeia in Boeotia.

Ateu. E'en as I know the means
To work your grace's freedom and your love.
Had I the mind, as many courtiers have, 220
To creep into your bosom for your coin,
And beg rewards for every cap and knee,
I then would say, 'If that your grace would give
This lease, this manor, or this patent sealed,
For this or that I would effect your love.' 225
But Ateukin is no parasite, O prince;
I know your grace knows scholars are but poor,
And therefore, as I blush to beg a fee,
Your mightiness is so magnificent,
You cannot choose but cast some gift apart 230
To ease my bashful need that cannot beg.
As for your love, O might I be employed,
How faithfully would Ateukin compass it!
But princes rather trust a smoothing tongue
Than men of art that can accept the time. 235
K. of Scot. Ateukin—if so thy name, for so thou say'st—
Thine art appears in entrance of my love;
And since I deem thy wisdom matched with truth,
I will exalt thee; and thyself alone
Shalt be the agent to dissolve my grief. 240

---

222. *cap and knee*] obeisance (made by removing the hat and bending the knee).
224. *lease*] grant of land; here one within a king's gift.
manor] landed estate.
patent sealed] Rights to property or office in the patronage of a monarch were conferred by means of letters-patent.
226. *parasite*] This is exactly what Ateukin would be recognized as by an Elizabethan audience. See Introduction, pp. xliv–xlv.
229. *magnificent*] royally lavish or munificent.
230. *cast . . . apart*] set aside for a special purpose.
233. *compass*] attain, achieve.
235. *men of art*] scholars.
accept the time] take the favourable moment for doing something.
237. *Thine . . . love*] Your skill presents itself as a right to be admitted to my favour.
238. *truth*] fidelity.
240. *dissolve*] disperse.

sc. I] JAMES THE FOURTH 25

  Sooth is, I love, and Ida is my love;
  But my new marriage nips me near, Ateukin,
  For Dorothea may not brook th' abuse.
Ateu. These lets are but as motes against the sun,
  Yet not so great; like dust before the wind,   245
  Yet not so light. Tut, pacify your grace:
  You have the sword and sceptre in your hand;
  You are the king, the state depends on you;
  Your will is law. Say that the case were mine,
  Were she my sister whom your highness loves,   250
  She should consent, for that our lives, our goods
  Depend on you; and if your queen repine,
  Although my nature cannot brook of blood,
  And scholars grieve to hear of murderous deeds,—
  But if the lamb should let the lion's way,   255
  By my advice the lamb should lose her life.

---

244. motes] *Dyce;* moaths *Q*.   245–6. like dust . . . Yet not] *Q;* the dust . . . Is not *conj.* Grosart.   255. But] *Q;* Yet *conj.* Deighton.

---

241. *Sooth is*] the truth is.
242. *nips me near*] vexes me greatly.
243. *brook th' abuse*] tolerate the injury.
244. *lets*] hindrances.
 motes] Despite the Q spelling it was the mote which was proverbial for its smallness, which seems to be the point here. 'Mote' was often spelt 'moth' during the period (e.g., *LLL.*, IV. iii. 157, First Folio text) and may have been pronounced in a similar manner; even as 'nothing' was probably a homophone of 'noting' (see P. A. Jorgensen, *Redeeming Shakespeare's Words* (1962), pp. 22–42).
249. *Your will is law*] This belief is in direct opposition to Elizabethan theory of monarchy, which stressed 'what power the king hath, he hath it by the law; and the bounds and limits of it are known' (R. Hooker, *Of the Laws of Ecclesiastical Polity* (1593–7), ed. C. Morris (1907), I, x). Ateukin is persuading the King to act in a manner which Hooker calls 'no better than mere tyranny' (p. 194).
251. *for that*] because.
252. *repine*] complain.
253. *brook of*] endure.
255–6. *But . . . life*] The same terminology for referring to the King and Dorothea is used in Sir Cuthbert Anderson's allegory of Jaques's attack on Dorothea at v. vi. 119–35.
255. *let*] hinder.

   Thus am I bold to speak unto your grace,
   Who am too base to kiss your royal feet;
   For I am poor, nor have I land nor rent,
   Nor countenance here in court; but for my love,   260
   Your grace shall find none such within the realm.
K. of Scot. Wilt thou effect my love? Shall she be mine?
Ateu. I'll gather moly, crocus, and the herbs
   That heals the wounds of body and the mind;
   I'll set out charms and spells, naught else shall be left 265
   To tame the wanton if she shall rebel:
   Give me but tokens of your highness' trust.
K. of Scot. Thou shalt have gold, honour, and wealth enough;
   Win my love, and I will make thee great.
Ateu. These words do make me rich, most noble prince;   270
   I am more proud of them than any wealth.
   Did not your grace suppose I flatter you,
   Believe me, I would boldly publish this:

263. moly, crocus] *conj. Mitford, Collins;* Moly-rocus *Q.*   265. else] *Q;* omitted *Dyce.*   269. Win my] *Q;* Win but my *conj. Dyce;* Win thou my *Grosart;* Win me my *Collins.*

---

259. *rent*] revenue, income (*O.E.D., sb.*¹ 1b).
260. *countenance*] patronage.
 for] as for.
262. *effect my love*] i.e., bring my love to its consummation.
 263–4. *moly, crocus ... mind*] Moly was a fabulous herb in Greek mythology which had a white bloom and a black root and was endowed with magical curative properties. It was, according to Homer (*Odyssey*, x. 301–6), given by Hermes to Odysseus as a charm against Circe's witchcraft. The choice of the word by Ateukin in this context is ironical if Greene believed with Golding 'And what is else herbe Moly than the gift of stayednesse / And temperance which dooth all fowle concupisence expresse?' (*Translation of Ovid's Metamorphoses*, ed. W. H. D. Rouse, The Epistle, ll. 278–9). Pliny lists the medicinal qualities of *crocus* in *Natural History*, XXI, lxxix, 137–8.
 265. *I'll set out*] Ateukin is using a hunting term employed to describe the setting of nets to catch animals or birds (*O.E.D., v.* 59).
 left] neglected.
 266. *the wanton*] i.e., Ida, who is here regarded as unmanageable. The word was also applied to an untrained bird in hawking, so that Ateukin is continuing his hunting metaphor in the previous line.
 272. *Did ... grace*] were it not that your grace would.
 273. *publish*] make public by report.

SC. I]   JAMES THE FOURTH   27

  Was never eye that saw a sweeter face,
  Nor never ear that heard a deeper wit— 275
  O God, how I am ravished in your worth!
K. of Scot. Ateukin, follow me; love must have ease.
Ateu. I'll kiss your highness' feet; march when you please. *Exeunt.*

[I. ii]
  Enter SLIPPER, NANO, *and* ANDREW, *with their bills,*
    ready written, in their hands.

And. Stand back, sir; mine shall stand highest.
Slip. Come under mine arm, sir, or get a footstool; or else, by
 the light of the moon, I must come to it.
Nano. Agree, my masters, every man to his height: though I
 stand lowest, I hope to get the best master. 5
And. Ere I will stoop to a thistle, I will change turns; as good
 luck comes on the right hand as the left; here's for me.
Slip. And me.
Nano. And mine. [*They put up their bills.*]

I. ii. 2–5.] *so Dyce; irregular verse in Q divided at* footstoole, / Or . . . it. / Agree . . . height, / Though. 6–9.] *so Grosart; irregular verse in Q divided at* turnes, / As . . . left: / Here's. 8. *Slip.*] *Grosart; assigned to And. in Q.* 9. *Nano.*] *Grosart; assigned to And. in Q.* They . . . bills] *Dyce (subst.); not in Q.*

---

276. *ravished in*] intoxicated with.
278. *march*] go.

I. ii. 0.1. *bills*] posters, advertisements.
1. *stand highest*] i.e., be hung in the topmost or most prominent position.
3. *come to it*] reach the best position. It is possible that bawdy puns are intended here on 'stand' and 'come to it', both of which had sexual connotations; see E. Partridge, *Shakespeare's Bawdy* (1948).
4. *every . . . height*] let each man hang his bill according to the height he can reach, with the overtone of 'according to his worth'.
5. *stand lowest*] The pun is on the two meanings: (1) am smallest in stature, (2) have my bill hanging third from the top.
6. *Ere . . . thistle*] a proverb: 'They have need of a blessing that kneel to a thistle' (Tilley N83).
change turns] change direction.
6–7. *as . . . me*] Andrew hangs his bill to the right of Slipper's; cf. Tilley L578: 'Left-handed luck is ill luck'.

28   JAMES THE FOURTH   [ACT I

And. But tell me, fellows, till better occasion come, do you   10
  seek masters?
Slip. ⎱
Nano. ⎰ We do.
And. But what can you do worthy preferment?
Nano. Marry, I can smell a knave from a rat.
Slip. And I can lick a dish before a cat.   15
And. And I can find two fools unsought,—how like you that?
  But, in earnest, now tell me of what trades are you two?
Slip. How mean you that, sir, of what trade? Marry, I'll tell
  you, I have many trades: the honest trade when I needs
  must, the filching trade when time serves, the cozening   20
  trade as I find occasion. And I have more qualities: I can-
  not abide a full cup unkissed, a fat capon uncarved, a full
  purse unpicked, nor a fool to prove a justice as you do.
And. Why, sot, why callest thou me fool?
Nano. For examining wiser than thyself.   25
And. So doth many more than I in Scotland.
Nano. Yea, those are such as have more authority than wit,
  and more wealth than honesty.

10–11.] *so Dyce; irregular verse in Q divided at* come, / Do.   12. *Slip. Nano.*] *Dyce; Ambo. Q.*   16–17.] *so Dyce; irregular verse in Q divided at* vnsought, / How . . . that? / But.   18–23.] *so Dyce; irregular verse in Q divided at* trade? / Marry . . . trades, / The . . . must, / The . . . serues, / The . . . occasion. / And . . . vnkist, / A . . . vncaru'd, / A . . . vnpickt, / Nor.   27–31.] *so Dyce; irregular verse in Q divided at* wit, / And . . . honestie. / This . . . him, / But.

---

10. *occasion*] opportunity, circumstances.
14. *smell . . . rat*] a variant of the two proverbs 'I smell him out' (Tilley S558) and 'I smell a rat' (Tilley R31).
15. *lick . . . cat*] a variant of the proverb 'That cat is out of kind that sweet milk will not lick' (Tilley C167).
before] sooner than, in the presence of.
20. *filching trade*] petty thieving.
time serves] the opportunity presents itself.
20–1. *cozening trade*] confidence trickery. Greene was the author of several pamphlets which described many of these tricks.
22. *unkissed*] untasted.
capon] a castrated cockerel.
23. *unpicked*] unstolen.
prove] turn out to be.

SC. II]   JAMES THE FOURTH   29

Slip. This is my little brother with the great wit: 'ware him!
    But what canst thou do, tell me, that art so inquisitive of 30
    us?
And. Anything that concerns a gentleman to do, that can I do.
Slip. So you are of the gentle trade?
And. True.
Slip. Then, gentle sir, leave us to ourselves; for here comes 35
    one as if he would lack a servant ere he went.
                                 [Andrew stands aside.]
                   Ent[er ATEUKIN].
Ateu. Why, so, Ateukin, this becomes thee best:
    Wealth, honour, ease, and angels in thy chest.
    Now may I say, as many often sing,
    'No fishing to the sea, nor service to a king'.   40
    Unto this high promotion doth belong
    Means to be talked of in the thickest throng.
    And first, to fit the humours of my lord,
    Sweet lays and lines of love I must record;
    And such sweet lines and love-lays I'll indite   45

35–6.] *so Dyce; irregular verse in Q divided at* our selues, / For.   36.1.]
Dyce; not in Q.   36.2. Enter Ateukin] *Dyce;* Ent. *before sp. h. in Q.*   37.
Ateukin,] *Dyce;* Ateukin? *Q.*   41. promotion] *Dyce;* promotions *Q.*

   33. *the gentle trade*] shoemaking; cf. T. Deloney's novel *The Gentle Craft*.
Andrew mistakes Slipper's insult for a compliment to his claimed gentility.
   36. *as . . . went*] as though he will be in the position of wanting a servant
while he is here. Lavin suggests 'as if he will hire a new servant and dismiss
an old one'; but this would appear to be Ateukin's first hiring since the
King has made him his confidant; see ll. 37 ff.
   38. *angels*] gold coins worth ten shillings each.
   40. *No . . . king*] a proverb: see Tilley F336; it means 'Nothing is superior
to sea fishing and the king's service.'
   42. *in the thickest throng*] among the largest number of people.
   43–6. *And . . . delight*] one of the traditional activities of the parasite: cf.
Gaveston in Marlowe's *Edward II*, I. i. 51–6: 'I must have wanton poets,
pleasant wits, / Musicians that with touching of a string / May draw the
pliant king which way I please. / Music and poetry is his delight; / Therefore I'll have Italian masks by night, / Sweet speeches, comedies, and
pleasing shows.'
   43. *fit the humours*] suit the moods.
   44. *record*] either 'get by heart' or 'call to mind', 'remember'; or perhaps
'sing': cf. *The Spanish Tragedy* (ed. P. Edwards, 1959), II. iv. 28.

As men may wish for and my liege delight;
And next, a train of gallants at my heels,
That men may say the world doth run on wheels;
For men of art, that rise by indirection
To honour and the favour of their king, 50
Must use all means to save what they have got,
And win their favours whom they never knew.
If any frown to see my fortunes such,
A man must bear a little, not too much.

[*He sees the posted bills.*]

But in good time, these bills portend, I think, 55
That some good fellows do for service seek.

[*He*] *read*[*s*].

'If any gentleman, spiritual or temporal, will entertain
out of his service a young stripling of the age of thirty
years, that can sleep with the soundest, eat with the
hungriest, work with the sickest, lie with the loudest, face 60
with the proudest, etc., that can wait in a gentleman's
chamber when his master is a mile off, keep his stable
when 'tis empty, and his purse when 'tis full, and hath
many qualities worse than all these,—let him write his
name and go his way, and attendance shall be given.' 65
By my faith, a good servant; which is he?

Slip. Truly, sir, that am I.

Ateu. And why dost thou write such a bill? Are all these
qualities in thee?

46. liege] *Dyce;* leech *Q.*   52. they] *Dyce;* he *Q.*   56.1. *He reads*] Read.
before l. 57 in Q.   60. sickest] *Q;* sickerest *or* stoutest *conj. Dyce.*

---

48. *the world ... wheels*] they live prosperously; a proverb (Tilley W893).
49. *by indirection*] by underhand or dishonest means.
54. *A man ... little*] i.e., a successful man can put up with some envious disapproval.
55. *in good time*] opportunely.
57–8. *entertain ... service*] i.e., will support by reason of or in return for his service.
59. *soundest*] healthiest, with the idea of 'sound asleep'.
60. *sickest*] Dyce's conjectures miss the point of the joke, which rests in Slipper's listing weaknesses as though they were qualifications.
face] show a bold face, swagger.

SC. II]   JAMES THE FOURTH   31

Slip. O Lord, ay, sir, and a great many more, some better, 70
 some worse, some richer, some poorer. Why, sir, do you
 look so? Do they not please you?
Ateu. Truly, no, for they are naught, and so art thou; if thou
 hast no better qualities, stand by.
Slip. O, sir, I tell the worst first; but, an you lack a man, I am 75
 for you; I'll tell you the best qualities I have.
Ateu. Be brief then.
Slip. If you need me in your chamber, I can keep the door at a
 whistle; in your kitchen, turn the spit and lick the pan and
 make the fire burn; but if in the stable— 80
Ateu. Yea, there would I use thee.
Slip. Why, there you kill me, there am I! And turn me to a
 horse and a wench, and I have no peer.
Ateu. Art thou so good in keeping a horse? I pray thee, tell me
 how many good qualities hath a horse? 85
Slip. Why, so, sir: a horse hath two properties of a man, that is

68–76.] *so Dyce; irregular verse in Q divided at* bill, / Are ... thee? / O ...
more, / Some ... porer, / Why ... you? / Trulie ... thou, / If ... by. / O ...
man, / I.   78–80.] *so Dyce; irregular verse in Q divided at* chamber, / I ...
kitchin, / Turne ... burne. / But.   80. stable—] *Dyce;* stable. *Q.*
82–91.] *so Dyce; irregular verse in Q divided at* I, / And ... peere. / Art ...
horse, / I ... horse? / Why ... man. / That ... stomacke, / Foure ...
docket, / Hold ... legs. / Nine ... Asse, / And.   82. there ... turn] *Manly;*
there am I, / And turne *Q;* there am I a per se, turn *conj. Mitford.*

---

74. *stand by*] stand aside.
75. *an you lack*] if you need.
75–6. *I am for*] I am (the one) for.
78–9. *keep ... whistle*] be always on call at the chamber door.
79. *lick the pan*] clean the pan by licking it; but the phrase also meant 'flatter'.
82. *there you kill me*] have me exactly. Lavin compares III. i. 45: 'I am dead at a pocket.'
  there am I] there you sum me up exactly.
  turn me to] employ me with, set me to work on.
86–100. *a horse ... bridle*] This passage is closely based on Sections 71–9 of John Fitzherbert's *Book of Husbandry* (first ed., 1523). The relevant passages are quoted in the following notes from W. W. Skeat's reprint of the 1534 edition published by the English Dialect Society in 1882.
86–7. *a horse ... stomach*] Cf. Fitzherbert, p. 63: 'The two properties, that a horse hath of a man. The fyrste is, to haue a proude harte; and the seconde is, to be bolde and hardy.'

a proud heart and a hardy stomach; four properties of a
lion, a broad breast, a stiff docket,—hold your nose, master,—a wild countenance, and four good legs; nine properties of a fox, nine of a hare, nine of an ass, and ten of a 90
woman.
Ateu. A woman! Why, what properties of a woman hath a
horse?
Slip. O master, know you not that? Draw your tables, and
write what wise I speak. First, a merry countenance; 95

94–100.] so Dyce; irregular verse in Q divided at that? / Draw . . . speake. /
First . . . countenance. / Second . . . pace. / Third . . . forehead. / Fourth
. . . buttockes. / Fift . . . warde. / Sixt . . . vpon. / Seuenth . . . iourney. / Eight
man. / Ninth . . . mouth. / Tenth.

87–9. *four properties . . . legs*] Cf. Fitzherbert, p. 64: 'The .iiii. properties
of a lyon. The fyrste is, to haue a brode breste; the seconde, to be styffe-
docked; the thyrde, to be wylde in countenaunce; the fourthe, to haue
foure good legges.'

88. *stiff docket*] O.E.D. glosses this as 'solid fleshy part of an animal's
tail' and records Greene's usage here as unique. Greene clearly derived the
noun from the 'styffe-docked' of his source and allows Slipper to make a
vulgar joke.

89–90. *nine . . . fox*] Cf. Fitzherbert, p. 64: 'The .ix. propertyes of a foxe.
The fyrste is, to be prycke-eared; the seconde, to be lyttel-eared; the
thyrde, to be rounde-syded; the fourthe, to be syde-tayled; the fyfte, to be
shorte-legged; the syxte, to be blacke-legged; the .vii. to be shorte-
trottynge; the .viii. to be well coloured; the .ix to have a lyttel heed.'

90. *nine of a hare*] Cf. Fitzherbert, p. 64: 'The .ix. propertyes of an hare.
The fyrste is styffe-eared; the seconde, to haue greate eyen; the thyrde,
round eyen; the fourthe, to haue a leane heed; the .v. to haue leane knees;
the syxte, to be wyght on foote; the .vii. to turne vpon a lyttell grounde; the
.viii. to haue shorte buttockes; the .ix. to haue two good fyllettes.'

nine . . . ass] Cf. Fitzherbert, p. 65: 'The .ix. propertyes of an asse. The
fyrste is to be small-mouthed; the seconde, to be long-rayned; the .iii. to
be thyn-cressed; the fourthe, to be streyght-backed; the fyfth, to haue
small stones; the syxte, to be lathe-legged; the .vii. to be rounde-foted; the
eyght, to be holowe-foted; the .ix. to haue a toughe houe.'

90–100. *ten . . . bridle*] Cf. Fitzherbert, p. 65: 'The .x. properties of a
woman. The fyrst is, to be mery of chere; the seconde, to be well paced; the
thyrde, to haue a brode foreheed; the fourth, to haue brode buttockes; the
fyfthe, to be harde of warde; the syxte, to be easye to lepe vppon; the .vii.
to be good at a longe iourneye; the .viii. to be well sturrynge vnder a man;
the .ix. to be alwaye besye with the mouthe; the tenth, euer to be chowynge
on the brydell.'

94. *Draw your tables*] take out your writing tablet.
95. *wise*] manner.

second, a soft pace; third, a broad forehead; fourth, broad
buttocks; fifth, hard of ward; sixth, easy to leap upon;
seventh, good at long journey; eighth, well moving under
a man; ninth, always busy with the mouth; tenth, ever
chewing on the bridle. 100
Ateu. Thou art a man for me; what's thy name?
Slip. An ancient name, sir, belonging to the chamber and the
nightgown; guess you that?
Ateu. What's that? Slipper?
Slip. By my faith, well guessed; and so 'tis indeed. You'll be 105
my master?
Ateu. I mean so.
Slip. Read this first.
Ateu. [*Reads*] 'Pleaseth it any gentleman to entertain a servant of more wit than stature, let them subscribe, and 110
attendance shall be given.'
What of this?
Slip. He is my brother, sir; and we two were born together,
must serve together, and will die together, though we be
both hanged. 115

98. eighth, well moving] *Lavin;* Eight, mouing *Q.* 102–3.] *so Dyce;
irregular verse in Q divided at* the / Chamber. 105–6.] *so Dyce; irregular
verse in Q divided at* indeed: / Youle. 109. Reads] *Dyce; not in Q.*
109–15.] *so Dyce; irregular verse in Q divided at* entertaine / A ... stature, /
Let ... giuen. / What ... this? / He ... togither, / Must ... togither, /
Though.

---

96. *a broad forehead*] This was considered a particularly beautiful attribute at the time, Queen Elizabeth's being very deep and therefore fashionable. Cf. *Wiv.*, III. iii. 59–61: 'The right arched beauty of the brow', and
Gent., IV. iv. 189: 'Ay, but her forehead's low, and mine's as high.'
    97. *hard of ward*] difficult to control. Lavin suggests a sexual innuendo in
a play on 'ward' meaning 'the inside of a lock' (*O.E.D.*, VI, 24a).
    leap upon] a common euphemism for sexual intercourse; cf. *Ado*, V.
iv. 49.
    98. *long journey*] i.e., sexual intercourse.
    well moving] I have emended with Lavin from the source which gives
point to the bawdy.
    99. *busy ... mouth*] talking or nagging.
    100. *chewing ... bridle*] reacting against restraint.
    102. *ancient name*] See note to Ind. 84.1.
    103. *nightgown*] dressing-gown.

Ateu. What's thy name?
Nano. Nano.
Ateu. The etymology of which word is 'a dwarf'. Art not thou the old stoic's son, that dwells in his tomb?
Slip. ⎱ We are. 120
Nano. ⎰
Ateu. Thou art welcome to me. Wilt thou give thyself wholly to be at my disposition?
Nano. In all humility I submit myself.
Ateu. Then will I deck thee princely, instruct thee courtly, and present thee to the queen as my gift; art thou 125 content?
Nano. Yes, and thank your honour too.
Slip. Then welcome, brother, and fellow now.
And. [*Coming forward*] May it please your honour to abase your eye so low as to look either on my bill or myself? 130
Ateu. What are you?
And. By birth a gentleman; in profession a scholar; and one that knew your honour in Edinburgh, before your worthiness called you to this reputation, by name Andrew Snoord. 135

118–19.] *so Dyce; irregular verse in Q divided at* dwarfe: / Art. 120. *Slip. Nano.*] *Dyce; Ambo. Q.* 121–2.] *so Dyce; irregular verse in Q divided at* me, / Wilt. 124–6.] *so Dyce; irregular verse in Q divided at* courtly, / And . . . gift. / Art. 129. *Coming forward*] *Dyce; not in Q.* 129–30.] *so Dyce; irregular verse in Q divided at* lowe, / As. 132–5.] *so Dyce; irregular verse in Q divided at* scholler, / And . . . *Edenborough*, / Before . . . reputation. / By. 134. by name] *Lavin;* By me *Q.*

---

118. *The etymology . . . dwarf*] See note to Ind. 84.1.
118–19. *Art . . . tomb*] For comment on this, see Introduction, pp. lii–liii.
122. *at my disposition*] under my control.
124–5. *Then . . . gift*] There is a long tradition in Europe of dwarf-servants of royalty. In England Mary I had a page John Jarvis, who was two feet tall, and Edward VI had a dwarf named Xit.
128. *fellow*] fellow-servant.
133. *Edinburgh*] The reference is to the university.
134. *reputation*] distinction.
by name] Q's 'By me' has been defended in that Andrew here points to his bill so signed; but this is rather strained and a palaeographical confusion is more likely the source of the error.

Ateu. Andrew, I remember thee; follow me, and we will con-
fer further; for my weighty affairs for the king commands me to be brief at this time. Come on, Nano;
Slipper, follow. *Exeunt.*

[I. iii]

Enter SIR BARTRAM, *with* EUSTACE, *and others, booted.*

Sir Bar. But tell me, lovely Eustace, as thou lovest me,
Among the many pleasures we have passed,
Which is the rifest in thy memory
To draw thee over to thine ancient friend?
Eust. What makes Sir Bartram thus inquisitive? 5
Tell me, good knight, am I welcome or no?
Sir Bar. By sweet Saint Andrew and may sale I swear,
As welcome is my honest Dick to me
As morning's sun, or as the wat'ry moon
In mirkest night when we the borders track. 10
I tell thee, Dick, thy sight hath cleared my thoughts
Of many baneful troubles that there wooned.
Welcome to Sir Bartram as his life!

136–9.] *irregular verse in Q divided at* me, / And ... affaires / For ... time. / Come.

I. iii. 13. Welcome] *Q*; As welcome *conj. Dyce*; Aye welcome *Grosart*.

137–8. *commands*] See note to I. i. 102.

I. iii. 0.1. *booted*] i.e., dressed for riding.
1. *lovely*] friendly, amicable (Scot.).
2. *passed*] experienced.
3. *rifest*] most frequent, most common.
4. *draw thee over to*] make you visit.
7. *Saint Andrew*] Bartram appropriately swears by the patron saint of Scotland.
   may sale] my soul (Scot.).
9. *wat'ry moon*] This connection between the moon and tides was often made.
10. *mirkest*] darkest (Scot.).
    track] trace, traverse.
11. *thy sight*] i.e., the sight of thee.
12. *wooned*] Scottish form of 'woned' meaning 'dwelt'; or possibly a form of 'wound'.

  Tell me, bonny Dick, hast got a wife?
Eust. A wife! God shield, Sir Bartram, that were ill,   15
  To leave my wife and wander thus astray;
  But time and good advice, ere many years,
  May chance to make my fancy bend that way.
  What news in Scotland? Therefore came I hither,
  To see your country and to chat together.   20
Sir Bar. Why, man, our country's blithe, our king is well,
  Our queen so-so, the nobles well, and worse
  And weel are they that are about the king,
  But better are the country gentlemen;
  And I may tell thee, Eustace, in our lives,   25
  We old men never saw so wondrous change—
  But leave this trattle, and tell me what news
  In lovely England with our honest friends?
Eust. The king, the court, and all our noble friends
  Are well; and God in mercy keep them so!   30
  The northern lords and ladies hereabouts,
  That knows I came to see your queen and court,
  Commends them to my honest friend, Sir Bartram,
  And many others that I have not seen.

14. Tell me, bonny] *Q;* But tell me, bonny *conj. Dyce;* Tell me, my bonny *Grosart.* 22. well, and worse] *Q;* well and worse *Dyce;* well, and worse, *Grosart;* well and worse; *Manly.* 23. are] *Dyce;* were *Q.*

---

14. *bonny*] handsome (Scot.).
22. *Our queen so-so*] i.e., she is indifferently well in health. Ruth Hudson (*P.M.L.A.*, XLVII (1932), 657–9) argues unconvincingly that this is a contemporary reference to the pregnancy of James VI's wife which was known in England in the summer of 1590; see Introduction, pp. xxxiv–xxxv.
22–3. *the nobles . . . king*] the nobles are 'well', but they that are about the king are 'worse' in disposition yet well-off ('weel').
23. *that are*] I take the reference to be to Ateukin and his train of flatterers. Lavin defends Q's 'were', suggesting that 'the king has probably already driven away some of his nobles before his dismissal of Douglas, Morton, and the Bishop of St. Andrews (II. ii).'
24. *But . . . gentlemen*] i.e., because they are away from court and the trouble brewing there.
27. *trattle*] chatter (Scot.).
28. *lovely*] See note to l. 1.
32, 33. *knows, Commends*] See note to I. i. 102.

SC. III]   JAMES THE FOURTH   37

  Among the rest, the Countess Elinor   35
  From Carlisle, where we merry oft have been,
  Greets well my lord, and hath directed me
  By message this fair lady's face to see. [*Shows a portrait.*]
Sir Bar. I tell thee, Eustace, lest mine old eyes daze,
  This is our Scottish moon and evening's pride;   40
  This is the blemish of your English bride.
  Who sails by her are sure of wind at will;
  Her face is dangerous, her sight is ill;
  And yet, in sooth, sweet Dick, it may be said
  The king hath folly, there's virtue in the maid.   45
Eust. But knows my friend this portrait ? Be advised.
Sir Bar. Is it not Ida, the Countess of Arran's daughter's ?
Eust. So was I told by Elinor of Carlisle;
  But tell me, lovely Bartram, is the maid
  Evil-inclined, misled, or concubine   50
  Unto the king or any other lord ?
Sir Bar. Should I be brief and true ? Then thus, my Dick:
  All England's grounds yields not a blither lass;
  Nor Europe cannot match her for her gifts
  Of virtue, honour, beauty, and the rest;   55
  But our fond king, not knowing sin in lust,
  Makes love by endless means and precious gifts;
  And men that see it dare not say 't, my friend,

35–6.] *so Dyce; divided in Q at Carlile* / Where.   38. *Shows a portrait*] *Dyce; not in Q.*   49–51.] *so Dyce; two lines in Q divided at* inclind, / Misled.   52. true ? Then thus, my Dick:] *This ed.;* true, then thus my Dicke, *Q;* true, then thus, my Dick. *Dyce.*   54. cannot match] *Manly;* can art *Q;* can surpass *Dyce.*

---

 39. *daze*] are dazzled.
 41. *the blemish . . . bride*] i.e., one who spoils the lot of Dorothea.
 42.] Those who navigate by reference to her (as their pole star) are sure of favourable weather conditions.
 43.] i.e., because of the effect they are having on the King.
 46. *Be advised*] reflect on it.
 53. *yields*] See note to I. i. 102.
 54. *cannot match*] Q's 'can art' is obviously corrupt. 'Match' seems to me to be more in keeping with the idea than the commonly accepted 'surpass' of Dyce.

But we may wish that it were otherwise.
But I rid thee to view the picture still,   60
For by the person's sights there hangs some ill.
Eust. O, good Sir Bartram, you suspect I love—
Then were I mad—her whom I never saw.
But howsoe'er, I fear not enticings:
Desire will give no place unto a king.   65
I'll see her whom the world admires so much,
That I may say with them, 'There lives none such.'
Sir Bar. Be Gad, and sall both see and talk with her;
And, when th' hast done, whate'er her beauty be,
I'll warrant thee her virtues may compare   70
With the proudest she that waits upon your queen.

[*Enter a* Servant.]

Serv. My lady entreats your worship in to supper.
Sir Bar. Guid bonny Dick, my wife will tell thee more:
Was never no man in her book before;
Be Gad, she's blithe, fair, lewely, bonny, etc.   *Exeunt.*   75

61. sights] *Q;* sight *Dyce.*   62. *Eust.*] *Dyce; assigned to Sir Bar. in Q.*   63. her] *Dyce;* hee *Q;* she *Lavin.*   71.1. *Enter a* Servant] *Dyce; not in Q.*   72. *Serv.*] *Dyce; assigned to Eust. in Q.*   74. no man] *Q;* woman *conj. Dyce*[1].

---

60. *I rid . . . still*] I advise you to keep looking at the picture.
61. *For by . . . ill*] because it is dangerous to expose yourself to the glances of the real woman; cf. Middleton and Rowley, *The Changeling* (ed. N. W. Bawcutt, 1961), II. i. 36: 'As if danger or ill luck hung in my looks'.
65. *give . . . unto*] not be denied even for.
68. *sall*] shall (Scot.).
72. Serv.] Dyce's emendation is obviously correct, as the phrasing is inappropriate coming from Eustace.
73. *Guid*] good (Scot.).
74. *her book*] her favour.
75. *Gad*] God (Scot.).
lewely] lovely (Scot.).
etc.] This is an indication for the actors to 'exit talking' or for Sir Bartram to *ad lib* as they leave the stage. For other examples, see *Orlando Furioso*, IV. ii. 1133; *Westward Ho!*, iv. 1; *Family of Love*, ii. 4. Thomas Heywood's *Edward IV* makes the device clear: 'Jockie is led to whipping ouer the stage, speaking some words, but of no importance' (Pearson reprint (1874), I, 180).

[Chorus 1]

Enter BOHAN *and* [OBERON,] *the fairy king, after the first act; to them a round of* Fairies, *or some pretty dance.*

Boh. Be Gad, gramercies, little king, for this;
 This sport is better in my exile life
 Than ever the deceitfuil werld could yield.
Ober. I tell thee, Bohan, Oberon is king
 Of quiet, pleasure, profit, and content, 5
 Of wealth, of honour, and of all the world;
 Tied to no place, yet all are tied to one.
 Live thou in this life, exiled from world and men,
 And I will show thee wonders ere we part.
Boh. Then mark my story, and the strange doubts 10
 That follow flatterers, lust, and lawless will;
 And then say I have reason to forsake
 The world and all that are within the same.
 Go shroud us in our harbour, where we'll see
 The pride of folly, as it ought to be. *Exeunt.* 15

Chorus 1. 7. one] *Q;* me *Dyce.* 8. in] *Q;* omitted *Dyce.* 10. story] *Dyce;* stay *Q.* doubts] *Q;* debates *conj. Dyce;* defeats *conj. Manly.* 12–13.] *so Dyce; divided in Q at* world, / And. 15. pride] *Q;* prize *conj. Dyce.* 15.] *This line in Q is followed by Choruses* VI, VII, VIII, V *of this ed., preceded by the words* 'After the first act.'

Chorus I. 0.2. round] a dance in which the performers move circularly.
 1. *little king*] The ordinary concept of a fairy at the time was, according to K. M. Briggs (*The Anatomy of Puck* (1959), pp. 14–15), a being 'the size of a three-years' child, like Oberon in *Huon of Bordeaux,* some . . . are three spans in height.'
 3. *deceitfuil werld*] deceitful world (Scot.).
 7. *one*] Some editors have emended to 'me' on the grounds that 'the emphasis of the whole speech is on Oberon's personal power' (Lavin). However, I take the point to be that Oberon is the exception to the rule of 'all being tied to one place'.
 10. *story*] Q's 'stay' makes no sense, particularly in view of the last lines of the three Additional Choruses which make use of this same formula.
 doubts] apprehensions, fears.
 14. *shroud*] conceal.
 harbour] resting-place rather than 'arbour' as some editors gloss; cf. Ind. 110 and Chor. II, 16.
 15. *as it ought to be*] according to the way things ought to work out.

Act II

[II. i]

Enter the COUNTESS OF ARRAN *with* IDA *her daughter in their porch, sitting at work. A song.*

Count. Fair Ida, might you choose the greatest good,
    Midst all the world in blessings that abound,
    Wherein, my daughter, should your liking be?
Ida. Not in delights, or pomp, or majesty.
Count. And why?
Ida.   Since these are means to draw the mind   5
    From perfect good, and make true judgment blind.
Count. Might you have wealth and fortune's richest store?
Ida. Yet would I (might I choose) be honest-poor;
    For she that sits at Fortune's feet a-low
    Is sure she shall not taste a further woe;   10
    But those that prank on top of Fortune's ball
    Still fear a change, and, fearing, catch a fall.
Count. Tut, foolish maid, each one contemneth need.
Ida. Good reason why, they know not good indeed.
Count. Many, marry, then, on whom distress doth lour?   15
Ida. Yes, they that virtue deem an honest dower.

II. i] *Actus Secundus. Schena Prima. Q.*   11. on] *Dyce;* one *Q.*   15.
Many, marry] *Dyce;* Many marrie *Q.*   lour?] *This ed.;* loure, *Q.*

0.2 at work] i.e., doing needlework.
7. *store*] treasures, gifts.
9. *a-low*] in humble condition.
11. *prank*] make ostentatious show.
    Fortune's ball] In many Renaissance emblematic representations of Fortune, the goddess is shown to be controlling a wheel or an orb which depicted the fickleness of her favour.
12. *catch*] take.
13. *need*] poverty; cf. *Bussy D'Ambois* (ed. N. Brooke, 1964), I. i. 3.

Madam, by right this world I may compare
Unto my work, wherein with heedful care
The heavenly workman plants with curious hand,
As I with needle draw, each thing on land, 20
Even as he list; some men like to the rose
Are fashioned fresh; some in their stalks do close,
And, born, do sudden die; some are but weeds,
And yet from them a secret good proceeds.
I with my needle, if I please, may blot 25
The fairest rose within my cambric plot;
God with a beck can change each worldly thing,
The poor to wealth, the beggar to the king.
What, then, hath man wherein he well may boast,
Since by a beck he lives, a lour is lost? 30

Enter EUSTACE *with letters.*

Count. Peace, Ida, here are strangers near at hand.
Eust. Madam, God speed.
Count.   I thank you, gentle squire.
Eust. The country Countess of Northumberland
Doth greet you well, and hath requested me
To bring these letters to your ladyship. 35
        He carries the letter[s].

20. on] *Dyce;* one *Q.*   28. wealth] *This ed.;* earth *Q;* rich *Dyce.*   30.
lour] *Dyce;* louer *Q.*   33. country] *Q;* courteous *conj. Manly.*   35.1.
letters] *Dyce;* letter *Q.*

---

18. *work*] needlework.
19. *curious*] ingenious, clever.
20. *draw*] depict (in embroidery).
21. *list*] wishes.
25. *blot*] efface.
26. *cambric*] a kind of fine white linen, originally made at Cambray in Flanders.
27. *beck*] slightest indication of command.
28. *wealth*] Emendation of Q's 'earth' is necessary to balance the latter half of the line. 'Wealth' seems to me more palaeographically likely than the more commonly accepted 'rich'.
30. *lour*] Q's spelling 'louer' is obviously phonetic.
33. *country*] i.e., who owns and resides on land.
35.1. carries] holds up, hands over.

Count. I thank her honour, and yourself, my friend.

She receives and peruseth them.

I see she means you good, brave gentleman.
Daughter, the Lady Elinor salutes
Yourself as well as me; then for her sake
'Twere good you entertained that courtier well. 40

Ida. As much salute as may become my sex,
And he in virtue can vouchsafe to think,
I yield him for the courteous countess' sake.
Good sir, sit down; my mother here and I
Count time misspent an endless vanity. 45

Eust. [*Aside*] Beyond report, the wit, the fair, the shape!
[*To her*] What work you here, fair mistress? May I see it?

Ida. Good sir, look on: how like you this compact?

Eust. Methinks in this I see true love in act:
The woodbines with their leaves do sweetly spread, 50
The roses blushing prank them in their red;
No flower but boasts the beauties of the spring;
This bird hath life indeed, if it could sing.
What means, fair mistress, had you in this work?

Ida. My needle, sir.

Eust.   In needles then there lurk 55
Some hidden grace I deem beyond my reach.

Ida. Not grace in them, good sir, but those that teach.

Eust. Say that your needle now were Cupid's sting—
[*Aside*] But, ah, her eye must be no less
In which is heaven and heavenliness, 60
In which the food of God is shut,

---

46. *Aside*] Dyce; not in Q. 47. *To her*] This ed.; not in Q. 55. lurk] Dyce; lurkes Q. 59. *Aside*] Dyce; not in Q.

---

37. *means you good*] intends good to you.
41. *salute*] greeting.
42. *vouchsafe*] condescend, be willing.
46. *fair*] beauty; cf. *Sonn.*, 16.11, 18.7, 21.4, 68.3, 83.2, 95.12.
48. *compact*] composition; the use antedates *O.E.D.*'s first citation.
51. *prank them*] See note to l. 11.
55. *lurk*] Dyce's emendation seems likely for the sake of the rhyme.
58. *sting*] arrow.

SC. I]   JAMES THE FOURTH   43

  Whose powers the purest minds do glut.
Ida. What if it were?
Eust.   Then see a wondrous thing:
  I fear me you would paint in Tereus' heart
  Affection in his power and chiefest parts.   65
Ida. Good Lord, sir, no! For, hearts but prickèd soft
  Are wounded sore; for so I hear it oft.
Eust. What recks the wound, where but your happy eye
  May make him live whom Jove hath judged to die?
Ida. Should life and death within this needle lurk, 70
  I'll prick no hearts, I'll prick upon my work.

    Enter ATEUKIN *with* SLIPPER, *the clown.*

Count. Peace, Ida, I perceive the fox at hand.
Eust. The fox? Why, fetch your hounds and chase him hence.
Count. O sir, these great men bark at small offence.
  Come, will it please you to enter, gentle sir? 75
  [*The Countess of Arran, Ida, and Eustace*] *offer to exeunt.*
Ateu. Stay, courteous ladies; favour me so much
  As to discourse a word or two apart.
Count. Good sir, my daughter learns this rule of me,
  To shun resort and strangers' company;

68. What . . . eye] *so Dyce; divided in Q at* second, / Where. wound]
Dyce; second *Q.* 75.] *so Dyce; assigned to Ateu. in Q.* 75. to] *Q;*
omitted Grosart.

---

 63. *What . . . were?*] This question is in response to Eustace's line 58.
 64. *paint*] depict.
 Tereus] King of Thrace and husband of Procne, he became enamoured
of his wife's sister Philomela whom he ravished and imprisoned; then he
cut out her tongue to prevent the revelation of his crime. Philomela, during
her captivity, depicted her misfortune on a piece of tapestry which she conveyed to her sister, with whom she planned revenge. The story is in Ovid,
Metamorphoses, VI.
 65. *Affection*] lust.
 chiefest parts] fullest amount.
 68. *What recks*] of what importance is.
 71. *prick upon*] i.e., use my needle on. Note the pun with 'prick' meaning
'pierce' or 'wound'.
 79. *shun resort*] avoid crowds.

    For some are shifting mates that carry letters,   80
Some, such as you, too good because our betters.
Slip. Now, I pray you, sir, what kin are you to a pickerel?
Ateu. Why, knave?
Slip. By my troth, sir, because I never knew a proper situation
    fellow of your pitch fitter to swallow a gudgeon.   85
Ateu. What meanest thou by this?
Slip. 'Shifting fellow', sir,—these be thy words, 'shifting
    fellow'; this gentlewoman, I fear me, knew your bringing
    up.
Ateu. How so?   90
Slip. Why, sir, your father was a miller that could shift for a
    peck of grist in a bushel, and you a fair-spoken gentleman
    that can get more land by a lie than an honest man by his
    ready money.
Ateu. Caitive, what sayest thou?   95
Slip. I say, sir, that if she call you shifting knave, you shall not
    put her to the proof.
Ateu. And why?
Slip. Because, sir, living by your wit as you do, shifting is
    your letters-patents; it were a hard matter for me to get   100

87–9.] *so Dyce; irregular verse in Q divided at* fellow: / This.   88. your]
Q corr. (BM, HN, VA); you *Q uncorr. (FO).*   91–2. Why . . . bushel,]
so Dyce; irregular verse in Q divided at Miller, / That . . . bushell, / And.
92. you] *Q;* you're *Dyce.*   96–7.] *so Dyce; irregular verse in Q divided at* knaue, / You.

---

80. *shifting mates*] false contriving fellows.
82. *pickerel*] young pike.
84–5. *situation fellow*] a man temporarily placed (*O.E.D.*, 3b). The point of Slipper's jibe seems to be that Ateukin will be baited.
85. *pitch*] status, level. There may be a pun here on 'pitch' meaning 'a net spread for catching fish' (*O.E.D.*, sb.² 6).
    swallow a gudgeon] be baited easily (by the Countess); cf. Tilley G473.
87. *thy words*] i.e., words which apply to thee.
91–2. *shift . . . bushel*] literally 'to obtain by cheating a quarter of corn from every bushel ground'.
97. *put her to the proof*] challenge her on the matter.
100. *letters-patents*] literally 'a document, usually from a sovereign, conferring some right or privilege'; here used figuratively to mean 'credentials'.

SC. I]   JAMES THE FOURTH   45

>   my dinner that day wherein my master had not sold a
>   dozen of devices, a case of cogs, and a suit of shifts, in the
>   morning. I speak this in your commendation, sir, and I
>   pray you so take it.
> *Ateu.* If I live, knave, I will be revenged. What gentleman 105
>   would entertain a rascal thus to derogate from his
>   honour?   [*Beats Slipper.*]
> *Ida.* My lord, why are you thus impatient?
> *Ateu.* Not angry, Ida; but I teach this knave
>   How to behave himself among his betters.   110
>   Behold, fair countess, to assure your stay,
>   I here present the signet of the king,
>   Who now by me, fair Ida, doth salute you;
>   And since in secret I have certain things
>   In his behalf, good madam, to impart,   115
>   I crave your daughter to discourse apart.
> *Count.* She shall in humble duty be addressed
>   To do his highness' will in what she may.
> *Ida.* Now, gentle sir, what would his grace with me?
> *Ateu.* Fair, comely nymph, the beauty of your face, 120
>   Sufficient to bewitch the heavenly powers,
>   Hath wrought so much in him that now of late
>   He finds himself made captive unto love;
>   And though his power and majesty requires
>   A straight command before an humble suit,   125
>   Yet he his mightiness doth so abase
>   As to entreat your favour, honest maid.
> *Ida.* Is he not married, sir, unto our queen?

102. cogs] *Q corr. (BM, HN, VA);* dogges *Q uncorr. (FO).*   103. your] *Q corr. (BM, HN, VA);* you *Q uncorr. (FO).*   107. Beats Slipper] *so* Manly *(subst.); not in Q.*

---

102. *case*] set (with a quibble on the legal term).
cogs] deceptions, frauds.
suit] number (with a quibble on the legal term).
111. *to assure ... stay*] to ensure you remain here.
125–7. *A straight ... favour*] a rhetorical commonplace; Lavin compares *LLL.*, IV. i. 75–7: 'Shall I command thy love? I may. Shall I enforce thy love? I could. Shall I entreat thy love? I will.' and *Ham.,* II. ii. 26–9.

Ateu. He is.
Ida.   And are not they by God accursed
    That sever them whom he hath knit in one? 130
Ateu. They be; what then? We seek not to displace
    The princess from her seat; but, since by love
    The king is made your own, he is resolved
    In private to accept your dalliance,
    In spite of war, watch, or worldly eye. 135
Ida. O, how he talks as if he should not die!
    As if that God in justice once could wink!
    Upon that fault I am ashamed to think.
Ateu. Tut, mistress, man at first was born to err;
    Women are all not formèd to be saints: 140
    'Tis impious for to kill our native king,
    Whom by a little favour we may save.
Ida. Better than live unchaste, to live in grave.
Ateu. He shall erect your state and wed you well.
Ida. But can his warrant keep my soul from hell? 145
Ateu. He will enforce, if you resist his suit.
Ida. What though? The world may shame to him account,
    To be a king of men and worldly pelf,
    Yet hath no power to rule and guide himself.
Ateu. I know you, gentle lady, and the care 150
    Both of your honour and his grace's health
    Makes me confusèd in this dangerous state.

---

133. he] *Dyce;* shee *Q.* 135. war, watch] *Q;* war, or watch *conj. Dyce, Collins;* wary watch *conj. Manly.* 137. wink!] *This ed.;* wink, *Q.* 143. live in] *Q;* lie in *Dyce.* 147. account] *Q;* impute *conj. Dyce.* 149.] *so Dyce; assigned to Ateu. in Q.* Yet hath] *Q;* Yet h' hath *Grosart.* no power to] *Dyce;* to power no *Q.*

---

135. *watch*] vigilance, surveillance.
137. *wink*] turn a blind eye.
139. *man . . . err*] Cf. Tilley E179: 'To err is human'.
143. *live in grave*] i.e., to die; Lavin glosses 'save one's soul'.
144. *erect your state*] raise you to a more dignified rank.
wed you well] provide you with a suitable husband.
146. *enforce*] force you to do as he wishes.
147. *What though*] even supposing that is so; or possibly 'What then': cf. Marlowe's *Ovid's Elegies* (*Poems*, ed. M. MacLure, 1968), I. ii. 3.

Ida. So counsel him, but soothe thou not his sin.
    'Tis vain allurement that doth make him love;
    I shame to hear, be you ashamed to move.   155
Count. [*Aside*] I see my daughter grows impatient;
    I fear me he pretends some bad intent.
Ateu. Will you despise the king and scorn him so?
Ida. In all allegiance I will serve his grace,
    But not in lust—O, how I blush to name it!   160
Ateu. [*Aside*] An endless work is this; how should I frame it?
                                  They discourse privately.
Slip. O, mistress, may I turn a word upon you?
Count. Friend, what wilt thou?
Slip. O, what a happy gentlewoman be you truly! The world
    reports this of you, mistress, that a man can no sooner   165
    come to your house, but the butler comes with a black-
    jack and says, 'Welcome, friend, here's a cup of the best
    for you.' Verily, mistress, you are said to have the best
    ale in all Scotland.
Count. Sirrah, go fetch him drink. [*A* Servant *brings drink.*]   170
    How likest thou this?
Slip. Like it, mistress? Why, this is quincy quarie, pepper
    de watchet, single goby, of all that ever I tasted. I'll
    prove in this ale and toast the compass of the whole
    world. First, this is the earth: it lies in the middle, a fair   175

---

156. *Aside*] Manly; not in Q.   161. *Aside*] Dyce; not in Q.   163.] so
Dyce; assigned to *Ateu.* in Q.   170. *A* Servant . . . *drink*] Dyce; not in Q.
175. lies] Dyce; ties Q.

---

   153. *soothe*] gloss over, render less objectionable.
   155. *move*] solicit.
   157. *pretends*] intends.
   161. *frame*] contrive.
   162. *turn . . . upon*] direct speech to.
   166–7. *black-jack*] leather jug shaped like a leg of an inverted boot.
   172–3. *quincy . . . goby*] nonce-words indicating Slipper's sensuous anticipation.
   174. *prove*] demonstrate.
   175–6. *a fair . . . toast*] Slipper is probably offered sack here in which a piece of toasted bread was often placed as an added delicacy; cf. *Wiv.*, III. v. 3.

brown toast, a goodly country for hungry teeth to dwell
upon; next, this is the sea, a fair pool for a dry tongue to
fish in. Now come I, and seeing the world is naught, I
divide it thus; and because the sea cannot stand without
the earth, as Aristotle saith, I put them both into their   180
first chaos, which is my belly; and so, mistress, you may
see your ale is become a miracle.

Eust. A merry mate, madam, I promise you.

Count. Why sigh you, sirrah?

Slip. Truly, madam, to think upon the world which, since I   185
denounced it, keeps such a rumbling in my stomach that,
unless your cook give it a counterbuff with some of your
roasted capons or beef, I fear me I shall become a loose
body, so dainty, I think I shall neither hold fast before
nor behind.   190

Count. [*To Servant*] Go, take him in and feast this merry swain.

[*To Slipper*] Sirrah, my cook is your physician;
He hath a purge for to digest the world.

[*Exit* SLIPPER *with the* Servant.]

Ateu. Will you not, Ida, grant his highness this?

180. Aristotle] *Dyce; Arist.* Q.   186. denounced it,] *Dyce;* denoŭced, it Q.   191. *To Servant*] *This ed.; not in* Q.   192. *To Slipper*] *This ed.; not in* Q.   193. digest] *Dyce;* disiest Q.   193.1. *Exit ... Servant*] *Dyce; not in* Q.

179–80. *because ... saith*] The reference is to Aristotle's critique of the theory of Thales of Miletus in *De Caelo*, II. xiii, in which he notes: 'this is to forget that the same thing may be said of water supporting the earth as was said of the earth itself. It is not the nature of water, any more than of earth, to remain suspended: it rests upon something.'

181. *first chaos*] i.e., the Greek χάος, 'the nether abyss, the first state of the universe'; cf. Webster's *The Duchess of Malfi* (ed. J. R. Brown, 1964), IV. i. 99.

182. *miracle*] wonder.

183. *mate*] fellow.

186. *denounced*] gave authoritative information about.

187. *counterbuff*] check.

188–9. *become a loose body*] have relaxed bowels.

189. *dainty*] delicate in health.

hold fast] be continent.

193. *digest*] help the digestion of.

SC. I] JAMES THE FOURTH 49

Ida. As I have said, in duty I am his;   195
   For other lawless lusts that ill beseem him,
   I cannot like, and good I will not deem him.
Count. Ida, come in; and, sir, if so you please,
   Come take a homely widow's entertain.
Ida. If he have no great haste, he may come nigh; 200
   If haste, though he be gone I will not cry.
         Exeunt [COUNTESS OF ARRAN, IDA, *and* EUSTACE].
Ateu. I see this labour lost, my hope in vain;
   Yet will I try another drift again.   [*Exit.*]

[II. ii]

   Enter the BISHOP OF ST ANDREWS, EARL DOUGLAS, MORTON,
      with others one way, the Queen [DOROTHEA,] *with* NANO,
                     another way.

B. of St And. [*Aside*] O, wrack of commonweal! O wretched
      state!
Doug. [*Aside*] O, hapless flock, whereas the guide is blind!
Mort. [*Aside*] O, heedless youth where counsel is despised!
                              They all are in a muse.
Dor. Come pretty knave, and prank it by my side;
   Let's see your best attendance out of hand.   5

---

197. him] *Q;* 'em *conj. Dyce.*   201.1. *Countess ... Eustace*] *Dyce; not in Q.*
203. *Exit*] *Dyce; not in Q.*

II. ii. 0.2. *Nano*] *Dyce; Dwarfes Q.*   1, 2, 3. *Aside*] *Dyce; not in Q.*
3.1. *They ... muse*] *so Dyce; follows l. 2 in Q.*

---

   198. *sir*] i.e., Eustace.
   199. *entertain*] entertainment; here more specifically 'a meal'.
   201. *though ... cry*] Ida, obviously attracted to Eustace, protests too much
here.
   203. *drift*] scheme, device.

   II. ii. 1, 2, 3. Aside] These seem to be called for by l. 22.
   2. *whereas*] where.
   3.1. a muse] a state of abstraction.
   4. *prank it*] strut, gambol.
   5. *out of hand*] immediately.

H

Nano. Madam, although my limbs are very small,
   My heart is good; I'll serve you therewithal.
Dor. How if I were assailed, what couldst thou do?
Nano. Madam, call help and boldly fight it too.
   Although a bee be but a little thing,   10
   You know, fair queen, it hath a bitter sting.
Dor. How couldst thou do me good, were I in grief?
Nano. Counsel, dear princess, is a choice relief:
   Though Nestor wanted force, great was his wit;
   And though I am but weak, my words are fit.   15
B. of St And. [*Aside*] Like to a ship upon the ocean seas,
   Tossed in the doubtful stream without a helm,
   Such is a monarch without good advice.
   I am o'erheard; cast rein upon thy tongue;
   Andrews, beware; reproof will breed a scar.   20
Mort. Good day, my lord.
B. of St And.   Lord Morton, well y-met.
   Whereon deems Lord Douglas all this while?
Doug. Of that which yours and my poor heart doth break,
   Although fear shuts our mouths: we dare not speak.
Dor. [*Aside*] What mean these princes sadly to consult? 25
   Somewhat, I fear, betideth them amiss,
   They are so pale in looks, so vexed in mind.
   [*To them*] In happy hour, ye noble Scottish peers,
   Have I encountered you: what makes you mourn?
B. of St And. If we with patience may attention gain,   30

6. *Nano.*] *Q has sp. h. 'Dwarfe. | Dwarf. | Dwar.' throughout the scene.*
16. *Aside*] *Dyce; not in Q.*   22. Whereon] *Q;* Whereupon *conj. Manly.*
deems] *Q;* dreams *Dyce.*   25. *Aside*] *Dyce; not in Q.*   28. *To them*] *This
ed.; not in Q.*   ye] *Dyce;* the *Q.*   30. attention] *Dyce;* attentiue *Q.*

---

9. *it*] that which threatened.
14. *Nestor*] the oldest and wisest of the Greek leaders at the siege of Troy.
wanted] lacked.
wit] wisdom.
15. *fit*] appropriate to the situation.
21. *y-met*] an archaic verb form used here for metrical purposes.
22. *deems*] ponders, considers.
28. *ye*] The MS. copy probably had this, which the compositor misread as 'y^e', the abbreviation for 'the'.

Your grace shall know the cause of all our grief.
Dor. Speak on, good father, come and sit by me;
    I know thy care is for the common good.
B. of St And. As fortune, mighty princess, reareth some
    To high estate and place in commonweal,   35
    So by divine bequest to them is lent
    A riper judgment and more searching eye,
    Whereby they may discern the common harm;
    For where our fortunes in the world are most,
    Where all our profits rise and still increase,   40
    There is our mind, thereon we meditate;
    And what we do partake of good advice,
    That we employ for to conserve the same.
    To this intent, these nobles and myself,
    That are (or should be) eyes of commonweal,   45
    Seeing his highness' reckless course of youth,
    His lawless and unbridled vain in love,
    His too intentive trust to flatterers,
    His abject care of counsel and his friends,
    Cannot but grieve; and, since we cannot draw   50
    His eye or judgment to discern his faults,
    Since we have spake and counsel is not heard,
    I, for my part (let others as they list),
    Will leave the court and leave him to his will,
    Lest with a ruthful eye I should behold   55
    His overthrow, which, sore I fear, is nigh.

39. our fortunes] *Dyce;* importunes *Q.*   43. conserve] *Manly;* concerne *Q.*   46. reckless] *Dyce;* reachlesse *Q.*   47. vain] *Q;* vein *Dyce.*

---

36. *bequest*] assignment, bestowal.
39. *our fortunes*] Q's reading was probably palaeographical in origin.
42.] and what powers to give good counsel we may have.
43. *conserve the same*] preserve the present condition of things.
47. *vain*] vanity (*O.E.D.*, 7a). It is possible that Q's spelling is a variant of 'vein', which could be defended as the reading here.
48. *intentive*] heedful, attentive.
49. *abject*] rejected.
    care] heedfulness.
54. *will*] The meaning here may be either 'self-will' (in preferring Ateukin) or 'sexual appetite' (with regard to Ida).

Dor. Ah, father, are you so estranged from love,
    From due allegiance to your prince and land,
    To leave your king when most he needs your help?
    The thrifty husbandmen are never wont,   60
    That see their lands unfruitful, to forsake them;
    But when the mould is barren and unapt,
    They toil, they plough, and make the fallow fat;
    The pilot in the dangerous seas is known;
    In calmer waves the silly sailor strives.   65
    Are you not members, lords, of commonweal,
    And can your head, your dear anointed king,
    Default, ye lords, except yourselves do fail?
    O, stay your steps, return and counsel him!
Doug. Men seek not moss upon a rolling stone,   70
    Or water from the sieve, or fire from ice,
    Or comfort from a reckless monarch's hands.
    Madam, he sets us light that served in court
    In place of credit, in his father's days;
    If we but enter presence of his grace,   75
    Our payment is a frown, a scoff, a frump;
    Whilst flattering Gnatho pranks it by his side,
    Soothing the careless king in his misdeeds;
    And if your grace consider your estate,

72. reckless] *Dyce;* rechlesse *Q.*

---

62. *mould*] surface soil.
63. *fat*] fertile.
64–5. *The pilot . . . strives*] W. P. Mustard, *M.L.N.*, XL (1925), 317, compares Seneca, *Epistulae Morales*, LXXXV, 34: 'It is indeed so far from hindering the pilot's art that it even exhibits the art; for anyone, in the words of the proverb, is a pilot on a calm sea.'
65. *silly*] simple.
68. *Default*] fail to perform his duty.
70.] a proverb (Tilley S885).
71. *water . . . sieve*] a proverb (Tilley W111).
73. *sets us light*] prizes us lightly, values us not at all.
76. *frump*] jeer.
77. *Gnatho*] the parasite in Terence's *Eunuchus* and a type-name. *pranks*] Cf. II. i. 11.
78. *Soothing*] encouraging (by expressing approval).
79. *estate*] situation.

SC. II]   JAMES THE FOURTH   53

  His life should urge you too, if all be true. 80
Dor. Why, Douglas, why?
Doug.   As if you have not heard
  His lawless love to Ida grown of late,
  His careless estimate of your estate.
Dor. Ah, Douglas, thou misconstrest his intent.
  He doth but tempt his wife, he tries my love: 85
  This injury pertains to me, not to you.
  The king is young; and, if he step awry,
  He may amend, and I will love him still.
  Should we disdain our vines because they sprout
  Before their time? Or young men, if they strain 90
  Beyond their reach? No, vines that bloom and spread
  Do promise fruits, and young men that are wild
  In age grow wise. My friends and Scottish peers,
  If that an English princess may prevail,
  Stay, stay with him; lo, how my zealous prayer 95
  Is pled with tears! Fie, peers, will you hence?
B. of St And. Madam, 'tis virtue in your grace to plead;
  But we that see his vain untoward course
  Cannot but fly the fire before it burn,
  And shun the court before we see his fall. 100
Dor. Will you not stay? Then, lordings, fare you well.
  Though you forsake your king, the heavens, I hope,
  Will favour him through mine incessant prayer.
Nano. Content you, madam; thus old Ovid sings,

81. *Dor.*] Dyce; assigned to Doug. in Q. 86. not to you] *Q;* not you *Dyce.*

---

 80. *life*] i.e., course of behaviour.
 urge] make you think of doing something.
 83. *estimate*] opinion.
 84. *misconstrest*] misconstruest.
 87–8. *The king . . . amend*] Cf. the proverb: 'He is young enough to amend' (Tilley A236).
 96. *pled*] pleaded.
 98. *untoward*] perverse, unruly. The accent is on the second syllable.
 101. *lordings*] The word indicates Dorothea's contempt.
 104–5. *thus . . . things*] Cf. Tilley A231: 'What cannot be altered must be borne not blamed,' and C922: 'What cannot be cured must be endured.' Collins suggests the reference is to *Remedia Amoris*, 91–2: 'Resist begin-

    'Tis foolish to bewail recureless things.'   105
Dor. Peace, dwarf; these words my patience move.
Nano. Although you charm my speech, charm not my love.
         Exeunt NANO [*and*] DOROTHEA.

Enter the KING OF SCOTS; *the* Nobles, *spying him* [*as they are about to go out*], *return.*

K. of Scot. Douglas, how now? Why changest thou thy cheer?
Doug. My private troubles are so great, my liege,
  As I must crave your licence for a while,   110
  For to intend mine own affairs at home.
K. of Scot. You may depart. [*Exit* DOUGLAS.] But why is Morton sad?
Mort. The like occasion doth import me too;
  So I desire your grace to give me leave.
K. of Scot. Well, sir, you may betake you to your ease.   115
            [*Exit* MORTON.]
[*Aside*] When such grim sirs are gone, I see no let
  To work my will.
B. of St And.   What, like the eagle, then,
  With often flight wilt thou thy feathers lose?
  O king, canst thou endure to see thy court

---

106. Peace, dwarf] *Q;* Peace, foolish dwarf *Grosart;* Peace, prating dwart *conj. Collins.* 107.2. Scots; the] *Dyce;* Scots; Arius, the *Q.* 107.2-3. as ... out] *Dyce; not in Q.* 107.3. return] *Dyce;* returnes *Q.* 112. Exit Douglas] *so Dyce;* 'Exit' *at l. 111 in Q.* 115.1. Exit Morton] *Dyce; not in Q.* 116. Aside] *Dyce; not in Q.* 117, 145. B. of St And.] 8. Atten. *Q.*

---

nings; too late is the medicine prepared, when the disease has gained strength by long delay.'
 105. *recureless*] irremediable.
 107. *charm*] subdue, control.
 107.2. *Scots*] Q's 'Arius' after the King's name also appears as the speech prefix of the King of England in v. iii.
 108. *thy cheer*] the expression on thy face.
 111. *intend*] attend to, look after.
 113. *import*] concern.
 116. *let*] hindrance.
 117-18. *like ... lose*] I have been unable to trace the source of this.

        Of finest wits and judgments dispossessed,   120
        Whilst cloaking craft with soothing climbs so high
        As each bewails ambition is so bad?
        Thy father left thee, with estate and crown,
        A learnèd council to direct thy court:
        These carelessly, O king, thou castest off,   125
        To entertain a train of sycophants.
        Thou well mayst see, although thou wilt not see,
        That every eye and ear both sees and hears
        The certain signs of thine incontinence.
        Thou art allied unto the English king   130
        By marriage: a happy friend indeed
        If usèd well; if not, a mighty foe.
        Thinketh your grace he can endure and brook
        To have a partner in his daughter's love?
        Thinketh your grace the grudge of privy wrongs   135
        Will not procure him change his smiles to threats?
        O, be not blind to good: call home your lords,
        Displace these flattering Gnathos, drive them hence!
        Love and with kindness take your wedlock wife,
        Or else (which God forbid) I fear a change: 140
        Sin cannot thrive in courts without a plague.
K. of Scot. Go pack thou too, unless thou mend thy talk!
        On pain of death, proud bishop, get you gone,
        Unless you headless mean to hop away!   144
B. of St And. Thou God of heaven prevent my country's fall!
                Exeunt [*the* BISHOP OF ST ANDREWS *and others*].
K. of Scot. These stays and lets to pleasure plague my thoughts,
        Forcing my grievous wounds anew to bleed;

---

124. court] *Q;* course *Dyce.*   145.1. the ... others] *Dyce (subst.); not in Q.*

---

  120. *wits*] wise men.
  121. *soothing*] flattering.
  133. *brook*] tolerate.
  134. *a partner ... love*] i.e., a rival to his daughter in her love.
  138. *Gnathos*] See note to l. 77.
  142. *pack*] go.
  146. *stays and lets*] checks and hindrances.

But care that hath transported me so far,
Fair Ida, is dispersed in thought of thee,
Whose answer yields me life or breeds my death. 150
Yond comes the messenger of weal or woe.

Enter ATEUKIN.

Ateukin, what news?
Ateu. The adamant, O king, will not be filed
But by itself, and beauty that exceeds
By some exceeding favour must be wrought. 155
Ida is coy as yet, and doth repine,
Objecting marriage, honour, fear, and death:
She's holy, wise, and too precise for me.
K. of Scot. Are these thy fruits of wits, thy sight in art,
Thine eloquence, thy policy, thy drift— 160
To mock thy prince? Then, caitiff, pack thee hence,
And let me die devourèd in my love.
Ateu. Good Lord, how rage gainsayeth reason's power!
My dear, my gracious, and belovèd prince,
The essence of my suit, my god on earth, 165
Sit down and rest yourself; appease your wrath,
Lest with a frown ye wound me to the death.
O, that I were included in my grave,

151.1. *Ateukin*] Dyce; *Gnato* Q.   158. holy, wise] Q; holy-wise *Dyce*.
165. suit] sute Q; soul *Dyce*.

---

148. *transported me*] put me beside myself.
153-4. *The adamant...itself*] Cf. Tilley D323: 'Diamond cuts diamond.'
153. *adamant*] diamond.
154. *exceeds*] excels.
155. *wrought*] won over.
157. *marriage*] i.e., the king's marriage; see II. i. 128.
158. *precise*] scrupulous, with a suggestion of 'puritanical'.
159. *sight*] knowledge, skill, insight.
160. *drift*] scheme, plot.
165. *essence*] substance. The word has religious overtones and thus accords with the blasphemy of the latter half of the line.
   suit] Many editors emend to 'soul', but Ateukin is referring to the errand from which he has just returned and in connection with which he has twice used this word (II. i. 125, 146).
168. *included in*] enclosed in.

SC. II]   JAMES THE FOURTH   57

  That either now, to save my prince's life,
  Must counsel cruelty or lose my king.   170
K. of Scot. Why, sirrah, is there means to move her mind?
Ateu. O, should I not offend my royal liege,—
K. of Scot. Tell all, spare naught, so I may gain my love.
Ateu. Alas, my soul, why art thou torn in twain,
  For fear thou talk a thing that should displease!   175
K. of Scot. Tut, speak whatso thou wilt, I pardon thee.
Ateu. How kind a word, how courteous is his grace!
  Who would not die to succour such a king?
  My liege, this lovely maid of modest mind
  Could well incline to love, but that she fears   180
  Fair Dorothea's power: your grace doth know
  Your wedlock is a mighty let to love.
  Were Ida sure to be your wedded wife,
  That then the twig would bow, you might command.
  Ladies love presents, pomp, and high estate.   185
K. of Scot. Ah, Ateukin, how should we displace this let?
Ateu. Tut, mighty prince,—O that I might be whist!
K. of Scot. Why dalliest thou?
Ateu.   I will not move my prince.
  I will prefer his safety before my life.
  Hear me, O king, 'tis Dorothea's death   190
  Must do you good.
K. of Scot.   What, murder of my queen!
  Yet, to enjoy my love, what is my queen?

172. liege,—] *Dyce;* liege. *Q.* 186. displace] *Dyce;* display *Q;* destroy *conj. Manly.*

---

 171. *move her mind*] change her opinion.
 182. *let*] check.
 184. *That*] so that.
 186. *displace*] Both Dyce's emendation and Manly's conjecture are attractive, but there was a contemporary medical usage of 'displace' meaning 'to dissipate', 'to disperse' and Greene was at one time a 'student of physick' at Cambridge.
  let] obstacle.
 187. *whist*] silent.
 188. *will not move*] do not wish to anger.

58   JAMES THE FOURTH   [ACT II

  O, but my vow and promise to my queen!
  Ay, but my hope to gain a fairer queen;
  With how contrarious thoughts am I withdrawn! 195
  Why linger I 'twixt hope and doubtful fear?
  If Dorothea die, will Ida love?
Ateu.   She will, my lord.
K. of Scot. Then let her die: devise, advise the means;
  All likes me well that lends me hope in love.
Ateu. What, will your grace consent? Then let me work. 200
  There's here in court a Frenchman, Jaques called,
  A fit performer of our enterprise,
  Whom I by gifts and promise will corrupt
  To slay the queen, so that your grace will seal
  A warrant for the man to save his life. 205
K. of Scot. Naught shall he want; write thou and I will sign.
  And, gentle Gnatho, if my Ida yield,
  Thou shalt have what thou wilt; I'll give thee straight
  A barony, an earldom for reward.
Ateu. Frolic, young king, the lass shall be your own; 210
  I'll make her blithe and wanton by my wit. *Exeunt.*

[Chorus II]

    Enter BOHAN *with* OBERON.

Boh. So, Oberon, now it begins to work in kind.
  The ancient lords by leaving him alone,

198.] *so Dyce; two lines in Q divided at* die. / Deuise.
Chorus II] *headed by* '3. *Act.' after l. 0.1 and followed by* 'Chorus' *in Q.*
2. alone] *Dyce;* aliue *Q.*

---

 195. *withdrawn*] distracted (*O.E.D.*, 5).
 201. *Jaques*] It is clear from this line that the pronunciation of the name was disyllabic.
 204. *so that*] on condition that.
 210. *Frolic*] be of good cheer.

 Chorus II. 1. *work in kind*] happen as is to be expected.
 2. *alone*] Q's reading is certainly an error of palaeographical origin.

Disliking of his humours and despite,
Lets him run headlong, till his flatterers,
Sweeting his thoughts of luckless lust 5
With vile persuasions and alluring words,
Makes him make way by murder to his will.
Judge, fairy king, hast heard a greater ill?
Ober. Nor seen more virtue in a country maid.
I tell thee, Bohan, it doth make me sorry 10
To think the deeds the king means to perform.
Boh. To change that humour, stand and see the rest:
I trow my son Slipper will show 's a jest.

Enter SLIPPER *with a companion, boy or wench, dancing a hornpipe, and dance out again.*

Now after this beguiling of our thoughts,
And changing them from sad to better glee, 15
Let's to our cell, and sit and see the rest;
For I believe this jig will prove no jest. *Exeunt.*

---

3. despite] *Dyce;* respight *Q*.   5. Sweeting] *Q;* Soliciting *Dyce;* Sweetening *Grosart;* Suiting *conj. Collier.*   luckless] *Q;* lawless *Dyce*.   9. seen] *Dyce;* send *Q;* found *conj. Manly.*   10. sorry] *Dyce;* merrie *Q*.   11. deeds] *Q;* deed *Thorndike.*   13.1. boy] *Dyce;* bog, *Q*.   16. the] *Dyce;* thee *Q*.

---

3. *humours*] capricious moods.
despite] contempt.
4. *Lets*] See note to I. i. 102.
5. *Sweeting*] gratifying, making pleasant, supporting.
luckless] ill-starred, unfortunate.
10. *sorry*] Q's 'merrie' is inappropriate in view of Bohan's reply in ll. 12–13.
11. *think*] think of.
13. *trow*] believe.
15. *glee*] entertainment.
16. *cell*] i.e., the gallery referred to in Ind. 110.
17. *jig*] a performance normally of a lively or comical nature usually applied to a piece given in the intervals or at the end of a play. Here it appears to mean simply 'a play', a meaning not recorded in *O.E.D.* See note to Ind. 94.1.

Act III

[III. i]

Enter SLIPPER *one way and* S[IR] BARTRAM *another way.*

Sir Bar. Ho, fellow! Stay and let me speak with thee.
Slip. Fellow! Friend, thou dost disbuse me; I am a gentleman.
Sir Bar. A gentleman? How so?
Slip. Why, I rub horses, sir.
Sir Bar. And what of that? 5
Slip. O, simple witted! Mark my reason: they that do good service in the commonweal are gentlemen, but such as rub horses do good service in the commonweal; *ergo*, tarbox, master courtier, a horse-keeper is a gentleman.
Sir Bar. Here is overmuch wit, in good earnest. But, sirrah, 10 where is thy master?
Slip. Neither above ground nor under ground, drawing out red into white, swallowing that down without chawing that was never made without treading.
Sir Bar. Why, where is he then? 15
Slip. Why, in his cellar, drinking a cup of neat and brisk claret

---

III. i] *Actus* 3. *Schena Prima. Q.*   2. disbuse] *Q;* abuse *Dyce.*   10–11. so *Dyce; irregular verse in Q divided at* earnest: / But.   12–14.] *so Dyce; irregular verse in Q divided at* ground, / Drawing ... white, / Swallowing ... chawing, / That.

---

1. *fellow*] a way of addressing an inferior in rank.
2. *disbuse*] a malapropism for 'abuse'.
8. ergo] Lat., therefore.
tarbox] a perfumed fellow.
12–13. *drawing ... white*] i.e., drawing red (wine) into a silver (white) bowl; see ll. 16–17.
13. *chawing*] chewing.
14. *treading*] i.e., the grapes.
16. *brisk*] agreeably sharp to the taste.

SC. I]   JAMES THE FOURTH   61

  in a bowl of silver. O sir, the wine runs trillill down his
  throat, which cost the poor vintner many a stamp before
  it was made. But I must hence, sir, I have haste.
Sir Bar. Why, whither now, I prithee?   20
Slip. Faith, sir, to Sir Silvester, a knight, hard by, upon my
  master's errand, whom I must certify this, that the lease of
  East Spring shall be confirmed; and therefore must I bid
  him provide trash, for my master is no friend without
  money.   25
Sir Bar. [*Aside*] This is the thing for which I sued so long,
  This is the lease which I, by Gnatho's means,
  Sought to possess by patent from the king;
  But he, injurious man, who lives by crafts,
  And sells king's favours for who will give most,   30
  Hath taken bribes of me, yet covertly
  Will sell away the thing pertains to me;
  But I have found a present help, I hope,
  For to prevent his purpose and deceit.
  [*To Slipper*] Stay, gentle friend.   35
Slip. A good word; thou hast won me: this word is like a warm
  caudle to a cold stomach.
Sir Bar. Sirrah, wilt thou, for money and reward,
  Convey me certain letters, out of hand,

18. vintner] *Dyce;* viutnerd *Q.* 26. Aside] *Dyce; not in Q.* 27. Gnatho's] *Dyce;* Guatoes *Q.* 35. To Slipper] *This ed.; not in Q.* 36–7.] *so Dyce; irregular verse in Q divided at* me, / This. 37. caudle] *Dyce;* candle *Q.* 38–40.] *so Q; Lavin prints as prose.*

---

 17. *trillill*] with the sound of flowing liquid.
 18. *stamp*] a reference to 'treading' grapes.
 23. *shall*] must.
 24. *trash*] money.
 27. *Gnatho's*] See note to II. ii. 77.
 29. *he*] i.e., Ateukin.
 30. *for who*] as the reward of whoever. 'For' was often used elliptically; for this usage see Abbott, 153.
 33. *present*] immediate.
 34. *prevent*] forestall.
 37. *caudle*] a thin warm gruel with ale or wine and sugar given to women, children, and invalids.
 39. *out of hand*] immediately.

From out thy master's pocket? 40
Slip. Will I, sir? Why, were it to rob my father, hang my mother, or any such like trifles, I am at your commandment, sir. What will you give me, sir?
Sir Bar. A hundred pounds.
Slip. I am your man; give me earnest. I am dead at a pocket, 45 sir. Why, I am a lifter, master, by my occupation.
Sir Bar. A lifter? What is that?
Slip. Why, sir, I can lift a pot as well as any man, and pick a purse as soon as any thief in my country.
Sir Bar. Why, fellow, hold; here is earnest, ten pound to as- 50 sure thee. [*Gives money.*] Go, despatch, and bring it me to yonder tavern thou seest; and assure thyself, thou shalt both have thy skin full of wine and the rest of thy money.
Slip. I will, sir. Now room for a gentleman, my masters! Who gives me money for a fair new angel, a trim new angel? 55
Exeunt.

50–3.] *so Dyce; irregular verse in Q divided at* earnest, / Ten ... dispatch, / And ... seest, / And ... haue / Thy. 51. *Gives money*] *Dyce; not in Q.*

---

45. *earnest*] a sum of money comprising part of an agreed payment which legally sealed a contract.
dead] sure, unerring.
46. *lifter*] an underworld term for a thief. Greene's *Second Part of Coney-Catching* has a section on the 'Discovery of the Lifting Law' (Grosart, x. 118–21).
48. *lift a pot*] drink. The pun is with 'lift' meaning 'steal'.
53. *skin full*] The reference is to leather jugs and bottles which were called 'skins'.
54. *room for*] make room for.
55. *money*] coins of smaller denomination, change. This use is not recorded in *O.E.D.* Cf. Fr. 'monnaie'.
angel] a gold coin worth about ten shillings.
trim] beautiful.

[III. ii]

Enter ANDREW *and* Purveyor.

Purv. Sirrah, I must needs have your master's horses; the king cannot be unserved.

And. Sirrah, you must needs go without them, because my master must be served.

Purv. Why, I am the king's purveyor, and I tell thee I will 5
have them.

And. I am Ateukin's servant, Signor Andrew, and I say thou shalt not have them.

Purv. Here's my ticket; deny it if thou darest.

And. There is the stable; fetch them out if thou darest. 10

Purv. Sirrah, sirrah, tame your tongue, lest I make you.

And. Sirrah, sirrah, hold your hand, lest I bum you.

Purv. I tell thee, thy master's geldings are good, and therefore fit for the king.

And. I tell thee, my master's horses have galled backs, and 15
therefore cannot fit the king. Purveyor, purveyor, purvey thee of more wit: darest thou presume to wrong my Lord Ateukin, being the chiefest man in court?

Purv. [*Aside*] The more unhappy commonweal, where flatterers are chief in court. 20

And. What sayest thou?

III. ii. 1–8.] *so Dyce; irregular verse in Q divided at* horses, / The ... vnserued. / Sirrha ... them, / Because ... serued. / Why ... Purueyor, / And ... them. / I ... *Andrew*, / And.   13–14.] *so Dyce; irregular verse in Q divided at* good, / And.   15–16. I tell ... king] *so Dyce; irregular verse in Q divided at* backes, / And.   19. *Aside*] Grosart (*subst.*); *not in* Q.   19–20.] *so Dyce; irregular verse in Q divided at* Common-weale, / Where.

III. ii. 0.1. *Purveyor*] the royal officer who requisitions horses, transport, and provisions for a sovereign.

2. *unserved*] unfurnished, unsupplied.

9. *ticket*] licence, warrant.

12. *bum*] beat, thump.

16. *fit*] be suitable for.

19–20. *The more ... court*] a commonplace of the period. Cf. Shakespeare's treatment of it in *R2*, and Marlowe's in *Edward II*.

19. *commonweal*] state.

64   JAMES THE FOURTH   [ACT III

Purv. I say thou art too presumptuous, and the officers shall
school thee.
And. A fig for them and thee, purveyor; they seek a knot in a
rush that would wrong my master or his servants in this   25
court.

Enter JAQUES.

Purv. The world is at a wise pass, when nobility is afraid of a
flatterer.
Jaqu. Sirrah, what be you that *parle contra Monsieur* my Lord
Ateukin? *En bonne foi,* prate you against Sir *Altesse,* me   30
maka your *tête* to leap from your shoulders, *par ma foi c'y
ferai-je.*
And. O signor captain, you show yourself a forward and
friendly gentleman in my master's behalf. I will cause him
to thank you.   35
Jaqu. Poltron, speak me one *parola* against my *bon gentil-
homme,* I shall *étampe* your guts and thump your backa
that you *ne point mange* this ten hours.

22–8.] *so Dyce; irregular verse in Q divided at* presumptuous, / And . . .
thee. / A . . . Purueyer, / They . . . wrong / My . . . Court. / The . . . passe, /
When.   25. rush] *conj. Bradley;* ring *Q.*   29. *parle*] *This ed.;* parley, *Q.
contra*] *Q;* contre *Dyce.*   31. *tête*] *Dyce;* test *Q.*   *c'y*] *Q; si conj. Manly.*
32. *ferai-je*] *Dyce;* fe-/re ie *Q.*   37. *étampe*] *This ed.;* estrampe *Q.*   38.
ne point] *Lavin;* no poynt *Q.*   *mange*] *This ed.;* mannage *Q;* manage *Dyce.*
hours] *Dickinson;* ours *Q.*

---

24. *A fig for*] an expression indicating contempt or little value, and
usually accompanied by a coarse gesture of thrusting the thumb between
the first and second fingers; cf. *2H6,* II. iii. 67.
24–5. *seek . . . rush*] make difficulties where none exist; a proverb (Tilley
K168). There is no recorded variant 'a knot in a ring' for which *O.E.D.*
cites this occurrence as its only authority for the existence of the phrase.
Greene uses the correct form in *A Quip for an Upstart Courtier,* XI, 219.
27. *at a wise pass*] in a fine state (ironical).
29. contra] against (Ital.).
30. Altesse] Highness.
31–2. par ma foi c'y ferai-je] upon my word, I will do it.
36. parola] word (Ital.).
37. étampe] stamp.
38. ne point mange] will not eat. Many editors retain 'manage' from Q;
but it is clear from the sense that the compositor has again misread the
French.

SC. II] JAMES THE FOURTH 65

Purv. Sirrah, come open me the stable and let me have the horses; and, fellow, for all your French brags I will do my duty. 40

And. I'll make garters of thy guts, thou villain, if thou enter this office.

Jaqu. Mort Dieu, take me that *cappa pour votre labeur*. [*To Purveyor*] Be gone, *vilain*, in the *mort*. 45

Purv. What, will you resist me then? Well, the council, fellow, shall know of your insolency. *Exit.*

And. Tell them what thou wilt, and eat that I can best spare from my back parts, and get you gone with a vengeance.

Enter ATEUKIN.

Ateu. Andrew. 50
And. Sir.
Ateu. Where be my writings I put in my pocket last night?
And. Which, sir? Your annotations upon Machiavel?
Ateu. No, sir, the letters-patents for East Spring.
And. Why, sir, you talk wonders to me, if you ask that question. 55
Ateu. Yea, sir, and will work wonders too with you, unless you find them out. Villain, search me them out and bring them me, or thou art but dead.

39–47.] *so Dyce; irregular verse in Q divided at* stable, / And . . . horses: / And . . . dutie. / Ile . . . guttes, / Thou . . . office. / Mort . . . cappa / Pour mort. / What . . . then? / Well.   44. *Mort Dieu*] *Dyce*; Mort lieu *Q.* votre] *Dyce*; nostre *Q.*   44–5. *To Purveyor*] *This ed.; not in Q.*   45.] *Dyce has Jaques exit.*   49.1. *Ateukin*] *Dyce*; Gnato *Q.*   53. Machiavel] *Dyce*; Matchauell *Q.*   57. too with] *Dyce*; too, which *Q.*

---

44. cappa] trifle (Ital.).
pour votre labeur] for your trouble.
45. *in the* mort] for ever (Fr. *à la mort*).
48–9. *that . . . parts*] i.e., excrement.
53. *annotations . . . Machiavel*] The Elizabethan stage version of Machiavelli was of the consummate Italianate villain, his *Il Principe* being considered the textbook for all political climbers. Perhaps the best illustration of the connotation this line would have for Greene's audience is to be found in the Prologue to Marlowe's *Jew of Malta*. Lavin notes (p. xv) that Flowerdale in *The London Prodigal* (1604) makes similar annotations.
59. *but*] nothing but.

I

And. A terrible word in the latter end of a sessions. Master, were you in your right wits yesternight? 60

Ateu. Dost thou doubt it?

And. Ay, and why not, sir? For the greatest clerks are not the wisest, and a fool may dance in a hood as well as a wise man in a bare frock. Besides, such as give themselves to *philautia*, as you do, master, are so choleric of complexion that that which they burn in fire over night they seek for with fury the next morning. Ah, I take care of your worship; this commonweal should have a great loss of so good a member as you are. 65

70

Ateu. Thou flatterest me.

And. Is it flattery in me, sir, to speak you fair? What is it then in you to dally with the king?

Ateu. Are you prating, knave? I will teach you better nurture! Is this the care you have of my wardrobe? of my accounts and matters of trust? 75

And. Why, alas, sir, in times past your garments have been so well inhabited as your tenants would give no place to a moth to mangle them; but since you are grown greater and your garments more fine and gay, if your garments are not fit for hospitality, blame your pride and commend my cleanliness—as for your writings, I am not for them nor they for me. 80

64. wisest] *Q*; wisest men *conj. Manly.*   66. philautia] *Dyce; Plulantia Q.* 72–6.] *so Dyce; irregular verse in Q divided at* faire? / What ... King? / Are ... knaue, / I ... nurture? / Is ... wardrop? / Of.

59–60. *thou ... sessions*] a reference to the pronouncement of the death sentence at the end of a capital trial.

63–4. *the greatest ... wisest*] a proverb (Tilley C409).

64. *a fool ... hood*] a variant of the proverb: 'The hood makes not the monk' (Tilley H586).

66. philautia] self-love, conceit (Gr. φιλαυτία).

choleric of complexion] quick-tempered by temperament. Choler was one of the four humours.

73. *dally*] behave in just such a wanton way.

74. *nurture*] breeding, manners.

77–9. *in times ... them*] i.e., Ateukin's garments were so full of lice that moth had not a chance to get in and reduce them to ribbons.

82–3. *I am ... me*] They are nothing to do with me.

SC. II] JAMES THE FOURTH 67

Ateu. Villain, go, fly, find them out; if thou losest them, thou
 losest my credit. 85
And. Alas, sir, can I lose that you never had?
Ateu. Say you so; then hold, feel you that you never felt.
 [*Beats him.*]
Jaqu. O, *monsieur, ayez patience,* pardon your *pauvre valet*;
 me be at your commandment.
Ateu. Signor Jaques, well met; you shall command me. [*To* 90
 Andrew] Sirrah, go cause my writings be proclaimed in
 the market-place, promise a great reward to them that
 finds them; look where I supped and everywhere.
And. I will, sir. [*Aside*] Now are two knaves well met, and
 three well parted, if you conceive mine enigma, gentle- 95
 men. What shall I be then? Faith, a plain harp shilling. *Exit.*
Ateu. Sieur Jaques, this our happy meeting rids
 Your friends and me of care and grievous toil;
 For I, that look into deserts of men
 And see among the soldiers in this court 100

84–5.] *so* Dyce; *irregular verse in* Q *divided at* out: / If. 87.1. Beats him]
Dyce; *not in* Q. 88.] Dyce *has* Jaques re-enter. 88–93.] *so* Dyce;
irregular verse in Q *divided at* vallet, / Me ... commaundement. / Signior
... me, / Sirra ... place, / Promise ... them, / Looke. 88. *ayez patience*]
Dyce; aies patient Q. *pauvre*] Dyce; pouure Q. 90–1. *To Andrew*]
This ed.; not in Q. 94. *Aside*] Manly; *not in* Q. 96. *Exit*] Dyce;
Exeunt Q. 97. rids] Manly; hides Q; hinders Dyce; prives Collins.

---

86. *that*] that which.
 88. Jaqu.] Some editors have Jaques exit at l. 45 and re-enter here, I take
it that he retires to one side of the stage while Ateukin is talking with
Andrew and comes forward to intervene when Ateukin beats his servant.
 91–2. *proclaimed ... market-place*] have the loss publicly announced (by
the town crier?).
 93. *finds*] See note to I. i. 102.
 94–5. *Now ... parted*] a proverb (Tilley K148). The 'two' are Ateukin
and Jaques, and the 'three' they and Andrew himself. This is the 'enigma'
he presents to the audience (i.e., the 'gentlemen'). He probably quibbles
on the two meanings of *parted*: 'separated' and 'furnished with good
parts' (ironically).
 95. *conceive*] comprehend.
 96. *plain harp shilling*] a brass coin bearing the figure of a harp on the
reverse side, current in Ireland during the late sixteenth century. It was
considered to be only worth a penny or twopence in England.

>   A noble forward mind and judge thereof,
>   Cannot but seek the means to raise them up
>   Who merit credit in the commonweal.
>   To this intent, friend Jaques, I have found
>   A means to make you great and well-esteemed,   105
>   Both with the king and with the best in court;
>   For I espy in you a valiant mind,
>   Which makes me love, admire, and honour you.
>   To this intent (if so your trust and faith,
>   Your secrecy, be equal with your force)   110
>   I will impart a service to thyself,
>   Which, if thou dost effect, the king, myself,
>   And what e'er he, and I with him, can work
>   Shall be employed in what thou wilt desire.
> *Jaqu.* Me sweara by my ten bones, my *signor*, to be loyal to 115
>   your lordship's intents, affairs; yea, my *monseigneur, que
>   non ferai-je pour* your pleasure? By my sworda me be no
>   *babillard*.
> *Ateu.* Then hoping on thy truth, I prithee see
>   How kind Ateukin is to forward thee: 120
>   Hold, take this earnest penny of my love,   [*Gives money*]
>   And mark my words. The king by me requires
>   No slender service, Jaques, at thy hands.
>   Thou must by privy practice make away
>   The queen, fair Dorothea, as she sleeps,   125
>   Or how thou wilt, so she be done to death.

---

113. e'er he, and I] *This ed.;* or hee, and I *Q;* or he or I *Manly.* 116. yea] *Dyce;* ye *Q.* que] *Dyce;* qui *Q.* 117. *ferai-je pour* your] *Dyce; fera ic pour.* Yea *Q.* 117–18. By . . . *babillard*] *so Dyce; printed as a verse line in Q.* 118. *babillard*] *Dyce;* babie Lords *Q.* 119. on] *Dyce;* one *Q.* 120. thee] *Dyce;* mee *Q.* 121. *Gives money*] *Dyce* (*subst.*)*; not in Q.*

---

113. *And . . . work*] and whatever either he himself or I with him can bring about.
115. *by my ten bones*] i.e., by my fingers, a common oath: cf. *2H6*, I. iii. 188.
118. *babillard*] chatterbox, tell-tale.
121. *earnest penny*] See note to III. i. 45.

Thou shalt not want promotion here in court.
Jaqu. Stabba the woman, *par ma foi!* *Monseigneur*, me thrusta
my weapon into her belly, so me may be guard *par le roi*.
Me do your service, but me no be hanged *pour* my labour. 130
Ateu. Thou shalt have warrant, Jaques, from the king;
None shall outface, gainsay, and wrong my friend.
Do not I love thee, Jaques? Fear not then:
I tell thee whoso toucheth thee in aught
Shall injure me. I love, I tender thee, 135
Thou art a subject fit to serve his grace.
Jaques, I had a written warrant once,
But that by great misfortune late is lost.
Come, wend we to St Andrews, where his grace
Is now in progress, where he shall assure 140
Thy safety and confirm thee to the act.
Jaqu. We will attend your nobleness.   *Exeunt.*

[III. iii]
   Enter SIR BARTRAM, DOROTHEA *the Queen,* NANO,
       LORD ROSS, Ladies, Attendants.

Dor. Thy credit, Bartram, in the Scottish court,
Thy reverend years, the strictness of thy vows—
All these are means sufficient to persuade,
But love, the faithful link of loyal hearts,
That hath possession of my constant mind, 5
Exiles all dread, subdueth vain suspect.
Methinks no craft should harbour in that breast

---

129. belly] *Dyce;* belle *Q.*   130. Me . . . labour] *so Dyce; irregular verse in Q divided at* seruice. / But. do] *Grosart;* de *Q.*   pour] *Dyce;* pur *Q.*

128–9. *me thrusta . . . belly*] common bawdy quibble on *weapon* (penis) and *belly* (womb).
132. *outface*] defy, put out of countenance.
135. *tender*] cherish a warm regard for.
140. *in progress*] on a state visit, made by monarchs normally to the houses of noblemen.

III. iii. 6. *suspect*] suspicion.

Where majesty and virtue is installed;
Methink my beauty should not cause my death.
Sir Bar. How gladly, sovereign princess, would I err 10
And blind my shame to save your royal life.
'Tis princely in yourself to think the best,
To hope his grace is guiltless of this crime;
But if in due prevention you default,
How blind are you that were forewarned before. 15
Dor. Suspicion without cause deserveth blame.
Sir Bar. Who see and shun not harms deserve the same:
Behold the tenor of this traitorous plot.
[*Displays the king's warrant.*]
Dor. What should I read? Perhaps he wrote it not.
Sir Bar. Here is his warrant under seal and sign 20
To Jaques, born in France, to murder you.
Dor. Ah careless king, would God this were not thine!
What though I read? Ah, should I think it true?
Ross. The hand and seal confirms the deed is his.
Dor. What know I though if now he thinketh this? 25
Nano. Madam, Lucretius saith that to repent
Is childish, wisdom to prevent.
Dor.   What though?
Nano. Then cease your tears that have dismayèd you,

---

8. installed] *Dyce;* mstaled *Q.*   11. blind] *Lavin;* binde *Q;* bide *Grosart;* find *conj. Dyce.*   17. see] *Dyce;* sees *Q.*   18.1. *Displays . . . warrant*] *Dyce (subst.); not in Q.*

---

11. *blind my shame*] close my eyes to my shame (in being wrong).
19. *What*] It is possible here that the sense intended was 'What! . . .'
22. *careless*] heedless, reckless.
23. *What though*] even if.
24. *hand*] handwriting.
25. *thinketh*] intends.
26–7. *Lucretius . . . prevent*] Cf. *De Rerum Natura,* iv. 1144–5: 'so that it is better to be on guard betimes as I have explained, and to take care that you be not enticed'.
27. *prevent*] take anticipatory steps to ensure that something undesirable does not happen.
What though] what then.

And cross the foe before he have betrayed you.
Sir Bar. What needs this long suggestions in this cause, 30
    When every circumstance confirmeth truth?
    First, let the hidden mercy from above
    Confirm your grace, since by a wondrous means
    The practice of your dangers came to light;
    Next, let the tokens of approvèd truth 35
    Govern and stay your thoughts, too much seduced,
    And mark the sooth and listen the intent.
    Your highness knows, and these my noble lords
    Can witness this, that whilst your husband's sire
    In happy peace possessed the Scottish crown, 40
    I was his sworn attendant here in court,
    In dangerous fight I never failed my lord.
    And since his death and this your husband's reign,
    No labour, duty have I left undone,
    To testify my zeal unto the crown; 45
    But now my limbs are weak, mine eyes are dim,
    Mine age unwieldy and unmeet for toil;
    I came to court, in hope for service past,
    To gain some lease to keep me, being old.
    There found I all was upsy-turvy turned, 50
    My friends displaced, the nobles loth to crave.

30. needs this] *Q;* need these *Dyce.*

---

29. *cross*] thwart.
30. *suggestions*] promptings; cf. *Gent.*, II. vi. 7.
33. *Confirm*] convince.
34. *practice*] planning (usually for evil purposes).
35. *approvèd truth*] demonstrated fact.
37. *sooth*] truth.
    listen] pay attention to.
    intent] meaning, import (*O.E.D.*, 5a).
47. *unwieldy*] attended by weakness or infirmity.
50. *upsy-turvy*] This version of 'topsy-turvy' is not recorded in *O.E.D.* Greene appears to have replaced the usual first element of the phrase with the word 'upsy', which meant in many phrases 'to excess'. 'Upsy' was a word much used by Thomas Nashe.
51. *crave*] beg for favour.

  Then sought I to the minion of the king,
  Ateukin, who allurèd by a bribe,
  Assured me of the lease for which I sought;
  But see the craft: when he had got the grant,   55
  He wrought to sell it to Sir Silvester
  In hope of greater earnings from his hands—
  In brief, I learnt his craft and wrought the means,
  By one, his needy servant, for reward
  To steal from out his pocket all the briefs,   60
  Which he performed, and, with reward, resigned.
  Them when I read (now mark the power of God)
  I found this warrant, sealed among the rest,
  To kill your grace whom God long keep alive.
  Thus in effect by wonder are you saved;   65
  Trifle not then, but seek a speedy flight;
  God will conduct your steps and shield the right.
Dor. What should I do? Ah, poor unhappy queen,
  Born to endure what fortune can contain!
  Alas, the deed is too apparent now.   70
  But O, mine eyes, were you as bent to hide
  As my poor heart is forward to forgive!
  Ah, cruel king, my love would thee acquit.
  O, what avails to be allied and matched
  With high estates that marry but in show?   75
  Were I baser born, my mean estate

---

59. servant] *Dyce;* seruants *Q.*   66. speedy] *Dyce;* speakie *Q.*   68. queen,] *Dyce;* Queen? *Q.*   69. contain!] *Dyce;* containe, *Q;* contrive. Grosart.   70. Alas] *Dyce;* Ah lasse *Q.*   76. Were I baser] *Q;* If I were baser *and* Were I more baser *conj. Dyce;* Were I but baser *conj.* Grosart.

---

52. *sought . . . to*] made an approach to.
56. *wrought*] contrived.
59. *one . . . servant*] i.e., Slipper; see III. i. 35 ff.
60. *briefs*] royal mandates.
61. *resigned*] passed on to me.
65. *wonder*] miraculous occurrence.
69. *what . . . contain*] all that Fate can hold.
72. *forward*] ready, eager.
75. *high estates*] men of high rank.

	Could warrant me from this impendent harm;
	But to be great and happy—these are twain.
	Ah, Ross, what shall I do, how shall I work?
Ross.	With speedy letters to your father send, 80
	Who will revenge you and defend your right.
Dor.	As if they kill not me, who with him fight!
	As if his breast be touched, I am not wounded!
	As if he wailed, my joys were not confounded!
	We are one heart, though rent by hate in twain; 85
	One soul, one essence doth our weal contain.
	What then can conquer him that kills not me?
Ross.	If this advice displease, then, madam, flee.
Dor.	Where may I wend or travel without fear?
Nano.	Where not, in changing this attire you wear? 90
Dor.	What, shall I clad me like a country maid?
Nano.	The policy is base, I am afraid.
Dor.	Why, Nano?
Nano.	Ask you why? What, may a queen
	March forth in homely weed and be not seen?
	The rose, although in thorny shrubs she spread, 95
	Is still the rose, her beauties wax not dead.
	And noble minds, although the coat be bare,
	Are by their semblance known how great they are.
Sir Bar.	The dwarf saith true.
Dor.	What garments likest thou then?

90. *Nano.*] *Q*; assigned to Ross by Grosart.

---

78. *But . . . twain*] a very common sentiment in Greene's works, best expressed in the lyric 'Sweet are the thoughts that sauour of content, / the quiet mind is richer than a crowne' (*Farewell to Folly*, IX, 279).
   twain] opposed, separate; this usage antedates the first citation in *O.E.D.*
79. *work*] act.
82. *him*] i.e., the King of Scots.
92. *The policy is base*] The plan is a bad one.
93–8. *What . . . are*] a common belief about innate nobility in Elizabethan England; cf. *Cymb.*, III. iii. 79 ff.
94. *weed*] clothing.
95. *spread*] grows, blooms.
96. *wax*] become.
98. *semblance*] outward appearance.

Nano. Such as may make you seem a proper man. 100
Dor. He makes me blush and smile, though I am sad.
Nano. The meanest coat for safety is not bad.
Dor. What, shall I jet in breeches like a squire?
    Alas, poor dwarf, thy mistress is unmeet.
Nano. Tut, go me thus, your cloak before your face, 105
    Your sword upreared with quaint and comely grace;
    If any come and question what you be;
    Say you a man, and call for witness me.
Dor. What, should I wear a sword? To what intent?
Nano. Madam, for show; it is an ornament. 110
    If any wrong you, draw; a shining blade
    Withdraws a coward thief that would invade.
Dor. But if I strike, and he should strike again,
    What should I do? I fear I should be slain.
Nano. No, take it single on your dagger so; 115
    I'll teach you, madam, how to ward a blow.
Dor. How little shapes much substance may include!
    Sir Bartram, Ross, ye ladies, and my friends,
    Since presence yields me death and absence life,
    Hence will I fly disguisèd like a squire, 120
    As one that seeks to live in Irish wars.
    You, gentle Ross, shall furnish my depart.

---

100. *proper*] complete or handsome.
103. *jet*] walk jauntily.
104. *unmeet*] unfitted. The break in the rhyme scheme may indicate that some lines are omitted here.
106. *quaint*] elegant.
112. *Withdraws*] causes to retreat.
invade] attack, make an assault.
115. *take ... so*] Nano demonstrates how a blow should be parried when fighting with a sword and dagger.
single] simply.
117. *shapes*] figures, with the suggestion of mere outward appearance.
much substance] large amount of good sense.
121.] taking great care for survival. The Irish wars were constantly breaking out during Elizabeth's reign as England sought to gain complete control of the island. There had been a fresh outbreak of activity in March 1589–May 1590. The wars were notorious for their savagery.
122. *furnish my depart*] make things ready for my departure.

Ross. Yea, prince, and die with you with all my heart.
   Vouchsafe me then in all extremest states
   To wait on you and serve you with my best. 125
Dor. To me pertains the woe, live then in rest.
   Friends, fare you well, keep secret my depart;
   Nano alone shall my attendant be.
Nano. Then, madam, are you manned, I warrant ye;
   Give me a sword, and if there grow debate, 130
   I'll come behind and break your enemy's pate.
Ross. How sore we grieve to part so soon away!
Dor. Grieve not for those that perish if they stay.
Nano. The time in words misspent is little worth;
   Madam, walk on and let them bring us forth. *Exeunt.* 135

Chorus [III]

Ent[er BOHAN].

Boh. So these sad motions makes the fairy sleep,
   And sleep he shall in quiet and content;
   For it would make a marble melt and weep
   To see these treasons 'gainst the innocent;
   But since she 'scapes by flight to save her life, 5
   The king may chance repent she was his wife.
   The rest is ruthful, yet to beguile the time,
   'Tis interlaced with merriment and rhyme. *Exit.*

126. then] *Q;* thou *Dyce.*
Chorus III. 0.1.] '*Ent.*' before sp. h. in l. *1 Q.*   1. fairy] *Dyce;* faire *Q.*
7. beguile] *Dyce;* beguilde *Q.*   8. Exit] *Dyce;* Exeunt *Q.*

---

126. *rest*] peace of mind, freedom from distress.
129. *manned*] The pun is on the two meanings: 'equipped with a manly attendant', and 'converted into a man'.
130. *debate*] quarrel.
135. *bring us forth*] see us off.

Chorus III. 1. *motions*] emotional agitations; with perhaps the suggestion of 'puppet shows'.
3. *marble . . . weep*] Cf. the proverb 'A heart as hard as marble' (Tilley H311).
6. *repent she was*] repent because he will remember she is.

Act IV

[IV. i]

After a noise of horns and shoutings, enter certain Huntsmen, *if you please, singing, one way; another way* ATEUKIN *and* JAQUES.

Ateu. Say, gentlemen, where may we find the king?
1 Hunt. Even here at hand on hunting;
　　And at this hour he taken hath a stand
　　To kill a deer.
Ateu. 　　　　A pleasant work in hand!
　　Follow your sport and we will seek his grace.　　　　5
1 Hunt. [*Aside*] When such him seek, it is a woeful case.
　　　Exeunt Huntsmen *one way,* ATEUKIN *and* JAQUES *another.*

[IV. ii]

Enter EUSTACE, IDA, *and the* COUNTESS [OF ARRAN].

Count. Lord Eustace, as your youth and virtuous life
　　Deserves a far more fair and richer wife,
　　So since I am a mother and do wit
　　What wedlock is and that which longs to it,

IV. i] *Actus Quartus. Schena Prima. Q.* 0.2. *Jaques*] Iaques, Gnato. *Q.* 2, 6. *1 Hunt.*] This ed.; Hunts. *Q.* 2. hunting] *Q;* hunting he is bent *conj.* Grosart. 6. *Aside*] Lavin; not in *Q.* 6.1. Huntsmen] Huntsman *Q.*

IV. ii. 2. far more] *Dyce;* faire, more *Q.*

---

3. *stand*] a standing place from which a hunter may shoot game.

IV. ii. 3. *wit*] know.
4. *longs*] belongs; no apostrophe is needed because this is a usual form of the word at this period.

sc. ii]   JAMES THE FOURTH   77

  Before I mean my daughter to bestow,   5
  'Twere meet that she and I your state did know.
Eust. Madam, if I consider Ida's worth,
  I know my portions merit none so fair;
  And yet I hold in farm and yearly rent
  A thousand pound, which may her state content. 10
Count. But what estate, my lord, shall she possess?
Eust. All that is mine, grave countess, and no less.
  But, Ida, will you love?
Ida.   I cannot hate.
Eust. But will you wed?
Ida.   'Tis Greek to me, my lord.
  I'll wish you well, and thereon take my word. 15
Eust. Shall I some sign of favour then receive?
Ida. Aye, if her ladyship will give me leave.
Count. Do what thou wilt.
Ida.   Then, noble English peer,
  Accept this ring wherein my heart is set,
  A constant heart with burning flames befret; 20
  But under written this: *O morte dura.*
  Hereon when so you look with eyes *pura,*
  The maid you fancy most will favour you.
Eust. I'll try this heart in hope to find it true.

   Enter certain Huntsmen *and* Ladies.

8. portions merit] *Q;* portion merits *Dyce.* 19. my] *Q;* a *conj. Walker.*

---

 6. *meet*] proper.
 your state] the state of your financial affairs.
 8. *portions*] inherited possessions.
 9. *in farm*] fixed yearly amount paid as rents.
 rent] income, revenue.
 10. *state*] position in life.
 14. '*Tis . . . me*] that is a subject I know nothing about; a proverb (Tilley G439).
 20. *with . . . befret*] either 'gnawed at by tongues of fire' or 'adorned with flames elaborately carved in decorative patterns'.
 21. O morte dura] O cruel death (Ital.).
 22. pura] chaste (Ital.).
 24. *try*] put to the test.

78   JAMES THE FOURTH   [ACT IV

Huntsmen. Widow countess well y-met; 25
　　　　　Ever may thy joys be many.
　　　　　Gentle Ida, fair beset,
　　　　　　Fair and wise, not fairer any;
　　　　　Frolic huntsmen of the game
　　　　　　Wills you well and gives you greeting. 30
Ida.　　Thanks, good woodmen, for the same
　　　　　And our sport and merry meeting.
Huntsmen. Unto thee we do present
　　　　　　Silver hart with arrow wounded.
Eust. [Aside] This doth shadow my lament 35
　　　　　　With both fear and love confounded.
Ladies. To the mother of the maid,
　　　　　　Fair as th' lilies, red as roses,
　　　　　E'en so many goods are said,
　　　　　　As herself in heart supposes. 40
Count. What are you, friends, that thus doth wish us well?
1 Hunt. Your neighbours nigh that have on hunting been,
　　　　Who, understanding of your walking forth,

25, 33. Huntsmen.] *This ed.*; Hunts. *Q.*　27. fair] *Q*; sair (*Scot.* 'sore') conj. *Walker.*　31. woodmen] *This ed.*; Woodman *Q.*　34. hart] *Dyce*; heart *Q.*　35. Aside] *Dyce; not in Q.*　36. With both] *Collins;* Both *Q;* Both with *Dyce.*　39. E'en] *This ed.*; Euen *Q.*　42. *1 Hunt.*] *Dyce;* Hunts. *Q.*

25–49.] Greene's exact intentions for the staging of this exchange are not clear from Q in which the speech headings at ll. 25, 33, 42, and 49 are all 'Hunts.'. For ll. 37–40 the speech heading in Q is '*Ladies.*', and in view of this it would appear that these lines were intended to be spoken in unison or perhaps even sung. To preserve the balance of the exchange suggested by the metrical changes, I have assumed that ll. 25–30 and 33–4 are also spoken or sung in unison by all the Huntsmen (which also entails the emending of Q's 'Woodman' to 'woodmen' in l. 31). I have also assumed that the answer to the Countess's question and the introductions effected in ll. 42–5 are provided by one member of the group and that a second member of the group speaks the general exit line at l. 49.

27. *fair beset*] either 'well bestowed in marriage' or 'well wooed'.
29. *Frolic*] merry.
35. *shadow my lament*] present an image of my disturbed state of mind.
39. *goods*] good things.
40. *supposes*] can imagine.

SC. II]   JAMES THE FOURTH   79

  Prepared this train to entertain you with.
  This Lady Douglas, this Sir Egmond is.   45
Count. Welcome, ye ladies, and thousand thanks for this;
  Come enter you a homely widow's house,
  And if mine entertainment please you, let us feast.
2 Hunt. A lovely lady never wants a guest.
     Exeunt [COUNTESS OF ARRAN, Huntsmen, Ladies].
Eust. Stay, gentle Ida, tell me what you deem,   50
  What doth this hart, this tender hart, beseem?
Ida. Why not, my lord, since nature teacheth art
  To senseless beasts to cure their grievous smart:
  Dictamnum serves to close the wound again.
Eust. What help for those that love?
Ida.   Why, love again.   55
Eust. Were I the hart—
Ida.   Then I the herb would be.
  You shall not die for help; come, follow me.   *Exeunt.*

49. *2 Hunt.*] *This ed.;* Hunts. *Q.* 49.1. *Exeunt* . . . Ladies] *Dyce; Exeunt Manet, Eustace, Ida Q.* 51. What] *Q;* What, *Lavin.* hart] *Dyce;* hast *Q;* haste *Lavin; omission conj. Grosart.* tender hart] *Dyce;* tender heart *Q.* 56. hart—] Hart, *Q.*

---

 49. *wants*] lacks.
 50. *deem*] judge, opine.
 51. *hart . . . hart*] I take this reference as being to the ornament presented in ll. 33–4, with Eustace seeking an emblematic meaning in the gift. Ida's reply is arch in keeping with her attitude in ll. 13–14, ironically referring to the image of the animal. Lavin has an alternative reading: 'The point of Eustace's question seems to be "What do you think, Ida, have we acted too hastily for your ladylike and gentle disposition?" . . . She replies, "Not at all, those who are wounded must seek immediate relief; even senseless beasts know that."'
 beseem] imply.
 53. *senseless*] devoid of intelligence, without reason.
 smart] physical pain caused by a wound.
 53.] Lavin suggests a line omitted after l. 53 which would be something like 'The struck deer feeds to ease her of her pain'.
 54. *Dictamnum*] a Cretan herb supposed to have the power to heal wounds by expelling the weapon; cf. *Aeneid,* XII, 411 ff., and Greene's *Card of Fancy*: 'The Deere beeing stroken, though neuer so deep, feedeth on the herb *Dictaninum* and forth is healed' (IV, 58). This was a common motif with emblem writers.
 56–7. *Then . . . me*] Ida here relents and reassures Eustace.

[IV. iii]

Enter ANDREW *and* JAQUES.

Jaqu. Mon Dieu, what *malheur* be this! Me come *à* the chamber, Signor Andrew, *mon Dieu*, taka my *poignard en ma main*, to give the *estocade* to the *damoisella; par ma foi,* there was no person; *elle s'est en allée.*

And. The worse luck, Jaques; but because I am thy friend, I 5
will advise thee somewhat towards the attainment of the gallows.

Jaqu. Gallows? What be that?

And. Marry, sir, a place of great promotion, where thou shalt by one turn above ground rid the world of a knave and 10
make a goodly ensample for all bloody villains of thy profession.

Jaqu. Que dites-vous, Monsieur Andrew?

And. I say, Jaques, thou must keep this path and hie thee, for the queen, as I am certified, is departed with her dwarf, 15
apparelled like a squire. Overtake her, Frenchman, stab her; I'll promise thee, this doublet shall be happy.

Jaqu. Pourquoi?

And. It shall serve a jolly gentleman, Sir Dominus Monsignor Hangman. 20

Jaqu. C'est tout un, me will rama *pour la monnaie.* *Exit.*

And. Go, and the rot consume thee! O, what a trim world is

IV. iii. 2. *ma*] Dyce; *mon* Q.   4. *s'est*] Dyce; *cest* Q.   13. *Jaqu.*] Dyce; not in Q.   *dites*] Dyce; *ditte* Q.   19–20.] *so* Dyce; *irregular verse divided in* Q *at* Gentleman, / Sir.   21. *la monnaie*] Lavin; *le monoy* Q.

IV. iii. 3. *estocade*] stab-wound.
damoisella] damsel (Italianate form).
9. *promotion*] quibble on 'elevation' (by hanging).
10. *one . . . ground*] i.e., being hanged; cf. *The Spanish Tragedy* (ed. P. Edwards, 1959), III. iv. 69.
11. *ensample*] practical warning.
17. *this doublet*] Andrew touches Jaques on the chest; but he is probably also alluding to the fact that a hanged man's clothes were a perquisite for the hangman; cf. ll. 19–20 below.
21. *rama*] thrust; an Italianized form of 'ram'.
22. *rot*] pox.
trim] well-ordered (ironical here).

SC. III]   JAMES THE FOURTH   81

this! My master lives by cozening the king, I by flattering
him, Slipper, my fellow, by stealing, and I by lying. Is not
this a wily accord, gentlemen? This last night, our jolly   25
horse-keeper, being well steeped in liquor, confessed to
me the stealing of my master's writings, and his great
reward. Now, dare I not bewray him lest he discover my
knavery; but thus have I wrought: I understand he will
pass this way to provide him necessaries; but if I and my   30
fellows fail not, we will teach him such a lesson as shall
cost him a chief place on penniless bench for his labour.
But yond he comes.

Enter SLIPPER *with a* Tailor, *a* Shoemaker, *and a* Cutler.

Slip. Tailor.
Tail. Sir.   35
Slip. Let my doublet be white northern, five groats the yard;
I tell thee, I will be brave.
Tail. It shall, sir.
Slip. Now sir, cut it me like the battlements of a custard, full

---

25. *wily accord*] artful agreement.
26. *horse-keeper*] i.e., Slipper.
28. *discover*] reveal.
29. *wrought*] arranged, contrived.
32. *chief . . . bench*] The Penniless Bench was a covered seat which formerly stood beside Carfax Church, Oxford. The name was apparently applied also to similar seats frequented by the destitute elsewhere.
36. *northern*] presumably a cloth manufactured in the north of England or perhaps Scotland; but I have been unable to discover exactly what kind of cloth it was. Mrs Madeline Ginsberg of the Department of Textiles of the Victoria and Albert Museum informs me that, as most of the silk textiles of the period are well known, it is likely that 'northern cloth' was a wool mixture or linen.

groats] coins worth 2d. during the fourteenth century but which fell much lower in value during the fifteenth century.
37. *brave*] finely dressed.
39. *battlements of a custard*] The reference is to the crenelation of the crust which was often used in the pastry decoration of a custard which at this period was a kind of open pie containing pieces of meat or fruit covered with a preparation of broth or milk, thickened with eggs, sweetened, and seasoned with spices. Slipper intends to have the sort of doublet ridiculed

K

of round holes; edge me the sleeves with Coventry-blue, 40
and let the linings be of tenpenny lockram.

Tail. Very good, sir.

Slip. Make it the amorous cut, a flap before.

Tail. And why so? That fashion is stale.

Slip. O, friend, thou art a simple fellow; I tell thee, a flap is a 45
great friend to a storre: it stands him in stead of clean
napery, and if a man's shirt be torn, it is a present penthouse to defend him from a clean housewife's scoff.

Tail. You say sooth, sir.

Slip. Hold, take thy money: there is seven shillings for the 50
doublet, and eight for the breeches—seven and eight.
Byrlady, thirty-six is a fair deal of money.

Tail. Farewell, sir.

Slip. Nay, but stay, tailor.

Tail. Why, sir? 55

---

41. lockram] *Dyce;* locorum *Q.*   46. storre] *This ed.;* storrie *Q;* sloven *conj. Bradley;* stoic *conj. Lavin.*

---

by Stubbes in *Anatomy of Abuses* (1583), and Harrison in his *Description of England* (1583); for these and other attacks made on the Englishman's love of sartorial finery, see P. Macquoid, 'Costume', *Shakespeare's England* (1916), II, 91–118.

40. *Coventry-blue*] a thread of vivid blue chiefly used for embroidery and manufactured at Coventry.

41. *lockram*] a coarse, loosely woven linen, with relatively finer varieties used for kerchiefs, household linen, and linings.

43. *amorous cut, a flap before*] Slipper appears to be describing the 'Peascod' or 'Dutch doublet'. This garment was long in the front, overhanging the girdle like the end of a peascod.

44. *That ... stale*] According to M. C. Linthicum (*Costume in the Drama of Shakespeare and his Contemporaries* (1936), p. 198) this fashion came in in the 1570s.

46. *storre*] I take Q's 'storrie' to be a misreading of 'storre' (or 'stour') meaning a 'stalwart or rough fellow' ('stour', *O.E.D.*, *a.* and $sb.^2$ 5).

47. *napery*] personal linen. This usage antedates the first citation in *O.E.D.*

47–8. *penthouse*] i.e., the flap will project over the shirt to conceal its deficiencies from the 'clean housewife'.

52. *thirty-six*] Slipper apparently pays the Tailor the total of fifteen shillings in this number of smaller coins, perhaps groats or testerns, or perhaps Slipper's arithmetic is simply faulty.

Slip. Forget not this special make: let my back parts be well
lined, for there come many winter storms from a windy
belly, I tell thee. [*Exit Tailor.*] Shoemaker.
Shoe. Gentleman, what shoe will it please you to have?
Slip. A fine neat calves' leather, my friend. 60
Shoe. O, sir, that is too thin, it will not last you.
Slip. I tell thee it is my near kinsman, for I am Slipper, which
hath his best grace in summer to be suited in lambs' skins.
Goodwife Calf was my grandmother and Goodman
Netherleather mine uncle; but my mother, good woman, 65
alas, she was a Spaniard, and being well tanned and
dressed by a good fellow, an Englishman, is grown to
some wealth: as when I have but my upper parts clad in
her husband's costly Spanish leather, I may be bold to
kiss the fairest lady's foot in this country. 70
Shoe. You are of high birth, sir, but have you all your mother's
marks on you?
Slip. Why, knave?
Shoe. Because if thou come of the blood of the Slippers, you
should have a shoemaker's awl thrust through your ear. 75

56–8.] *so Dyce; irregular verse in Q divided at* mate, / Let... linde, / For...
bellie. / I.   56. make] *Dyce;* mate *Q.*   58. Exit Tailor] *Dyce; not in Q.*
63. lamb's] *Lavin;* lakus *Q;* Jack-ass' *Dyce;* calves' *Manly.*   64. Calf]
Dyce; Clarke *Q;* Bark *conj. Manly;* calves' *Manly.*   71–2.] *so Dyce;
irregular verse in Q divided at* sir, / But.

---

56. *make*] design, style.
60. *neat calves' leather*] a fine leather made from calf hide.
63. *lambs' skins*] Q's 'lakus' has provoked various editorial suggestions;
but the reference would appear to be to fur-lined slippers.
65. *Netherleather*] covering in leather for the legs.
66. *was a Spaniard*] The reference is to Spanish leather, a fine soft
leather for making boots.
66–7. *tanned and dressed*] The quibbles are on the meanings 'turned into
leather and dressed for use' and 'thrashed and chastised'. There is almost
certainly an allusion here to the Spanish Armada which had been defeated
only three or four years previously.
68. *as*] so that.
71–2. *your mother's marks*] The allusion is probably to the 'Spanish pox',
a common name for syphilis at the time ('pox', *O.E.D., sb.* 1e).
75. *awl...ear*] The Shoemaker may well be referring to the practice of
marking a felon in the pillory by cutting his ears.

Slip. Take your earnest, friend, and be packing, and meddle not with my progenitors. [*Exit* Shoemaker.] Cutler.
Cut. Here, sir.
Slip. I must have a rapier and dagger.
Cut. A rapier and dagger, you mean, sir? 80
Slip. Thou sayest true; but it must have a very fair edge.
Cut. Why so, sir?
Slip. Because it may cut by himself; for truly, my friend, I am a man of peace and wear weapons but for fashion.
Cut. Well, sir, give me earnest, I will fit you. 85
Slip. Hold, take it. I betrust thee, friend, let me be well armed.
Cut. You shall. *Exit.*
Slip. Now what remains? There's twenty crowns for a house, three crowns for household stuff, sixpence to buy a constable's staff; nay, I will be the chief of my parish. There 90 wants nothing but a wench, a cat, a dog, a wife, and a servant to make an whole family. Shall I marry with Alice, Goodman Grimshave's daughter? She is fair, but indeed her tongue is like clocks on Shrove Tuesday, always out of

---

76–7.] so Dyce; irregular verse in Q divided at packing, / And.   77. *Exit Shoemaker*] so Dyce; '*Exit*.' follows l. 75 in Q.   80. rapier and dagger] Q; reaper and digger Dyce; rape 'er and dig 'er *conj. Lavin*.   93. Grimshave's] Q; Grimshaw's Dyce.

---

76. *earnest*] See note to III. i. 45.
80. *rapier and dagger*] The words are obviously mispronounced by Slipper. Collier suggests *reaper* and *digger*, and Lavin *rape 'er* and *dig 'er*.
81. *fair*] Lavin glosses 'blunt' and notes that the meaning is not recorded in *O.E.D.* However, I think Slipper is asking for so fine or sharp an edge that the sword may cut without his help because he 'wears weapons but for the fashion'.
85. *fit you*] provide you with what you need.
86. *betrust*] have confidence in.
88. *crowns*] coins originally minted by Henry VIII worth a quarter of a sovereign at the end of the sixteenth century.
89–90. *constable's staff*] a staff with some kind of insignia borne by the chief officer of a parish as a sign of his authority.
94–5. *her tongue . . . temper*] The connection between clocks striking and tongues wagging was a common one in the writing of the period; Lavin cites Heywood's *The First Hundred Epigrammes*, sig. O4^r. Shrove Tuesday was a day notorious for the wild antics of apprentices including the tampering with the mechanism of the clocks of the City.

SC. III] JAMES THE FOURTH 85

 temper. Shall I wed Cicely of the Whighton? O no; she is 95
different from the one I love. like a frog in a parsley bed, as skittish as an eel: if I seek to
hamper her, she will horn me. But a wench must be had,
Master Slipper; yea, and shall be, dear friend.
And. [*Aside*] I now will drive him from his contemplations.
O, my mates, come forward; the lamb is unpent, the fox 100
shall prevail.

 Enter three Antics, *who dance round and take Slipper
with them.*

Slip. I will, my friends, and I thank you heartily. Pray keep
your curtsy; I am yours in the way of an hornpipe. [*Aside*]
They are strangers, I see they understand not my language: wee, wee. [*To them*] Nay, but my friends, one 105
hornpipe further, a refluence back and two doubles forward. What, not one cross-point against Sundays? What

---

99. *Aside*] Dyce; *not in* Q.   102. friends] Dyce; friend Q.   103. curtsy] curtesie Q; courtesy Dyce.   *Aside*] Dyce; *not in* Q.   105. wee, wee] Q; *oui, oui* Lavin.   To them] *This ed.; not in* Q.

---

 95. *Cicely of the Whighton*] Cicely was a stock name for a servant or country girl; Whighton (or Wigton) was a maritime county in the southwest of Scotland. Lavin interestingly conjectures that the reference may be to Ye Olde Dick Whittington, a fifteenth-century London tavern in Cloth Fair.
 96. *as skittish . . . eel*] i.e., strongly sexed; a proverb (Tilley E60).
 97. *hamper*] restrain by confinement. Greene also uses this word in the sense of 'beat' in *Friar Bacon*, II. iv. 900.
 horn] cuckold.
 100. *unpent*] released from an enclosure.
 101.1. round] i.e., 'a round', a popular dance in which the performers moved in a circle.
 102. *keep*] pay attention to.
 105. *wee, wee*] Slipper's English imitation of *oui, oui*.
 106. *refluence*] a *démarche*, a dance-step in which the dancers sway backwards without moving their feet.
 doubles] *pas doubles*, in which the dancer moves the left foot, swings the right foot past it, and follows it with the left.
 107. *cross-point*] a *contrapasso*, a dance-step in which the feet are crossed, sometimes in the air.
 against] in preparation for.
 Sundays] i.e., days of recreation.

ho, sirrah, you yon, you with the nose like an eagle: an you be a right Greek, one turn more.

Whilst they are dancing, ANDREW *takes away Slipper's money, and [he and] the other* Antics *depart.*

Thieves, thieves! I am robbed! Thieves! Is this the 110 knavery of fiddlers? Well, I will then bind the whole credit of their occupation on a bagpiper, and he for my money. But I will after and teach them to caper in a halter that have cozened me of my money. *Exit.*

[IV. iv]

Enter NANO [*and*] DOROTHEA, *in man's apparel.*

Dor. Ah, Nano, I am weary of these weeds,
Weary to wield this weapon that I bear,
Weary of love from whom my woe proceeds,
Weary of toil, since I have lost my dear.
O weary life, where wanteth no distress, 5
But every thought is paid with heaviness.

---

108. yon] *conj. Manly;* gone *Q;* gome *Dyce.* an] *Dyce;* and *Q.* 109.
1–2.] *so Dyce; follows* 'wee', *l. 105, in Q.* 109.1. Slipper's] *Dyce;* his *Q.*
109.2. he and] *Dyce; not in Q.* 114. Exit] *Dyce;* Exeunt *Q.*

IV. iv. 5. wanteth] *Dyce;* wanted *Q.*

---

109. *right Greek*] quite unable to understand me; see note to IV. ii. 14.
turn] bout or 'go'; but perhaps 'revolution' (of the dance).
110–12. *Is . . . bagpiper*] Slipper characteristically prizes the homely bagpiper more highly than the courtly fiddler.
111. *fiddlers*] The pun is with the meaning 'triflers'.
112–13. *he for my money*] I prefer him; a proverb (Tilley M1040).
113. *caper in a halter*] be hanged.

IV. iv. 1–6.] This passage is as good an example as the play has to offer of the passion for rhetorical repetition common to many of the plays written during the 1580s and 1590s. Perhaps the best-known exponent of the device is Thomas Kyd; and the clearest Shakespearian example is to be found in Henry VI's soliloquy at the Battle of Towton (*3H6*, II. v. 21–40).

1. *weeds*] clothes.
5. *wanteth*] there lacks.
6. *heaviness*] sadness.

SC. IV] JAMES THE FOURTH 87

Nano. Too much of 'weary', madam; if you please,
  Sit down, let 'weary' die, and take your ease.
Dor. How look I, Nano? Like a man or no?
Nano. If not a man, yet like a manly shrow. 10
Dor. If any come and meet us on the way,
  What should we do if they enforce us stay?
Nano. Set cap a-huff and challenge him the field;
  Suppose the worst, the weak may fight to yield.
Dor. The battle, Nano, in this troubled mind 15
  Is far more fierce than ever we may find.
  The body's wounds by medicines may be eased,
  But griefs of minds by salves are not appeased.
Nano. Say, madam, will you hear your Nano sing?
Dor. Of woe, good boy, but of no other thing. 20
Nano. What if I sing of fancy, will it please?
Dor. To such as hope success, such notes breed ease.
Nano. What if I sing like Damon to my sheep?
Dor. Like Phyllis I will sit me down to weep.
Nano. Nay, since my songs afford such pleasure small, 25
  I'll sit me down and sing you none at all.
Dor. O, be not angry, Nano.
Nano.   Nay, you loathe
  To think on that which doth content us both.
Dor. And how?

29. And] *Q;* As *Dyce;* An' *Grosart.*

---

10. *shrow*] i.e., shrew, here meaning 'person' (*O.E.D.*, sb.² 3a).
13. *Set cap a-huff*] set your hat at a swaggering angle; a *huff-cap* was a swashbuckler.
15–26. *The battle . . . all*] R. Walker (*T.L.S.*, 10 Aug. 1951, p. 501) compares *R2*, III. iv. 13–22: 'Queen. . . . For if of joy, being altogether wanting, / It doth remember me the more of sorrow; / Or if of grief, being altogether had, / It adds more sorrow to my want of joy; / For what I have I need not to repeat, / And what I want it boots not to complain. / *Lady.* Madam, I'll sing. / *Queen.* 'Tis well that thou hast cause; / But thou shouldst please me better wouldst thou weep. / *Lady.* I could weep, madam, would it do you good. / *Queen.* And I could sing, would weeping do me good.'
21. *fancy*] love.
23–4. *Damon . . . Phyllis*] type-names of pastoral lovers deriving from Virgil and Horace.

Nano. You scorn disport when you are weary,
And loathe my mirth, who live to make you merry. 30
Dor. Danger and fear withdraw me from delight.
Nano. 'Tis virtue to contemn false Fortune's spite.
Dor. What should I do to please thee, friendly squire?
Nano. A smile a day is all I will require,
And if you pay me well the smiles you owe me, 35
I'll kill this cursèd care or else beshrow me.
Dor. We are descried. O, Nano, we are dead.

Enter JAQUES, *his sword drawn.*

Nano. Tut, yet you walk; you are not dead indeed.
Draw me your sword, if he your way withstand,
And I will seek for rescue out of hand. 40
Dor. Run, Nano, run; prevent thy prince's death.
Nano. Fear not, I'll run all danger out of breath. [*Exit.*]
Jaqu. Ah, you *calletta*, you *strumpetta, Maitressa Dorétie,
êtes-vous surprise*? Come, say your paternoster, *car vous
êtes morte, par ma foi.* 45
Dor. Callet? No strumpet, caitiff as thou art,

37. Dor.] Dyce; Doug. Q.   40.] assigned to Dor. in Q.   41. prince's] Lavin; princes Q; princess' Dyce.   43. strumpetta] Collins; strumpet, ta Q; strumpet, la Grosart; strumpet! ha conj. Manly.   44. surprise] Dyce; surprius Q.   46. Callet? No strumpet] Lavin; Callet, me strumpet Q; Callest me strumpet? conj. Dyce; Callet! me strumpet! Collins.

---

29. *disport*] diversion, entertainment.
31. *withdraw*] debar.
36. *beshrow me*] the devil take me.
40. *out of hand*] at once.
41. *prince's*] The Q reading 'princes' has often been taken to be a common form of 'princess' and some editors have so emended. However, the word is a possessive here and Compositor B, who set this page of Q, favoured the '-esse' form for 'princess'.
43. calletta . . . strumpetta] Greene has merely Italianized the English words. 'Callet' means 'drab', 'trull'.
Maitressa] Italianized form of *Maîtresse*.
46.] Dyce suggested 'callest me strumpet?' and Collins and Dickinson attempted to make sense of Q's wording by reading 'Callet! me strumpet!' However, I think Lavin's emendation produces the best sense in the context.

SC. IV]   JAMES THE FOURTH   89

>But even a princess born who scorn thy threats.
>Shall never Frenchman say an English maid
>Of threats of foreign force will be afraid.
Jaqu. You no *dites votres prières? Morbleu, méchante femme,*   50
>guarda your bresta, there me make you die on my morglay.
Dor. God shield me, hapless princess and a wife,
>And save my soul, although I lose my life.
>   *They fight and she is sore wounded.*
>Ah, I am slain! Some piteous power repay
>This murderer's cursèd deed, that doth me slay.   55
Jaqu. Elle est toute morte; me will run *pour* a wager, for fear me
>be *surpris* and *pendu* for my labour. *Bien, je m'en allerai au
>roi lui dire mes affaires. Je serai un chevalier* for this day's
>travail.   *Exit.*

>   *Enter* NANO [*and*] S[IR] CUTHBERT ANDERSON,
>   *his sword drawn.*

Sir Cuth. Where is this poor distressèd gentleman?   60
Nano. Here laid on ground and wounded to the death.
>Ah gentle heart, how are these beauteous looks
>Dimmed by the tyrant cruelties of death.
>O weary soul, break thou from forth my breast
>And join thee with the soul I honoured most.   65
Sir Cuth. Leave mourning, friend, the man is yet alive.
>Come, help me to convey him to my house;

50. *dites*] Grosart; *dire* Q.   *prières*] Dyce; *prieges* Q.   Morbleu, méchante] Dyce; vrbleme merchants. Q.   53.1.] so Dyce; follows l. 52 in Q.   55. slay] Dyce; stay Q.   57. Bien] Dyce; Be in Q.   m'en] Dyce; meu Q.   58. lui dire mes] Dyce; auy cits me Q.   67. Come] conj. Manly; Some Q.

48–9. Shall ... afraid] For comment on these lines see Introduction, pp. xxvi–xxvii.
51. *morglay*] sword; originally the name of the sword belonging to Sir Bevis of Southampton in the romance of that name.
55. *slay*] Q's 'stay' is possible but not likely.
56. pour *a wager*] as if there were a wager on my speed.
67. *Come*] Q's 'Some' is possibly an address to servants offstage, or could mean 'some help'. However, Sir Cuthbert's whole speech seems to be addressed to Nano.

> There will I see him carefully recured
> And send privy search to catch the murderer.

Nano. The God of heaven reward thee, courteous knight.   70

Exeunt. And they bear out DOROTHEA.

[IV. v]

Enter the KING OF SCOTS, JAQUES, ATEUKIN, ANDREW;
JAQUES *running with his sword [drawn] one way, the* KING
with his train another way.

K. of Scot. Stay, Jaques, fear not; sheathe thy murdering blade:
  Lo, here thy king and friends are come abroad
  To save thee from the terrors of pursuit.
  What, is she dead?
Jaqu. Oui, monsieur, *elle* is blessée par la tête over les épaules; I   5
  warrant she no trouble you.
Ateu. O then, my liege, how happy art thou grown,
  How favoured of the heavens and blessed by love!
  Methinks I see fair Ida in thine arms,
  Craving remission for her late contempt;   10
  Methinks I see her blushing steal a kiss,
  Uniting both your souls by such a sweet,
  And, you, my king, suck nectar from her lips.
  Why then delays your grace to gain the rest
  You long desired? Why lose we forward time?   15
  Write, make me spokesman now, vow marriage;
  If she deny your favour, let me die.

69. send privy] *Q;* send forth privy *Grosart.*

IV. v. 0.2. *drawn*] *This ed.; not in* Q.   5. Oui] *Dyce;* Wee *Q.*   la] *Dyce;*
lake *Q.*   over] *Dyce;* oues *Q.*   épaules] *Dyce;* espanles *Q.*   10. contempt] *Dyce;* attempt *Q.*   17. your] *Q;* you *Dyce.*

---

68. *recured*] restored to health.
69. *privy*] secret, private.

IV. v. 10. *remission*] pardon.
contempt] scornful refusal.
15. *forward time*] the propitious moment.

And. Mighty and magnificent potentate, give credence to
  mine honourable good lord; for I heard the midwife
  swear at his nativity that the fairies gave him the property
  of the Thracian stone; for who toucheth it is exempted
  from grief, and he that heareth my master's counsel is
  already possessed of happiness; nay, which is more
  miraculous, as the noble man in his infancy lay in his
  cradle, a swarm of bees laid honey on his lips in token of
  his eloquence, for *melle dulcior fluit oratio.*
Ateu. Your grace must bear with imperfections:
  This is exceeding love that makes him speak.
K. of Scot. Ateukin, I am ravished in conceit,
  And yet depressed again with earnest thoughts.
  Methinks this murder soundeth in mine ear
  A threatening noise of dire and sharp revenge;
  I am incensed with grief, yet fain would joy.
  What may I do to end me of these doubts?
Ateu. Why, prince, it is no murder in a king
  To end another's life to save his own;
  For you are not as common people be,
  Who die and perish with a few men's tears;
  But if you fail, the state doth whole default,
  The realm is rent in twain in such a loss.

38. men's] *Dyce;* mans *Q.*

20–2. *the property...grief*] Cf. John Lyly's *Euphues and his England* (ed. R. W. Bond (1902), II. 90): 'There is a stone in the floud of Thracia, y^t whosoeuer findeth it, is neuer after grieued.'

24–6. *as the...oratio*] Greene appears to be blending two passages from Cicero here: *De Senectute*, x. 31: 'For as Homer says, "Speech sweeter than honey flowed from his tongue"'; and *De Divinatione*, I. xxxvi. 76–8: 'Again, while Plato was an infant, asleep in his cradle, bees settled on his lips and this was interpreted to mean that he would have a rare sweetness of speech.'

29. *ravished in*] carried away with pleasure by.
conceit] fancies.
31. *soundeth*] utters.
33. *incensed*] inflamed, excited.
35–9. *Why...default*] R. Walker (*T.L.S.*, 10 Aug. 1951, p. 501) compares Rosencrantz's flattery of Claudius in *Ham.*, III. iii. 11–23.
39. *default*] collapse, suffer failure.

      And Aristotle holdeth this for true,
      Of evil needs we must choose the least:
      Then better were it that a woman died
      Than all the help of Scotland should be blent.
      'Tis policy, my liege, in every state,   45
      To cut off members that disturb the head,
      And by corruption generation grows,
      And contraries maintain the world and state.
K. *of Scot.* Enough, I am confirmed. Ateukin, come,
      Rid me of love and rid me of my grief,   50
      Drive thou the tyrant from this tainted breast,
      Then may I triumph in the height of joy.
      Go to mine Ida, tell her that I vow
      To raise her head and make her honours great.
      Go to mine Ida, tell her that her hairs   55
      Shall be embellishèd with orient pearls,
      And crowns of sapphires compassing her brows
      Shall war with those sweet beauties of her eyes.
      Go to mine Ida, tell her that my soul
      Shall keep her semblance closèd in my breast,   60
      And I, in touching of her milk-white mould,
      Will think me deified in such a grace.
      I like no stay; go write and I will sign.

42. needs] *Q;* needeth *conj. Dyce;* needful *Grosart;* twain needs *Manly.*
50. Rid] *Q;* Rede *Grosart.*   58. war] *Dyce;* weare *Q.*

41–2. *And Aristotle . . . least*] The reference is to *Nicomachean Ethics,* II. ix. 4: 'Hence, inasmuch as to hit the mean extremely well is difficult, the second best way to sail, as the saying goes, is to take the least of the evils'; and cf. Tilley E207.
  44. *blent*] disrupted, troubled ('blend', *O.E.D.*, $v.^2$ 2b).
  47. *generation grows*] fruitfulness increases.
  51. *tainted*] afflicted, contaminated.
  54. *raise her head*] promote her to higher rank.
  56. *orient pearls*] pearls from the Indian seas as distinguished from those of less beauty found in European mussels; hence, brilliant or very precious pearls.
  60. *semblance*] image.
  61. *mould*] body.
  63. *stay*] delay.

SC. V]   JAMES THE FOURTH   93

   Reward me Jaques; give him store of crown;
   And sirrah Andrew, scout thou here in court   65
   And bring me tidings if thou canst perceive
   The least intent of muttering in my train;
   For either those that wrong thy lord or thee
   Shall suffer death.
Ateu.   How much, O mighty king,
   Is thy Ateukin bound to honour thee!   70
   Bow thee, Andrew, bend thine sturdy knees;
   Seest thou not here thine only God on earth?
          Exit the KING [OF SCOTS].
Jaqu. Mais, où est mon argent, signor?
Ateu. Come, follow me; his grace, I see, is mad
   That thus on sudden he hath left us here.   75
   Come, Jaques, we will have our packet soon despatched,
   And you shall be my mate upon the way.
Jaqu. Comme vous plaira, monsieur. Exeunt [ATEUKIN *and* JAQUES].
And. Was never such a world, I think, before,
   When sinners seem to dance within a net: 80
   The flatterer and the murderer they grow big;
   By hook or crook promotion now is sought.
   In such a world where men are so misled,

---

64. crown] *Q;* crowns *Dyce.* 68. thee] *Q;* me *conj. Manly.* 71. thee,] *Q;* thee then, *Grosart.* 72.1.] *so Dyce; follows* 'death', *l.* 69, *in Q.* 73. Mais, où] *Dyce;* Mes on *Q.* Signor] *Q;* Seigneur *Dyce.* 74–5. his ... here] *so Q; Aside in Dyce.* 74. grace] *conj. Manly;* graue *Q.* mad] *conj. Manly;* made *Q.* 78. plaira] *Dyce;* plera *Q.* 83. misled] *Dyce;* missed *Q.*

---

64. *store*] an abundance.
crown] See note to IV. iii. 88; here it is used as a collective.
67. *muttering*] complaining, criticism.
74. *mad*] beside himself with anger (*O.E.D.*, a5).
75. *on sudden*] abruptly.
76. *packet*] parcel of state despatches or commissions. Cf. *Ham.*, v. ii. 15.
77. *mate*] companion.
80. *When ... net*] act with concealment, while expecting to escape notice; a proverb (Tilley N130). The allusion is ultimately to Vulcan's trapping the adulterous Venus with Mars in a net.
82. *By ... crook*] See Tilley H588.

What should I do ? But as the proverb saith,
Run with the hare and hunt with the hound ? 85
To have two means beseems a witty man.
Now here in court I may aspire and climb
By subtlety before my master's death;
And if that fail, well fare another drift.
I will in secret certain letters send 90
Unto the English king and let him know
The order of his daughter's overthrow,
That if my master crack his credit here
(As I am sure long flattery cannot hold),
I may have means within the English court 95
To 'scape the scourge that waits on bad advice. *Exit.*

Chorus [IV]

Enter BOHAN *and* OBERON.

Ober. Believe me, bonny Scot, these strange events
　　Are passing pleasing; may they end as well.
Boh. Else say that Bohan hath a barren skull,
　　If better motions yet than any past
　　Do not more glee to make the fairy greet; 5

85. hunt with] *Q;* hunt too with *Grosart.*　　88. before] *conj. Dyce;* for *Q.*
Chorus IV. 5. greet] *Q;* gree *Grosart.*

---

　85. *Run . . . hound*] See Tilley H158.
　86. *means*] schemes, modes of action.
　witty] clever.
　88. *subtlety*] ingenuity.
　89. *drift*] scheme, plan.
　92. *order of*] sequence of events (leading to).
　overthrow] destruction.
　93. *crack*] exhaust, ruin.
　96. *bad advice*] evil counsel, evil influence.

　Chorus IV. 2. *passing*] surpassingly.
　4. *motions*] stage actions; with possibly an allusion to 'puppet shows'. Cf. note to Chor. III, I.
　5.] do not give more delight to provide a greeting for the fairy. For a similar use of *greet*, see *Friar Bacon*, III. ii. 1291.

But my small son made pretty handsome shift
To save the queen his mistress by his speed.
Ober. Yea, and yon laddie, for his sport he made
Shall see, when least he hopes, I'll stand his friend,
Or else he capers in a halter's end. 10
Boh. What, hang my son? I trow not, Oberon;
I'll rather die than see him woebegone.

Enter a round or some dance at pleasure.

Ober. Bohan, be pleased, for, do they what they will,
Here is my hand, I'll save thy son from ill. *Exeunt.*

8. Yea, and yon laddie] *Dyce;* Yea you Ladie *Q.*   14. *Exeunt*] *Dyce; Exit Q.*

8. *yon laddie*] i.e., Slipper; see v. vi. 40 ff.
9–10. *I'll . . . end*] See v. vi. 57.1–2.
11. *trow*] believe.
12.1. round] See note to IV. iii. 101.1.
at pleasure] i.e., at the actors' discretion.

Act V

[v. i]

Enter the Queen [DOROTHEA] *in a nightgown,* LADY ANDERSON, *and* NANO.

L. And. My gentle friend, beware, in taking air,
Your walks grow not offensive to your wounds.
Dor. Madam, I thank you of your courteous care;
My wounds are well-nigh closed, though sore they are. 4
L. And. Methinks these closèd wounds should breed more grief,
Since open wounds have cure and find relief.
Dor. Madam, if undiscovered wounds you mean,
They are not cured because they are not seen.
L. And. I mean the wounds which do the heart subdue.
Nano. O, that is love, madam; speak I not true? 10

SIR CUTHBERT ANDERSON [*enters and*] *overhears.*

L. And. Say it were true, what salve for such a sore?
Nano. Be wise and shut such neighbours out of door.
L. And. How if I cannot drive him from my breast?
Nano. Then chain him well and let him do his best.
Sir Cuth. [*Aside*] In ripping up their wounds, I see their wit; 15
But if these wounds be cured, I sorrow it.

v. i.] *Actus Quintus. Schena Prima. Q.*   10.1. *Sir Cuthbert Anderson*] *conj.*
Manly; Ladie Anderson Q.   *enter and*] *conj. Manly; not in Q.*   15.
Aside] *Dyce; not in Q.*

   0.1. nightgown] dressing-gown.
   3. *of*] for.
   5. *grief*] suffering.
   14. *let . . . best*] however hard he tries he will be harmless.
   15. *ripping up*] disclosing.
   16. *sorrow it*] shall experience sorrow for it.

Dor. Why are you so intentive to behold
   My pale and woeful looks, by care controlled?
L. And. Because in them a ready way is found
   To cure my care and heal my hidden wound.   20
Nano. Good master, shut your eyes, keep that conceit;
   Surgeons give coin to get a good receipt.
Dor. Peace, wanton son, this lady did amend
   My wounds; mine eyes her hidden grief shall end.
Nano. Look not too much; it is a weighty case.   25
   Whereas a man puts on a maiden's face,
   For many times, if ladies wear them not,
   A nine months' wound with little work is got.
Sir Cuth. [*Aside*] I'll break off their dispute, lest love proceed
   From covert smiles to perfect love indeed.   30
                              [*He comes forward.*]
Nano. The cat's abroad; stir not, the mice be still.
L. And. Tut, we can fly such cats, when so we will.
Sir Cuth. How fares my guest? Take cheer, naught shall default
   That either doth concern your health or joy.
   Use me, my house, and what is mine is yours.   35
Dor. Thanks, gentle knight, and if all hopes be true,
   I hope ere long to do as much for you.

24. grief] *Q;* griefs *Dickinson.*   25.] *so Manly; assigned to 'Doro.' in Q.*
27. wear] *Q;* 'ware *Dyce.*   29. *Aside*] *Dyce; not in Q.*   30.1.] *Dyce;
not in Q.*   35. is yours] *Q;* as yours *Dyce.*

---

17. *intentive*] heedful, attentive.
18. *controlled*] dominated.
21. *conceit*] idea, conception.
22.] In view of Dorothea's 'Peace, wanton son', and Nano's subsequent quibble in ll. 25–8, it is possible that the dwarf may be referring to pregnancy-eluding devices.
25. *weighty case*] serious matter.
26. *Whereas*] where, when.
27. *wear*] Most editors emend to ''ware', taking *them* to refer to 'men who put on maidens' faces' (i.e., assume innocence). However, the sense of Q seems to be 'it behoves ladies to wear maidens' faces [i.e., remain modest] and so avoid the nine-months' wound [i.e., pregnancy].'
30. *perfect*] fully developed.
31.] a variation of the proverb; see Tilley C175.
33. *Take cheer*] take heart, cheer up.

L

Sir Cuth. Your virtue doth acquit me of that doubt.
  But, courteous sir, since troubles calls me hence,
  I must to Edinburgh unto the king, 40
  There to take charge and wait him in his wars.
  Meanwhile, good madam, take this squire in charge
  And use him so as if it were myself.
L. And. Sir Cuthbert, doubt not of my diligence.
  Meanwhile, till your return, God send you health. 45
Dor. God bless his grace, and if his cause be just,
  Prosper his wars; if not, he'll mend, I trust.
  Good sir, what moves the king to fall to arms?
Sir Cuth. The king of England forageth his land
  And hath besieged Dunbar with mighty force. 50
Dor. What other news are common in the court?
Sir Cuth. [*Giving letters to Lady Anderson*] Read you these
    letters, madam; tell the squire
  The whole affairs of state, for I must hence. *Exit.*
Dor. God prosper you and bring you back from thence.
  Madam, what news?
L. And.   They say the queen is slain. 55
Dor. Tut, such reports more false than truth contain.
L. And. But these reports have made his nobles leave him.
Dor. Ah, careless men, and would they so deceive him?
L. And. The land is spoiled, the commons fear the cross,
  All cry against the king, their cause of loss: 60
  The English king subdues and conquers all.
Dor. Alas, this war grows great on causes small!

41. wait] *Dyce;* waight *Q.*   50. Dunbar] *Dyce;* Dambac *Q.*   51.] *so Dyce;* assigned to 'S. Cutb.' in *Q.*   52. Giving ... Anderson] *Dyce; not in Q.*   62. Alas] *Dyce;* Ah lasse *Q.*

---

38. *acquit ... doubt*] make me certain that you will do as you say.
41. *take charge*] undertake responsibility, here a military commission.
wait him] escort, accompany him.
47. *mend*] reform himself, improve morally.
58. *careless*] thoughtless, irresponsible.
deceive] be false to.
59. *cross*] misfortune, adversity (*O.E.D., sb.* 10b); or perhaps the reference is to the English banner bearing the Cross of St George.

L. And. Our court is desolate, our prince alone,
  Still dreading death.
Dor.   Woe's me, for him I moan.
  Help, now help, a sudden qualm 65
  Assails my heart.
Nano.   Good madam, stand his friend;
  Give us some liquor to refresh his heart.
L. And. Daw thou him up, and I will fetch thee forth
  Potions of comfort to repress his pain. *Exit.*
Nano. Fie, princess, faint on every fond report? 70
  How well-nigh had you opened your estate.
  Cover these sorrows with the veil of joy
  And hope the best; forwhy this war will cause
  A great repentance in your husband's mind.
Dor. Ah, Nano, trees live not without their sap, 75
  And Clytia cannot blush but on the sun;
  The thirsty earth is broke with many a gap,
  And lands are lean where rivers do not run.
  Where soul is reft from that it loveth best,
  How can it thrive or boast of quiet rest? 80
  Thou know'st the prince's loss must be my death,
  His grief, my grief; his mischief must be mine.
  O, if thou love me, Nano, hie to court,
  Tell Ross, tell Bartram that I am alive.
  Conceal thou yet the place of my abode; 85

65. Help . . . a] *Q;* Help me now help me, for a *Grosart.* 66, 67. his] *Dyce;* her *Q.* 68. him] *Dyce;* her *Q.* 69. his] *Dyce;* h r *Q.* 76. Clytia] *Clitia Q;* Clytie *Dyce.* 81. know'st] *Dyce;* knowest *Q.*

---

68. *Daw*] rouse, revive from a swoon (*O.E.D.*, $v.^1$ 3).
70. *fond*] idle, trifling.
71. *opened . . . estate*] revealed your true position.
73. *forwhy*] because.
76. *Clytia*] the ocean nymph beloved of Apollo who deserted her. She was transformed into a sunflower, which was supposed always to turn its head in the direction of the sun and was thus a common symbol of unwavering affection; see Ovid, *Metamorphoses,* IV. 234–70.
78. *lean*] barren.
82. *mischief*] misfortune.

      Will them even as they love their queen,
      As they are chary of my soul and joy,
      To guard the king, to serve him as my lord.
      Haste thee, good Nano, for my husband's care
      Consumeth me and wounds me to the heart.   90
Nano. Madam, I go, yet loth to leave you here.   *Exit.*
Dor. Go thou with speed; even as thou hold'st me dear,
      Return in haste.

              Enter LADY ANDERSON.

L. And. Now, sir, what cheer? Come, taste this broth I bring.
Dor. My grief is past, I feel no further sting.   95
L. And. Where is your dwarf? Why hath he left you, sir?
Dor. For some affairs; he is not travelled far.
L. And. If so you please, come in and take your rest.
Dor. Fear keeps awake a discontented breast.   *Exeunt.*

[v. ii]

After a solemn service, enter from the Countess of Arran's house a service, musical songs of marriage, or a masque, or what pretty triumph you list; to them ATEUKIN *and* JAQUES [*who approach one of the Servants*].

Ateu. What means this triumph, friend? Why are these feasts?

86. Will] *Q;* But will *or* And will *conj. Dyce.*   91. *Exit*] *Dyce; Exeunt Q.*
92. speed;] *This ed.;* speed, *Q.*

v. ii. o.1. *Countess of Arran's*] *Dyce;* widdowes *Q.*   o.2. marriage] *This ed.;* marriages *Q.*   o.3. *Jaques*] *Dyce;* Gnato *Q;* his Gnato *Grosart.*

---

86. *Will*] enjoin, order.
87. *chary*] careful in the preservation.
89. *my husband's care*] care for my husband.
95. *sting*] pain, distress.
99. *discontented*] deprived of peace.

    v. ii. 0.1. solemn service] marriage ceremony. Presumably Greene wants this celebration to be seen or at least heard by the audience.
    0.2. service] Greene clearly desires some kind of religious display, perhaps ritual or procession, to start off the scene.
    triumph] spectacle, pageant.
    0.3. list] like, choose.

SC. II]   JAMES THE FOURTH   101

Serv. Fair Ida, sir, was married yesterday
  Unto Sir Eustace, and for that intent
  We feast and sport it thus to honour them;
  And if you please, come in and take your part;   5
  My lady is no niggard of her cheer.   *Exit.*
Jaqu. *Monseigneur*, why be you so sadda? *Faites bonne chère,*
  foutre de ce monde!
Ateu. What, was I born to be the scorn of kin?
  To gather feathers like to a hopper crow   10
  And lose them in the height of all my pomp?
  Accursèd man, now is my credit lost!
  Where is my vows I made unto the king?
  What shall become of me, if he shall hear
  That I have caused him kill a virtuous queen   15
  And hope in vain for that which now is lost?
  Where shall I hide my head? I know the heavens
  Are just and will revenge; I know my sins
  Exceed compare. Should I proceed in this?
  This Eustace must amain be made away—   20
  O, were I dead, how happy should I be!
Jaqu. *Est-ce donc à tel point votre état?* Faith, then *adieu*, Scot-

---

7. *Faites*] Dyce; *fette* Q.   8. *foutre*] Dyce; *fontre* Q.   10. a] Q; Grosart omits.   20. amain] Dyce; *a man* Q.

---

  3. *for that intent*] to that end, for that reason.
  7–8. Monseigneur ... Faites bonne chère, foutre de ce monde] My lord ... be merry, a fig for the world; see note to III. ii. 24.
  9. *kin*] my family.
  10–11. *To gather ... pomp*] O.E.D. suggests 'a crow that follows a seed-hopper during sowing' but the allusion is unexplained. 'To gather feathers' could mean 'become augmented, grow bigger'. R. Walker (*T.L.S.*, 10 Aug. 1951, p. 501) points to this as being a version of Greene's later accusation in *Greene's Groatsworth of Wit* that Shakespeare was 'an upstart crow beautified with our feathers'.
  13. *is*] See Abbott, 335.
  17–18. *the heavens Are just*] Cf. *Wisdom*, XI. 16, XII. 23; and also *Lr.*, V. iii. 170.
  19. *Exceed compare*] are without equal, beyond comparison.
  20. *amain*] immediately.
  22. *Est-ce ... état*] Has your position then reached such a point?

land, *adieu*, Signor Ateukin: me will homa to France and
no be hanged in a strange country. *Exit.*

Ateu. Thou dost me good to leave me thus alone, 25
That galling grief and I may yoke in one.
O, what are subtle means to climb on high,
When every fall swarms with exceeding shame?
I promised Ida's love unto the prince,
But she is lost and I am false forsworn: 30
I practised Dorothea's hapless death,
And by this practice have commenced a war.
O, cursèd race of men that traffic guile,
And in the end themselves and kings beguile!
Ashamed to look upon my prince again, 35
Ashamed of my suggestions and advice,
Ashamed of life, ashamed that I have erred,
I'll hide myself, expecting for my shame.
Thus God doth work with those that purchase fame
By flattery, and make their prince their gain. *Exit.* 40

[v. iii]

Enter the KING OF ENGLAND, LORD PERCY, SAMLES,
and others.

K. of Eng. Thus far, ye English peers, have we displayed

40. gain] *Q;* game *Dyce.*   *Exit*] *Dyce; Exeunt Q.*

v. iii. 1. *K. of Eng.*] '*Arius, Ari.*' *throughout the scene in Q.*   ye] *Dyce;* the *Q.*

---

24. *strange*] foreign (cf. Fr. *étrange*).
26. *yoke in one*] be fastened together.
28.] a proverb; see Tilley F132: 'He went out with shift and came home with shame.'
31. *practised*] plotted, contrived.
33–4.] a proverb; see Tilley S334.
33. *traffic*] deal in.
36. *suggestions*] See note to III. iii. 30.
38. *expecting for*] awaiting.
40. *gain*] source of gain.

v. iii. 0.1. *Samles*] a ghost character; see Introduction, p. lix.

> Our waving ensigns with a happy war;
> Thus nearly hath our furious rage revenged
> My daughter's death upon the traitorous Scot.
> And now before Dunbar our camp is pitched,   5
> Which, if it yield not to our compromise,
> The plough shall furrow where the palace stood
> And fury shall enjoy so high a power
> That mercy shall be banished from our swords.

[Enter DOUGLAS *and others above.]*

Doug. What seeks the English king?   10
K. of Eng. Scot, open those gates and let me enter in;
> Submit thyself and thine unto my grace,
> Or I will put each mother's son to death
> And lay this city level with the ground.

Doug. For what offence? For what default of ours?   15
> Art thou incensed so sore against our state?
> Can generous hearts in nature be so stern
> To prey on those that never did offend?
> What though the lion, king of brutish race,
> Through outrage sin, shall lambs be therefore slain?   20
> Or is it lawful that the humble die

---

5. Dunbar] *Dyce;* Dambar *Q.*   7. plough] *Dyce;* place *Q.*   8. enjoy] *Dyce;* enuy *Q.*   9.1.] Enter Douglas and others on the walls *Dyce; not in Q.*

---

2. *happy*] successful.
3. *nearly*] thoroughly.
6. *compromise*] proffered terms (*O.E.D., sb.* 4a).
7. *plough*] *O.E.D.* records no occurrence of 'furrow' used intransitively, which would be necessary if Q's 'place' were allowed to stand.
9.1. *above*] This scene clearly utilizes some upper-level acting area which apparently most Elizabethan theatres possessed but the exact nature of which is still a subject of discussion; see note to Ind. 110.
12. *grace*] mercy, clemency (*O.E.D., sb.* 15).
15. *default*] failing, defect.
19. *lion . . . race*] This comparison between king and lion was a natural one in view of the correspondences between primacies in the 'Elizabethan World Picture' (see E. M. W. Tillyard, *Elizabethan World Picture* (1950), pp. 27–8).
brutish] animal.

Because the mighty do gainsay the right?
O English king, thou bearest in thy breast
The king of beasts that harms not yielding ones;
The roseal cross is spread within thy field,   25
A sign of peace not of revenging war.
Be gracious then unto this little town
And, though we have withstood thee for a while
To show allegiance to our liefest liege,
Yet since we know no hope of any help,   30
Take us to mercy, for we yield ourselves.
K. of Eng. What, shall I enter then and be your lord?
Doug. We will submit us to the English king.
   They descend down, open the gates, and humble them[selves].
K. of Eng. Now life and death dependeth on my sword;
This hand now reared, my Douglas, if I list,   35
Could part thy head and shoulders both in twain.
But since I see thee wise and old in years,
True to thy king and faithful in his wars,
Live thou and thine. Dunbar is too too small
To give an entrance to the English king: 40
I, eagle-like, disdain these little fowls
And look on none but those that dare resist.

23. breast] *Q*; crest *Dyce*.   39. Dunbar] *Dyce*; Dambar *Q*.

---

  22. *gainsay*] oppose.
  23. *breast*] All editors emend to 'crest' except Lavin, who correctly explains: 'In a coat of arms the crest is that part above the shield and helmet. The royal arms contains the lions not in the crest but on the shield. As the following line makes clear, Douglas is referring to the king's coat-armour, and is therefore correct in his phrase *in* [i.e., on] *thy breast*.'
  24. *yielding ones*] those prepared to submit.
  25. *roseal*] rose-red.
  field] the surface of the shield in a coat of arms on which the 'charge' (i.e., heraldic device) is displayed.
  29. *liefest liege*] dearest overlord.
  33.1. descend down] See note to line 9.1.
  35. *list*] desired, chose.
  41. *I, eagle-like . . . fowls*] The eagle/king comparison, like that of the lion/king in l. 19, was a common one and for the same reason. Cf. Tilley E1.

SC. III]   JAMES THE FOURTH   105

  Enter your town as those that live by me:
  For others that resist, kill, forage, spoil.
  Mine English soldiers, as you love your king,   45
  Revenge his daughter's death and do me right. *Exeunt.*

[v. iv]
    Enter the Lawyer, *the* Merchant, *and the* Divine.

Law. My friends, what think you of this present state?
 Were ever seen such changes in a time?
 The manners and the fashions of this age
 Are like the ermine skin, so full of spots
 As sooner may the Moor be washèd white   5
 Than these corruptions banished from this realm.
Merch. What sees Mas Lawyer in this state amiss?
Law. A wresting power that makes a nose of wax
 Of grounded law, a damned and subtle drift
 In all estates to climb by others' loss,   10
 An eager thirst of wealth, forgetting truth.
 Might I ascend unto the highest states
 And by descent discover every crime,
 My friends, I should lament and you would grieve
 To see the hapless ruins of this realm.   15

v. iv. 4. ermine] *Q;* ermine's *Dyce.* 5. sooner] *Dyce;* soone *Q.* 11. thirst] *Dyce;* thrift *Q.*

---

43. *by me*] by my favour.

v. iv] See Introduction, p. xli.
4. *ermine . . . spots*] a proverb (Tilley L206).
ermine] Ermine fur was often used in heraldic designs, marked with black spots at regular intervals.
5. *As . . . white*] a proverb (Tilley E186).
7. *Mas*] a vulgar shortening of 'Master'.
8. *wresting*] distorting.
a nose of wax] a proverbial expression to indicate something easily moulded; see Tilley H531, L104, N226.
9. *grounded*] well-established.
drift] process.
11. *truth*] loyalty.
13. *discover*] reveal.

Div. O lawyer, thou hast curious eyes to pry
　　Into the secret maims of their estate;
　　But if thy veil of error were unmasked,
　　Thyself should see your sect do maim her most.
　　Are you not those that should maintain the peace, 20
　　Yet only are the patrons of our strife?
　　If your profession have his ground and spring
　　First from the laws of God, then country's right,
　　Not any ways inverting Nature's power,
　　Why thrive you by contentions? Why devise you 25
　　Clauses and subtle reasons to except?
　　Our state was first, before you grew so great,
　　A lantern to the world for unity;
　　Now they that are befriended and are rich
　　Oppress the poor: come Homer without coin, 30
　　He is not heard. What shall we term this drift?
　　To say the poor man's cause is good and just,
　　And yet the rich man gains the best in law.
　　It is your guise (the more the world laments)
　　To coin provisoes to beguile your laws, 35

17. *secret*] Dyce; *secrets* Q.　　30. *Oppress*] Dyce; *Or presse* Q.

16. *curious*] unduly inquisitive.
17. *maims*] defects.
19. *sect*] profession.
22. *ground and spring*] basis and source.
24. *inverting*] perverting, upsetting.
26. *Clauses*] legal term meaning 'provisoes', 'stipulations' (*O.E.D.*, *sb.* 2).
　　subtle reasons] Lavin cites Barnabe Riche, *My Ladies Looking Glass* (1616), sig. I1r: '[Lawyers] haue such a number of subtill subtillties, that they do yet make more subtill by their subtill handling, that they be able to set the Lawes themselues togither by the eares.'
　　except] make objections (a legal term).
28. *lantern*] a shining example.
30. *Homer*] proverbial for his 'sweet tongue'; see Tilley H537 and note to IV. v. 24–6.
31. *What . . . term*] how shall we describe.
　　drift] process.
32–3. *To say . . . law*] a proverb (Tilley L116).
33. *gains the best*] comes off best.
34. *guise*] habit, usual practice.
35. *provisoes*] clauses inserted in a legal document making some con-

  To make a gay pretext of due proceeding,
  When you delay your common-pleas for years.
  Mark what these dealings lately here have wrought:
  The crafty men have purchased great men's lands,
  They poll, they pinch, their tenants are undone;   40
  If these complain, by you they are undone;
  You fleece them of their coin, their children beg,
  And many want because you may be rich.
  This scar is mighty, Master Lawyer;
  Now war hath gotten head within this land,   45
  Mark but the guise: the poor man that is wronged
  Is ready to rebel; he spoils, he pills;
  We need no foes to forage that we have:
  The law (they say) in peace consumèd us,
  And now in war we will consume the law.   50
  Look to this mischief, lawyers: conscience knows
  You live amiss; amend it, lest you end.
Law. Good Lord, that these divines should see so far
  In others' faults without amending theirs!
  Sir, sir, the general defaults in state   55
  (If you would read before you did correct)
  Are, by a hidden working from above,

---

41. complain, ... undone;] *Dyce;* complaine ... vndone, *Q.* 45. war] *Dyce;* man *Q.* 53. these] *Dyce;* their *Q.*

---

dition or exception upon which the validity of the document depends.
 beguile] cheat, get round.
36. *gay*] merry, irresponsible.
pretext ... proceeding] pretence of properly administering the law.
37. *common-pleas*] civil law suits.
40. *poll*] practise extortion.
pinch] synonymous with 'poll'.
45. *gotten head*] gained power or ascendancy.
46. *guise*] manner (of it).
47. *pills*] plunders, pillages.
48. *forage*] plunder.
51. *mischief*] See note to v. i. 82.
53–4. *that ... theirs*] a proverb (Tilley F107).
55. *defaults*] See note to v. iii. 15.
56. *read*] understand properly, comprehend.
57. *working*] operation.

By these successive changes still removed.
Were not the law by contraries maintained,
How could the truth from falsehood be discerned? 60
Did we not taste the bitterness of war,
How could we know the sweet effects of peace?
Did we not feel the nipping winter frosts,
How should we know the sweetness of the spring?
Should all things still remain in one estate, 65
Should not in greatest arts some scars be found;
Were all upright and changed, what world were this?
A chaos, made of quiet, yet no world,
Because the parts thereof did still accord;
This matter craves a variance not a speech. 70
But, Sir Divine, to you: look on your maims,
Divisions, sects, your simonies, and bribes,
Your cloaking with the great for fear to fall,
You shall perceive you are the cause of all.
Did each man know there were a storm at hand, 75
Who would not clothe him well to shun the wet?
Did prince and peer, the lawyer and the least,

58. removed] *Dyce;* remainde *Q*.   67. and] *Q;* nor *Dyce*.   70. speech] *Q;* peace *conj. Manly*.   72. simonies] *Dyce;* summonies *Q*.   77. least] *Q;* Priest *Collins*.

59–67. *Were ... this*] This was a common kind of argument of the period, and was used for a variety of purposes; cf. Sidney, *Defence of Poesie* (*Works*, ed. A. Feuillerat, 1912), III. 23: 'Now as in *Geometrie*, the oblique must be knowne as well as the right, and in *Arithmetick*, the odde as well as the even, so in the actions of our life, who seeth not the filthinesse of evill, wanteth a great foile to perceive the bewtie of vertue.'

65. *still*] ever, always.
estate] condition.
66. *arts*] branches of learning.
67. *upright*] in conformity.
changed] altered from its present condition.
69. *accord*] agree, harmonize.
70. *variance*] debate.
71. *maims*] grave defects, blemishes.
72. *simonies*] the buying and selling of ecclesiastical offices.
73. *cloaking*] pretending, dissembling.

  Know what were sin without a partial gloss,
  We'd need no long discovery then of crimes,
  For each would mend, advised by holy men.   80
  Thus I but slightly shadow out your sins;
  But if they were depainted out for life,
  Alas, we both had wounds enough to heal.
Merch. None of you both, I see, but are in fault;
  Thus simple men as I do swallow flies.   85
  This grave divine can tell us what to do,
  But we may say, 'Physician, mend thyself.'
  This lawyer hath a pregnant wit to talk;
  But all are words, I see no deeds of worth.
Law. Good Merchant, lay your fingers on your mouth;   90
  Be not a blab, for fear you bite yourself.
  What should I term your state, but even the way

---

79. We'd] *Dyce;* Wee *Q.*   discovery] *Q;* discoursing *Dyce.*   81. Thus
I but] *Dyce;* Thus but *Q.*   82. for] *Q;* of *Manly.*

---

 78. *partial gloss*] biased interpretation.
 79. *discovery*] revelation.
 81. *shadow out*] outline, depict.
 82. *depainted out*] described graphically.
 for life] to the life, exactly.
 85. *swallow flies*] Cf. Tilley B451: 'The blind eat many a fly,' and H622:
'To wear a horn and not know it will do one no more harm than to eat a fly
and not see it.'
 87. *Physician . . . thyself*] Cf. *Luke*, iv. 23.
 91. *blab*] tatler, uncontrolled talker.
 92–104. *What . . . beguiled*] All of these were common topics of discussion
at the time. There was general agreement that usury was a great evil,
although some commentators argued that it should be tolerated and controlled in a modern commonwealth. While the Church Fathers and the
Scriptures condemned it, Calvin, Beza, and other Divines agreed that it
was a necessity. Bacon in his essay 'Of Usury' saw it as 'inevitable', and the
English law, while calling it sinful and aiming at its repression, allowed
borrowing up to the ten per cent rate. Noblemen were often considered to
be particularly victimized: Sidney, Essex, Leicester, and Southampton all
had debts running to thousands of pounds. The topic was dealt with in
many plays of the period; with A. B. Stone (*P.M.L.A.*, XXXI (1916), 190–
210) finding seventy-one plays written between 1553 and 1640 in which
attacks were made on usurers. Intermarriage between the aristocratic and
merchant classes was also sufficiently common to encourage dramatic

To every ruin in this commonweal?
You bring us in the means of all excess,
You rate it and retail it as you please, 95
You swear, forswear, and all to compass wealth,
Your money is your god, your hoard your heaven.
You are the groundwork of contention:
First, heedless youth by you is overreached,
We are corrupted by your many crowns; 100
The gentlemen, whose titles you have bought,
Lose all their fathers' toil within a day,
Whilst Hob, your son, and Sib, your nutbrown child,
Are gentlefolks and gentles are beguiled.
This makes so many noble minds to stray 105
And take sinister courses in the state.

Enter a Scout.

Scout. My friends, begone, and if you love your lives;
The King of England marcheth here at hand;

95. retail] *Dyce;* retalde *Q.*   105. minds] *Dyce;* maides *Q.*

---

treatment of the subject such as the Lacy–Rose episodes in Dekker's *The Shoemakers' Holiday*.
   94. *means of*] way to.
   95. *rate*] assign a price to.
   96. *compass*] attain.
   100. *crowns*] See note to IV. iii. 88.
   101–2. *The gentlemen . . . day*] Cf. Tilley F91: 'A sparing father and a spending son.'
   103. *nutbrown*] of reddish-brown complexion, and thus by Elizabethan standards of beauty 'dark and coarse complexioned', particularly typical of sunburnt country-girls. Cf. Lyly, *Euphues, The Anatomy of Wit*, I. 254: 'If she be well sette, then call hir a Bosse . . . if Nutbrowne, as blacke as a coale'; and also *Gent.*, IV. iv. 148–9, 152: 'But since she did neglect her looking-glass / And threw her sun-expelling mask away, / The air hath starv'd the roses in her cheeks. . . / That now she is become as black as I'; and *Sonn.*, 127.
   104. *gentles*] people of gentle birth.
   105. *minds*] Q's reading makes sense, but the attack seems to require a general conclusion rather than a specific reference to class-intermarriage.
   106. *sinister*] corrupt, dishonest.
   107. *and if*] if.

SC. IV] JAMES THE FOURTH 111

    Enter the camp for fear you be surprised.
Div. Thanks, gentle scout. God mend that is amiss   110
    And place true zeal whereas corruption is.   *Exeunt.*

[v. v]

    Enter DOROTHEA [*in man's apparel*], LADY ANDERSON,
    and NANO.

Dor. What news in court, Nano? Let us know it.
Nano. If so you please, my lord, I straight will show it:
    The English king hath all the borders spoiled,
    Hath taken Morton prisoner, and hath slain
    Seven thousand Scottish lads not far from Tweed.   5
Dor. A woeful murder and a bloody deed.
Nano. The king, our liege, hath sought by many means
    For to appease his enemy by prayers;
    Naught will prevail unless he can restore
    Fair Dorothea, long supposèd dead.   10
    To this intent he hath proclaimèd late
    That whosoever return the queen to court
    Shall have a thousand marks for his reward.
L. And. He loves her then, I see, although enforced,
    That would bestow such gifts for to regain her.   15
    Why sit you sad, good sir? Be not dismayed.
Nano. I'll lay my life this man would be a maid.

---

v. v. 0.1. *in man's apparel*] Dyce; not in Q.   5. lads] *Dyce;* Lords Q.
Tweed] *Dyce;* Twearde Q.   7. The king] *Dyce;* Thinking Q.

---

  109. *surprised*] unexpectedly captured by sudden attack; cf. Marlowe's *Dido Queen of Carthage* (ed. H. J. Oliver, 1968), I. i. 72.
  111. *whereas*] where.

  v. v. 5. *lads*] Q's 'Lords' is obviously an impossibility.
  Tweed] the river Tweed which constitutes part of the border between England and Scotland. The Battle of Flodden, in which the historical James IV was slain, was fought near to it on 9 September 1513.
  8. *prayers*] petitions, entreaties.
  13. *marks*] Scottish coins worth 13s. 4d.
  14. *enforced*] pressed hard by physical force.

112   JAMES THE FOURTH   [ACT V

Dor. [*Aside to Nano*] Fain would I show myself and change my
   tire.
L. And. Whereon divine you, sir?
Nano.   Upon desire.
   Madam, mark but my skill: I'll lay my life   20
   My master here will prove a married wife.
Dor. [*Aside to Nano*] Wilt thou bewray me, Nano?
Nano. [*Aside to Dorothea*]   Madam, no.
   You are a man and like a man you go,
   But I that am in speculation seen
   Know you would change your state to be a queen.   25
Dor. [*Aside to Nano*] Thou art not, dwarf, to learn thy mistress'
   mind.
   Fain would I with thyself disclose my kind,
   But yet I blush.
Nano. [*Aside to Dorothea*] What, blush you, madam, then,
   To be yourself, who are a feignèd man?
   Let me alone.
Dor. [*Aside to Nano*] Good Nano, stay awhile.   30

18. Aside to Nano] *Lavin; not in Q.*   22. Aside to Nano] *Dyce; not in Q.*
Aside to Dorothea] *Dyce; not in Q.*   26. Aside to Nano] *Dyce; not in Q.*
27. with] *Q;* wish *conj. Dyce.*   28. Aside to Dorothea] *Dyce; not in Q.*
30–45. Good Nano . . . again] *so Lavin; these lines stand between ll. 59 and 60 in Q, with* 'Let me alone.' *repeated after l. 59.*

---

18. *show myself*] reveal my true identity.
tire] habit, dress.
19. *divine*] conjecture.
23. *like . . . go*] you are habitually attired like a man.
24. *in speculation seen*] well versed in observation or understanding.
25. *state*] condition.
27. *kind*] true nature.
29. *feignèd*] Nano's pun on Dorothea's 'Fain would' (l. 27) is more evident in Q's spelling 'fayned'.
30. *Let me alone*] Do not interfere with me.
30–59. *Good . . . more*] In Q, ll. 46–59 follow Nano's 'Let me alone' (l. 29) as the last lines of Sig. I4ʳ. Ll. 30–45 are set in Q as the first 16 lines of Sig. I4ᵛ and are headed by the phrase 'Let me alone'. It is clear from the sense of the exchange and the repeated 'Let me alone' that the two passages were interchanged either during the composition of the type or in the imposition of the forme. I4ʳ and I4ᵛ are two of the pages on which the two compositors who set the play collaborated (see Introduction, pp. lvi–lvii)

SC. V]　　　　　JAMES THE FOURTH　　　　　　113

  Were I not sad, how kindly could I smile
  To see how fain I am to leave this weed;
  And yet I faint to show myself indeed.
  But danger hates delay, I will be bold.
  [*To Lady Anderson*] Fair lady, I am not, as you suppose,　35
  A man, but even that queen, more hapless I,
  Whom Scottish king appointed hath to die.
  I am the hapless princess for whose right
  These kings in bloody wars revenge despite.
  I am that Dorothea whom they seek,　　　　　　　40
  Yours bounden for your kindness and relief;
  And since you are the means that save my life,
  Yourself and I will to the camp repair,
  Whereas your husband shall enjoy reward,
  And bring me to his highness once again.　　　　45
L. And. Deceitful beauty, hast thou scorned me so?
Nano. Nay, muse not, madam, for she tells you true.
L. And. Beauty bred love, and love hath bred my shame.
Nano. And women's faces work more wrongs than these;
  Take comfort, madam, to cure your disease.　　50
  And yet she loves a man as well as you,
  Only this difference, she cannot fancy too.

35. *To Lady Anderson*] This ed.; not in *Q*.　not, as you suppose] *Dyce;* not, suppose *Q*.　37. hath] *Q;* had *Grosart.*　47. madam] *Dyce;* maiden *Q*.　50. your] *Dyce;* our *Q*.　51. she] *Manly;* he *Q*.　52. too] *Q;* two *Dyce*.

---

and the composing error may have been due to this. One possible explanation is that one compositor had set the first 'Let me alone' on Sig. I4ʳ and then continued correctly following the copy with Dorothea's reply (ll. 30–45). The second compositor, helping out at this point, may have started setting at l. 46, taking the relevant section of the copy, and leaving the first compositor to continue with Lady Anderson's speech at l. 60 as if it were a reply to the speech by Dorothea that he had just completed setting.

32. *weed*] habit, dress.
37. *appointed*] ordained.
39. *revenge despite*] inflict punishment for outrages or injuries.
44. *Whereas*] where.
47. *muse not*] do not be astonished.
52. *fancy*] entertain a casual liking for.
 too] Many editors emend to 'two'; but the sense is that Dorothea (like

M

L. And. Blush, grieve, and die in thine insatiate lust!
Dor. Nay, live and joy that thou hast won a friend
    That loves thee as her life by good desert.   55
L. And. I joy, my lord, more than my tongue can tell,
    Although not as I desired, I love you well;
    But modesty that never blushed before
    Discover my false heart. I say no more.
    Pardon, most gracious princess, if you please,   60
    My rude discourse and homely entertain;
    And if my words may savour any worth,
    Vouchsafe my counsel in this weighty cause:
    Since that our liege hath so unkindly dealt,
    Give him no trust, return unto your sire;   65
    There may you safely live in spite of him.
Dor. Ah, lady, so would worldly counsel work,
    But constancy, obedience, and my love,
    In that my husband is my lord and chief,
    These call me to compassion of his estate;   70
    Dissuade me not, for virtue will not change.
L. And. What wondrous constancy is this I hear!
    If English dames their husbands love so dear,
    I fear me in the world they have no peer.
Nano. Come, princess, wend, and let us change your weed;   75
    I long to see you now a queen indeed.   *Exeunt.*

---

55. her] *Lavin;* his *Q.*   good] *Dyce;* god *Q.*   57. Although] *Q;*
Though *Dyce.*   desired] *Q;* wished *conj. Manly.*   60, 72.] *sp. h.* 'An.'
Q.   70. estate] *Q;* state *Dyce.*

Lady Anderson) loves a man, but (unlike Lady Anderson) she cannot 'fancy' *as well.*

56. *my lord*] Lady Anderson cannot yet, in her embarrassment, think of Dorothea as a woman. She dismisses the matter abruptly in l. 59 and thereafter treats Dorothea as a queen.

    59. *Discover*] let it reveal.
    61. *entertain*] hospitality.
    67. *work*] operate.

[V. vi]

Enter the KING OF SCOTS, *the* English Herald, *and* Lords.

K. of Scot. He would have parley, lords. Herald, say he shall,
And get thee gone: go, leave me to myself.
                    [*Exit* Herald; *the* Lords *retire.*]
'Twixt love and fear continual is the wars;
The one assures me of my Ida's love,
The other moves me for my murdered queen.   5
Thus find I grief of that whereon I joy,
And doubt in greatest hope, and death in weal.
Alas, what hell may be compared with mine,
Since in extremes my comforts do consist?
War then will cease when dead ones are revived,   10
Some then will yield when I am dead for hope.
Who doth disturb me? Andrew?

ANDREW *enter[s] with* SLIPPER.

And.   Ay, my liege.
K. of Scot. What news?
And.   I think my mouth was made at first
To tell these tragic tales, my liefest lord.
K. of Scot. What, is Ateukin dead? Tell me the worst.   15
And. No, but your Ida—shall I tell him all?—
Is married late—ah, shall I say to whom?—
My master sad—forwhy he shames the court—
Is fled away! Ah, most unhappy flight!
Only myself—ah, who can love you more?—   20
To show my duty, duty past belief,

---

v. vi. 2.1. *Exit . . . retire*] Dyce; *not in* Q.   8. Alas] Dyce; Ah lasse Q.

---

v. vi. 7. *weal*] happiness.
10–11.] War will stop when Dorothea is alive again and the King of England will then make peace when I am without hope.
13. *made at first*] primarily created.
14. *liefest*] dearest.
18. *forwhy*] for which reason.
shames] is ashamed (to show himself at).

　　　　Am come unto your grace, O gracious liege,
　　　　To let you know—O, would it were not thus—
　　　　That love is vain and maids soon lost and won.
K. of Scot. How have the partial heavens, then, dealt with me, 25
　　　　Boding my weal for to abase my power!
　　　　Alas, what thronging thoughts do me oppress!
　　　　Injurious love is partial in my right,
　　　　And flattering tongues, by whom I was misled,
　　　　Have laid a snare to spoil my state and me. 30
　　　　Methinks I hear my Dorothea's ghost
　　　　Howling revenge for my accursèd hate:
　　　　The ghosts of those my subjects that are slain
　　　　Pursue me crying out, 'Woe, woe to lust!'
　　　　The foe pursues me at my palace door; 35
　　　　He breaks my rest and spoils me in my camp.
　　　　Ah, flattering brood of sycophants, my foes!
　　　　First shall my dire revenge begin on you.
　　　　I will reward thee, Andrew.
Slip. Nay, sir, if you be in your deeds of charity, remember 40
　　　　me. I rubbed Master Ateukin's horse-heels when he rid to
　　　　the meadows.
K. of Scot. And thou shalt have thy recompense for that.
　　　　Lords, bear them to the prison, chain them fast,
　　　　Until we take some order for their deaths. 45
And. If so your grace in such sort give rewards,
　　　　Let me have naught; I am content to want.
Slip. Then, I pray, sir, give me all; I am as ready for a reward
　　　　as an oyster for a fresh tide; spare not me, sir.
K. of Scot. Then hang them both as traitors to the king. 50

33. ghosts] *Dyce;* gifts *Q.*　　42. meadows] *Q;* widow's *conj. Manly.*

　　25. *partial*] biased.
　　26. *Boding my weal*] promising my joy.
　　33. *ghosts*] Q's 'gifts' makes no sense.
　　45. *take some order*] make the necessary arrangements.
　　46. *sort*] manner.
　　47. *want*] lack.
　　49. *as an . . . tide*] gaping like an oyster for the tide; a proverb (Tilley
O114).

SC. VI] JAMES THE FOURTH 117

Slip. The case is altered, sir; I'll none of your gifts. What, I
take a reward at your hands, master? Faith, sir, no; I am a
man of a better conscience.
K. of Scot. Why dally you? Go draw them hence away.
Slip. Why, alas, sir, I will go away. [*To the Lords*] I thank you, 55
gentle friends; I pray you spare your pains. I will not
trouble his honour's mastership; I'll run away.

Enter OBERON *and* Antics, *and carry away the Clown*[, SLIPPER].
He makes pots, and sports, and scorns.

K. of Scot. Why stay you? Move me not. Let search be made
For vile Ateukin; whoso finds him out
Shall have five hundred marks for his reward. 60
Away with ye! Lords, troop about my tent;
Let all our soldiers stand in battle 'rray,
For, lo, the English to their parley come.

March over [*the stage*] *bravely first the English host, the sword carried
before the* KING [OF ENGLAND] *by* PERCY. *The Scottish* [*host*] *on the
other side* [*of the stage*], *with all their pomp bravely.*

55. To the Lords] This ed.; not in Q.   57.1. Oberon] *Dyce;* Adam
Q.   57.2. pots] *Q;* mops *Dyce;* pouts *conj. Dyce*[1].   58. K. of Scot.]
Dyce; not in *Q.*   61. ye] *Lavin;* the *Q;* them *Dyce.*   troop] *Dyce;*
troupes *Q.*

---

51. *The case is altered*] a proverb (Tilley C111). Lavin compares the
anonymous *Appius and Virginia* (1564), ll. 1128 ff., for an extended treatment of the same type of comic situation.
57.1. Enter *Oberon*] Q's 'Enter Adam' has been taken by Grosart as a reference to a contemporary actor who may have played the part of Oberon; but it is more likely to be a misprint for 'Enter a dance'. See Introduction, p. xxix.
57.2. pots] grimaces (*O.E.D.*, *sb.*[3] 1a).
sports] comical actions.
scorns] mocking gestures.
60. *marks*] See note to v. v. 13.
61. *troop*] assemble in a military troop or company, or perhaps 'march in rank'.
63.1. *March over*] Greene is indicating that a certain amount of pageantry is desirable for the entry of the two armies. It has been argued that such entrances may have been effected from the theatre yard to the stage (see A. Nicoll, 'Passing over the Stage', *Shakespeare Survey*, 12 (1959), pp. 47–

What seeks the King of England in this land?
K. of Eng. False traitorous Scot, I come for to revenge 65
    My daughter's death; I come to spoil thy wealth,
    Since thou hast spoiled me of my marriage joy;
    I come to heap thy land with carcasses
    That this thy thirsty soil, choked up with blood,
    May thunder forth revenge upon thy head; 70
    I come to quit thy lawless love with death.
    In brief, no means of peace shall e'er be found,
    Except I have my daughter or thy head.
K. of Scot. My head, proud king? Abase thy pranking plumes;
    So striving fondly mayst thou catch thy grave. 75
    But if true judgment do direct thy course,
    These lawful reasons should divide the war:
    Faith, not by my consent thy daughter died.
K. of Eng. Thou liest, false Scot; thy agents have confessed it.
    These are but fond delays; thou canst not think 80
    A means to reconcile me for thy friend.
    I have thy parasite's confession penned;
    What, then, canst thou allege in thy excuse?
K. of Scot. I will repay the ransom for her blood.
K. of Eng. What, think'st thou, caitiff, I will sell my child? 85
    No, if thou be a prince and man-at-arms,

69. thirsty] *Dyce;* thriftie *Q.*   71. lawless] *Dyce;* louelesse *Q.*   74. plumes] *Dyce;* plaines *Q.*   77. These... reasons... divide] *Q;* This... reason... divert *conj. Dyce.*   81. to] *Dyce;* for to *Q.*

---

55). Greene demands a similar effect in *Alphonsus King of Aragon*, between Acts I and II.
63.1, 3. bravely] in a showy manner.
66. *spoil*] destroy.
67. *spoiled*] robbed, deprived.
71. *quit*] repay.
74. *pranking*] ostentatious.
75. *fondly*] foolishly.
catch thy grave] meet thy death.
77. *divide*] determine.
80. *fond*] foolish.
think] devise.
81. *for*] as.
84. *repay the ransom*] pay what is due.

SC. VI]   JAMES THE FOURTH   119

  In single combat come and try thy right,
  Else will I prove thee recreant to thy face.
K. of Scot. I brook no combat, false injurious king;
  But since thou needless art inclined to war,   90
  Do what thou darest; we are in open field.
  Arming my battles, I will fight with thee.
K. of Eng. Agreed. Now, trumpets sound a dreadful charge,
  Fight for your princess, brave English men!
K. of Scot. Now for your lands, your children, and your wives, 95
  My Scottish peers, and lastly for your king!

Alarum sounded. Both the battles offer to meet, and as the Kings [of Scotland and England] are joining battle, enter SIR CUTHBERT [ANDERSON] *to his* LADY [ANDERSON], *with the queen* DOROTHEA, *richly attired [and veiled, and* NANO].

Sir Cuth. Stay, princes; wage not war: a privy grudge
  'Twixt such as you, most high in majesty,
  Afflicts both nocent and the innocent.
  How many swords, dear princes, see I drawn!   100
  The friend against his friend, a deadly friend;
  A desperate division in those lands
  Which, if they join in one, command the world.

---

89. brook] *Dyce;* tooke *Q;* seek *conj. Manly.* 92. Arming my] *Dyce;* Arming thy *Q;* Among thy *conj. Manly.* battles] *Q;* battle *Dyce.* 94. princess, brave] *Q;* princess my brave *Dyce.* 95–6.] *so Dyce;* assigned to 'K. of E.' *in Q.* 96.3. to] *Q;* and *Dyce.* Lady Anderson] *Dyce;* Lady Cutbert *Q.* 96.4. *and veiled*] *conj. Lavin; who stands concealed Dickinson;* not in *Q.* and Nano] *Dyce;* not in *Q.* 101. deadly friend] *Q;* deadly fiend *Dyce;* deadly feud *or* deadly field *conj. Manly.*

---

 88. *prove*] demonstrate.
 89. *brook*] tolerate.
 92. *battles*] battalions.
 96.1. battles] armies.
 96.3. to] beside.
 96.4. veiled] This stage direction seems necessary in view of Q's stage direction at l. 135.1. Cf. Appendix, p. 141.
 99. *nocent*] guilty.
 101. *deadly*] bringing or threatening death.
 103.] The allusion is to the possible unification of Scotland and England

    O stay! With reason mitigate your rage,
    And let an old man, humbled on his knees,   105
    Entreat a boon, good princes, of you both.
K. of Eng. I condescend, forwhy thy reverend years
    Import some news of truth and consequence.
K. of Scot. I am content, for, Anderson, I know
    Thou art my subject and dost mean me good.   110
Sir Cuth. But by your gracious favours grant me this:
    To swear upon your sword to do me right.
K. of Eng. See, by my sword and by a prince's faith,
    In every lawful sort I am thine own.
K. of Scot. And by my sceptre and the Scottish crown,   115
    I am resolved to grant thee thy request.
Sir Cuth. I see you trust me, princes, who repose
    The weight of such a war upon my will.
    Now mark my suit. A tender lion's whelp,
    This other day, came straggling in the woods   120
    Attended by a young and tender hind,
    In courage haughty yet tired like a lamb.
    The prince of beasts had left this young in keep,

109.] *so Dyce; assigned to 'K. of E.' in Q.*   122. haughty] *Q;* haught *Dyce.*

---

which, together with the question of succession, was much discussed during the 1590s. Relations between the two countries had been stabilized optimistically, since James VI was induced to sign the Treaty of Berwick in July 1586, thereby becoming a pensioner and ally of England, although James's aspirations to the English throne and his intrigues with England's enemies occupied Elizabeth and her ministers until her death. See J. B. Black, *The Reign of Elizabeth* (2nd ed., 1959), pp. 357–71, 441–60.

 107. *condescend*] am willing to listen.
 forwhy] because.
 108. *consequence*] importance.
 112. *To swear . . . sword*] a common method of taking an oath, the blade and hilt of the sword forming a cross; see *Ham.*, I. iii. 154.
 114.] in every lawful way I am on your side.
 121. *hind*] There may be a pun on the meanings 'female deer' and 'household servant'.
 122. *haughty*] exalted.
 tired] dressed.
 123–5. *in keep . . . Unto*] in the charge of, under the protection of.

SC. VI]   JAMES THE FOURTH   121

    To foster up as love-mate and compeer,
    Unto the lion's mate, a neighbour friend.   125
    This stately guide, seducèd by the fox,
    Sent forth an eager wolf, bred up in France,
    That gripped the tender whelp and wounded it.
    By chance as I was hunting in the woods,
    I heard the moan the hind made for the whelp;   130
    I took them both and brought them to my house.
    With chary care I have recured the one
    And, since I know the lions are at strife
    About the loss and damage of the young,
    I bring her home; make claim to her who list.   135
                He discovereth [Dorothea].

Dor. I am the whelp, bred by this lion up,
    This royal English king, my happy sire;
    Poor Nano is the hind that tended me;
    My father, Scottish king, gave me to thee,
    A hapless wife. Thou, quite misled by youth,   140
    Hast sought sinister loves and foreign joys.
    The fox Ateukin, cursèd parasite,
    Incensed your grace to send the wolf abroad,
    The French-born Jaques, for to end my days;
    He, traitorous man, pursued me in the woods   145
    And left me wounded, where this noble knight
    Both rescued me and mine and saved my life.
    Now keep thy promise: Dorothea lives.
    Give Anderson his due and just reward;
    And since, you kings, your wars began by me,   150

---

125. a] *Q;* and *conj. Dyce.*   135.1. Dorothea] *Dyce;* her *Q.*

---

    124. *foster up*] cherish, harbour.
    125. *mate*] fellow.
    126. *guide*] adviser, governor.
    132. *chary*] See note to V. i. 87.
    recured] See note to IV. iv. 68.
    141. *sinister*] erring.
    foreign] outside marriage; cf. *Oth.*, IV. iii. 25–6: 'They . . . pour our treasures into foreign laps.'

   Since I am safe returned, surcease your fight.
K. of Scot. Durst I presume to look upon those eyes
   Which I have tirèd with a world of woes?
   Or did I think submission were enough,
   Or sighs might make an entrance to thy soul,   155
   You heavens, you know how willing I would weep;
   You heavens can tell how glad I would submit;
   You heavens can say how firmly I would sigh.
Dor. Shame me not, prince, companion in thy bed;
   Youth hath misled—tut, but a little fault: 160
   'Tis kingly to amend what is amiss.
   Might I with twice as many pains as these
   Unite our hearts, then should my wedded lord
   See how incessant labours I would take.
   My gracious father, govern your affects;   165
   Give me that hand, that oft hath blessed this head,
   And clasp thine arms, that have embracèd this,
   About the shoulders of my wedded spouse.
   Ah, mighty prince, this king and I am one!
   Spoil thou his subjects, thou despoilest me;   170
   Touch thou his breast, thou dost attaint this heart;
   O, be my father, then, in loving him!

---

151. returned] *This ed.;* returne *Q.*   155. thy] *Grosart;* my *Q.*   160. misled] *Dyce;* missed *Q.*   167. this] *Q;* this neck *Dyce.*

---

 151. *returned*] This reading makes more sense than those of previous editors. In Elizabethan handwriting final 'd' and 'e' were often indistinguishable, and I take the printer's copy to have read 'returnd'.
 surcease] desist from, abandon.
 153. *tirèd*] 'attacked' with perhaps the suggestion of 'adorn'; the word is derived from the French *tirer* and was a term used in falconry. Cf. *Ven.*, 56, and *3H6*, I. i. 268 ff.
 155. *thy*] Some editors have taken this to be a reference to the King of Scots' soul and have retained Q's 'my'. However, he is clearly addressing Dorothea.
 158. *firmly*] strongly.
 160.] a proverb (Tilley M533).
 165. *affects*] emotions.
 167. *this*] i.e., her neck.
 171. *attaint*] strike.

SC. VI] JAMES THE FOURTH 123

K. of Eng. Thou provident kind mother of increase,
  Thou must prevail, ah, Nature, thou must rule.
  Hold, daughter, join my hand and his in one; 175
  I will embrace him for to favour thee;
  I call him friend and take him for my son.
Dor. Ah, royal husband, see what God hath wrought:
  Thy foe is now thy friend. Good men-at-arms,
  Do you the like. These nations, if they join, 180
  What monarch with his liegemen in this world
  Dare but encounter you in open field?
K. of Scot. All wisdom, joined with godly piety,
  Thou English king, pardon my former youth;
  And pardon, courteous queen, my great misdeed; 185
  And for assurance of mine after-life,
  I take religious vows before my God
  To honour thee for father, her for wife.
Sir Cuth. But yet my boons, good princes, are not past.
  First, English king, I humbly do request 190
  That by your means our princess may unite
  Her love unto mine aldertruest love,
  Now you will love, maintain, and help them both.
K. of Eng. Good Anderson, I grant thee thy request.
Sir Cuth. But you, my prince, must yield me mickle more: 195
  You know your nobles are your chiefest stays
  And long time have been banished from your court;

188. father] *Dyce;* fauour *Q.*   189–93.] *so Dyce; assigned to L. And. in Q.*   195–205.] *so Dyce; assigned to L. And. in Q.*   196. stays] *Q;* states *conj. Dyce*[1].

---

173. *provident*] foreseeing and making provision for the future; the word often had religious overtones.
  increase] enlargement of natural prosperity.
  180–2. *These . . . field*] See note to l. 103.
  182. *but*] even, merely.
  186. *after-life*] future conduct.
  191–3.] i.e., that through your influence our princess's love may be joined with the King's.
  192. *aldertruest*] truest of all.
  195. *mickle*] much, a great deal.
  196. *stays*] supports.

  Embrace and reconcile them to yourself;
They are your hands whereby you ought to work.
As for Ateukin and his lewd compeers,   200
That soothed you in your sins and youthly pomp,
Exile, torment, and punish such as they;
For greater vipers never may be found
Within a state than such aspiring heads,
That reck not how they climb, so that they climb.   205
K. of Scot. Guid knight, I grant thy suit. First, I submit
And humble crave a pardon of your grace;
Next, courteous queen, I pray thee by thy loves
Forgive mine errors past and pardon me.
My lords and princes, if I have misdone   210
(As I have wronged indeed both you and yours),
Hereafter, trust me, you are dear to me.
As for Ateukin, whoso finds the man,
Let him have martial law and straight be hanged,
As all his vain abettors now are dead.   215
And Anderson our treasurer shall pay
Three thousand marks for friendly recompense.
Nano. But, princes, whilst you friend it thus in one,

215. As all . . . dead] *Dyce;* As (all . . . diuided) *Q.*   218. *Nano*] *Dyce;*
L. Andr. Q.

---

200. *lewd*] evil, worthless.
compeers] associates.
201. *soothed*] encouraged.
206. *Guid*] good (Scot.).
210. *misdone*] done amiss.
214. *martial law*] judgment without trial.
215.] Although there has been no indication of the death of Jaques, this reference is clarified by the source, where the counterpart of Jaques, the Captain, is killed in battle by Arenopia's (Dorothea's) brother; see Appendix, p. 139.
 dead] Q's reading 'diuided' could be defended but it is unlikely to be correct on both metrical and dramatic grounds, as we know this not to be true.
 217. *marks*] See note to v. v. 13.
 218. *friend it*] make friends; this occurrence antedates the first citation in *O.E.D.*
 in one] together.

  Methinks of friendship Nano shall have none.
Dor. What would my dwarf that I will not bestow? 220
Nano. My boon, fair queen, is this: that you would go;
  Although my body is but small and neat,
  My stomach after toil requireth meat,
  An easy suit, dread princess; will you wend?
K. of Scot. Art thou a pigmy born, my pretty friend? 225
Nano. Not so, great king, but Nature, when she framed me,
  Was scant of earth, and Nano therefore named me;
  And when she saw my body was so small,
  She gave me wit to make it big withal.
K. of Scot. Till time when—
Dor.   Eat then.
K. of Scot.   My friend, it stands with wit
  To take repast when stomach serveth it. 231
Dor. Thy policy, my Nano, shall prevail.
  Come, royal father, enter we my tent;
  And soldiers, feast it, frolic it like friends.
  My princes, bid this kind and courteous train 235
  Partake some favours of our late accord.
  Thus wars have end and, after dreadful hate,
  Men learn at last to know their good estate. *Exeunt.*

---

 227. *Nano . . . me*] See note to Ind. 84.1.
 230–1.] As Dyce notes, there seems to be a hiatus in the text here.
 230–1. *it stands . . . it*] i.e., it is up to the wit to eat when the stomach has provided it with material for a joke.
 232. *policy*] prudence, shrewdness.
 234. *frolic it*] rejoice, make merry.
 234–8.] Manly thinks these lines are more appropriate to one of the kings present than to Dorothea; but, as Lavin notes, 'as Rosalind herself demonstrates and points out: "it is no more unhandsome than to see the lord the prologue" (*AYL.*, Epilogue)'.

[Chorus v]

[*Enter* BOHAN *and* OBERON.]

Boh. And here we'll make ends. The mirk and sable night
    Doth leave the peering morn to pry abroad;
    Thou nill me stay: hail then, thou pride of kings!
    I ken the world and wot well worldly things.
    Mark thou my jig, in mirkest terms that tells   5
    The loath of sins and where corruption dwells.
    Hail me ne mere with shows of guidly sights;
    My grave is mine, that rids me from despites.
    Accept my jig, guid king, and let me rest;
    The grave with guid men is a gay-built nest.   10
Ober. The rising sun doth call me hence away;

Chorus v] *These lines in Q follow on l. 8 of Chor. VIII.*   1. And . . . make]
Lavin; An he weele meete Q.   9–14.] *Manly prints these lines as a separate Chorus.*   10. gay-built] *Dyce;* gay built *Q.*

Chorus V] These lines appear in Q immediately after the Additional Choruses VI–VIII, between Acts I and II. G. L. Kittredge (in Manly's edition) first made the suggestion that the lines constitute a separate Chorus from Chorus VIII, but went on wrongly to suggest a further division at l. 8. As Lavin notes, it is clear from ll. 1 and 2 and 11 that this Chorus is a single unit and was obviously intended as a fitting conclusion to the play and an effective balancing of the opening Induction. In Q the speech prefix *Boh.* appears at the beginning of l. 1, although the final two lines of Chorus VIII are spoken by this character; this too I take to be an additional indication of the separateness of Chorus v.

    1. *And . . . ends*] Lavin's emendation makes sense and is also palaeographically possible.
    mirk] dark (Scot.).
    2. *leave*] allow, give leave to.
    3. *Thou . . . stay*] You are unwilling to stay with me; see Abbott, 220.
    4. *ken*] know (Scot.).
    5. *jig*] entertainment; see note to Chor. II. 17.
    mirkest] See note to l. 1 above.
    6. *loath*] disgust, hatred.
    7. *Hail*] greet.
    ne mere] no more, no further (Scot.).
    guidly] goodly (Scot.).
    8. *despites*] outrages, injuries.
    10. *gay-built*] This is not recorded in *O.E.D.*, but the meaning appears to be 'built so as to appear attractive'.
    11.] It was a common belief that fairies and other supernatural beings

Thanks for thy jig, I may no longer stay;
But if my train did wake thee from thy nest,
So shall they sing thy lullaby to rest.
[*Exit* BOHAN *into the tomb. Exit* OBERON.]

[*Some* Fairies *enter, sing a lullaby, and exeunt.*]

---

13. nest] *Lavin;* rest Q.   14. rest] *Grosart;* nest Q.   14.1–2.] *This ed.;* not in Q.

---

vanished at cock-crow; see *Ham.*, I. i. 150–64. Shakespeare's Oberon is unusual in that he boasts he is not so limited as other spirits in this respect; see *MND.*, III. ii. 388–93.
    13.] The reference is to Ind. 0.1–4.
    13–14. *nest . . . rest*] The transposition of these words in Q was almost certainly due to the close proximity of the same order in ll. 9 and 10.

[ADDITIONAL CHORUSES]

[Chorus VI]

[*Enter* BOHAN *and* OBERON.]

Ober. Here see I good fond actions in thy jig,
And means to paint the world's inconstant ways;
But turn thine eyen, see which I can command.

Enter two battles strongly fighting; the one [*led by*] SEMIRAMIS, *the other* [*by*] STABROBATES. *She flies, and her crown is taken, and she* [*is*] *hurt.*

Boh. What gars this din of mirk and baleful harm,
Where everywean is all betaint with bloud? 5

Chorus VI] *This occurs in Q following Chor. I and is headed 'After the first act.'.* 3. which I] *This ed.;* which for I *Q;* what I *Dyce.* 3.1. one led by] *Dyce;* one *Q.* Semiramis] *Dyce;* Simi Ranus *Q.* 3.2. Stabrobates] *Dyce;* Staurobates *Q.*

Chorus VI] In Q these lines follow Chorus I under the heading '*After the first act*' between Acts I and II. This phrase, which has been taken by many editors to refer to these additional choruses, could just as well have been intended as a reference to Chorus I, as its position is similar to the word '*Chorus*' printed after rather than before Chorus II in Q. The tone of the first two lines suggests that this Chorus was designed to occur early in the play at a point where Oberon, with limited knowledge, begins to perceive the drift of the story. If Greene, after the manner of some users of framework material, intended to start the framework off in the Induction and then follow this up with some early reminders to the audience of Bohan's and Oberon's presence, then these lines may have been designed to follow I. i. The dumb show would also be appropriate at this point, showing another ruler (Semiramis) overreaching herself as the King of Scots is about to do at this point in the play.

1. *fond*] foolish.
jig] play; see note to Chor. II. 17.
2. *paint*] depict.
3. *which*] that which.
3.1. battles] armies, bodies of fighting men.
4. *gars*] causes (Scot.).
mirk] atrociously wicked; cf. the use at Chor. V. 1, 5.
5. *everywean*] everyone (Scot.).

Ober. This shows thee, Bohan, what is worldly pomp:
Semiramis, the proud Assyrian queen,
When Ninus died, did levy in her wars
Three millions of footmen to the fight,
Five hundred thousand horse, of armèd chars 10
A hundred thousand more; yet in her pride
Was hurt and conquered by Stabrobates.
Then what is pomp?
Boh. I see thou hast thine eyen,
Thou bonny king, if princes fall from high;
My fall is past, until I fall to die. 15
Now mark my talk and prosecute my jig. [*Exeunt.*]

7. Semiramis] *Dyce; Simeranus Q.* 8. levy] *Dyce;* tene *Q;* tire *conj. Lavin;* tend *conj. this ed.* in] *Q;* into *conj. Manly.* 10. chars] *Q;* cars *Dyce.* 12. Stabrobates] *Dyce; S. Taurobates Q.* 13. hast] *conj. Grosart;* art *Q.* eyen] *conj. Grosart;* ene *Q.*

7–12.] Collins notes that the expedition of Semiramis against Stabrobates is recorded by Diodorus Siculus (II. xvi–xviii), which had been translated in 1569 by Thomas Stocker. 'But Stocker's version was in fact a translation from Claude de Seisset's *L'histoire des successeurs d'Alexandre le Grand,* itself a translation from a Latin version by Janus Lascaris of books 18–20 of Diodorus' *Bibliotheca Historica*... It does not contain the relevant material' (Lavin).

8. *Ninus*] King of Assyria and the legendary founder of Nineveh, he was the second husband of Semiramis.

levy] Q's 'tene' may have been due to a misreading of 'leuie'. Lavin suggests 'tire' (equip), which is possible, as are 'lead' and 'tend' (furnish, supply).

10. *chars*] chariots.

13. *hast thine eyen*] All editors allow Q's 'art thine ene' to stand but provide no gloss of the meaning. I take the meaning to be 'can see clearly [the results of overproud actions by rulers]'. Cf. Q's similar spelling 'ene' at l. 3 above.

15. *fall to*] begin to.
16. *prosecute*] continue to attend to.
jig] See note to Chor. II. 17.

[Chorus VII]

[*Enter* BOHAN *and* OBERON.]

Ober. How should these crafts withdraw thee from the world?
But look, my Bohan, pomp allureth.

Enter CYRUS, Kings *humbling themselves; himself crowned by olive, that at last dying* [is] *laid in a marble tomb with this inscription:*

Whoso thou be that passest, for I know one shall pass,
know I am Cyrus of Persia, and I prithee envy me not
this little clod of clay wherewith my body is covered.
                                                        All exeunt.

Chorus VII] This follows Chor. VI in Q and is headed '2.'.   2. pomp allureth] Q; pomp again allureth Grosart; pomp allureth thee Manly. 2.1. Cyrus, Kings] Dyce; Cirus king, Q.   2.1–2. olive, that] This ed.; Oliue Pat Q corr. (BM, VA, HN); Oliue Pat, Q uncorr. (FO); Olive and Palm Grosart; Aspatia Manly; olive, but Lavin.   2.3–5.] so Lavin; irregular verse in Q divided at passest, / For . . . I / I . . . Persia, / And . . . clay / Wherewith.   2.4. I am] Dyce; I / I am Q.   2.4–5. envy . . . little] Lavin; leaue me not thus like a Q.   2.5. body] Q corr. (BM, VA, HN); bydy Q uncorr. (FO).

Chorus VII] In Q these lines follow Chorus VI with the figure '2.' at their head. The expression of surprise by Oberon in ll. 1–2 would indicate that this Chorus was to follow a scene quite early in the play, as they refer back to Bohan's description of his retirement from the world described in the Induction. If I am right in my suggestion that Greene intended to follow up the Induction with one or two extra choruses within the acts in the early part of the play (see note to Chor. VI), then these lines may well have been designed to follow I. ii, which shows Ateukin's 'crafts' exercising themselves in no desperately serious fashion, which would account for Oberon's puzzlement in the first line. The dumb show is also appropriate at this point, illustrating that for Ateukin, as well as for Cyrus, 'pomp allureth'.

1. *crafts*] frauds.

2.1–8. Enter Cyrus . . . meum] Plutarch tells the story of Alexander's seeing the tomb of Cyrus: 'When he had red the inscription . . . he would needes also have it written in the Greeke tongue: and this it was: "O man, what so thou art, and whencesoever thou commest, for I knowe thou shalt come: I am Cyrus that conquered the Empire of Persia, I pray thee envy me not for this little earth that covereth my body." These words pearced Alexanders hart, when he considered the uncertainty of worldly things' (Thomas North's trans., *Plutarch's Lives* (Tudor Translations (1895), IV, 377).

Enter the King *in great pomp who reads it, and issueth,* [*and*] *crieth,* '*Ver meum*'.

Boh. What meaneth this?
Ober.   Cyrus of Persia,
 Mighty in life, within a marble grave
 Was laid to rot; whom Alexander once   5
 Beheld entombed, and weeping, did confess
 Nothing in life could 'scape from wretchedness:
 Why then boast men?
Boh.   What reck I then of life,
 Who makes the grave my home, the earth my wife.
 But mark me more.   [*Exeunt.*] 10

2.8. *Ver meum*] Dyce; *vermeum Q; vermium* conj. Dyce.   6. entombed] in tombde *Q corr. (BM, VA, NH)*; in tombe *Q uncorr. (FO).*   confess] *Q corr. (BM, VA, HN)*; confesse, *Q uncorr. (FO).*   9. makes] *Q corr. (BM, VA, HN)*; make *Q uncorr. (FO).*   home] Dyce; tomb *Q corr. (BM, VA, HN)*; tumbe *Q uncorr. (FO).*   10.] so *Q*; Dyce assigns to Ober.

2.1–2. olive, that] Q's 'Oliue Pat' is susceptible of a palaeographical explanation; 'that' refers back to Cyrus.

2.4. envy] See quotation in note to 2.1–8.

2.5. this little] See quotation in note to 2.1–8.

2.7. issueth] goes out, exits.

2.8. Ver meum] Lat. 'my spring' or 'my youth'; presumably the opening words of some phrase lamenting the passing of youth and the transience of life. Dyce suggests 'vermium', beginning a phrase on the futility of human grandeur, and the genitive as exclamation was used in Latin, for example, by Plautus. It is possible that the MS. may have had something like '& issueth, esca vermium' (and utters 'food for worms'), which the compositor set up as Q's '*& issueth, crieth vermeum*'.

[Chorus VIII]

[*Enter* BOHAN *and* OBERON.]

Boh. I can no more; my patience will not warp
  To see these flatterers how they scorn and carp.
Ober. Turn but thy head.

Enter four Kings *carrying crowns,* Ladies *presenting odours to* [a]
Potentate *enthroned, who suddenly is slain by his* Servants *and thrust
  out; and so they* [*sit and*] *eat.* [*Then*] *exeunt.*

Boh. Sike is the werld; but whilk is he I saw?
Ober. Sesostris, who was conqueror of the world,   5
  Slain at the last, and stamped on by his slaves.
Boh. How blest are peur men, then, that know their graves!
  Now mark the sequel of my jig.   [*Exeunt.*]

Chorus VIII] *This follows Chor. VII in Q and is headed* '3.'.   2. flatterers]
Dyce; flatteries Q.   3.1. *four*] Dyce; *our* Q.   *carrying*] Dyce; *carring*
Q.   3.1–2. *a* Potentate] Dyce; *Potentates* Q.   3.3. *sit and*] *This ed.;
not in* Q.   4.] *so* Dyce; *assigned to* Ober. *in* Q.   Sike] Q *corr. (BM,
VA, HN);* Sicke Q *uncorr. (FO)*.   7. graves] Dyce; graue Q.

Chorus VIII] In Q these lines follow Chorus VII and are headed by the
numeral '3.'. Again, the opening lines appear to refer to a specific scene in
the play. The most obvious choice is III. ii where Jaques, Ateukin, and
Andrew 'scorn and carp'.

1. *can*] can endure.

warp] endure, submit (*O.E.D., v.* 19b, of which this the first citation).

3.1–3. Enter four . . . eat] I have been unable to find any source for this
episode. See note to l. 5.

4. *Sike*] such (Scot.). Some editors read 'Sick' which makes sense. However, 'Sicke' is the reading which occurs in the Folger copy of Q and it is
this copy which has the uncorrected state of the outer forme of Sheet D.
Cf. Introduction, p. lvii.

werld] world (Scot.).

whilk] who (Scot.).

5. *Sesostris*] the Greek name for the Egyptian king Rameses, legendary
conqueror of Ethiopia, Asia, and Thrace, whose empire was more extensive
than that of Alexander. His death was not as Greene has it here; he committed suicide after becoming blind.

7. *peur*] poor (Scot.).

8. *jig*] See note to Chor. II. 17.

APPENDIX
G. B. Giraldi Cinthio's *Hecatommithi*
Decade III, Novel I

This story is the first novel of the third decade of the *Hecatommithi*, and is here translated from the French version produced by Gabriel Chappuys, and published by A. L'Angier in Paris in 1583-4. It is told by Quinto, a character in the framework material. The translation and paragraphing are those of the present editor.

I realize that if I were to start today's discussion and pastime with the disloyalty of some woman to her husband, Fulvia, who has complained greatly that such a matter should be spoken of, might think that I wished to do it in order to make her more bitter in her wrath. For this reason, so that she may listen to me with more tranquillity, I will tell you the story of the disloyalty of a king to a very noble woman, his wife, who having fallen in love with another woman not only disdains his wife but tries to have her killed; and she with utmost loyalty, when he is in great need, delivers him from a troublesome siege, and makes him realize how loyally she loves him.

In the isle of Ireland there once reigned a king named Astatio, a brave man but truly and very much more subject to satisfying his desires than to being guided by reason. This same king took for his wife a lovely and gracious daughter of the King of Scotland of most virtuous bearing, with whom he lived peacefully for a few years. It happened that, as he had left Ireland to go to Scotland to his father-in-law, he was cast by a sudden tempest on to a near-by island called Mona, where he was amiably received by a widow, the lady of the Isle, who had a daughter of fifteen, not less beautiful than charming and virtuous, whose name was Ida. As soon as Astatio saw her, she entered his heart with such force that he completely forgot his wife, who almost in spite of the king her father, who wanted to marry her to the King of England, had desired Astatio for her husband. The latter, affected by this new passion, turned all his thoughts to Ida. And since the storm which lasted ten days gave him occasion to remain there, he began to wait for an opportunity to speak in private with Ida.

The mother, who had only the one daughter and who was wise and far-seeing, did not let her once out of her sight, as all women who have daughters should, for if these women who ought to take special care of them give them free rein, being simple, they are sometimes, when one thinks least, waited and watched for by a man who, finding occasion either to talk to them or to make lascivious advances to them, gives them afterwards matter either for scandal or some dishonour. This wise mother then watched all the more carefully over her daughter because, seeing the storm at an end and the water very calm, Astatio did not give any orders for his departure; which made her think that the long stay of this man stemmed from the fact that he had conceived a passion for her daughter.

Astatio, perceiving the diligence of the mother, well knew that the means of speaking to Ida alone were denied him; because of this he bethought himself of employing another plan. Two years before the sea had so flooded the island more than usual that with great loss and death it had destroyed the humblest homes and had come right into the midst of the most exalted ones, in such a way as to have consumed and devoured everything which was good both in the court and in the island, and the fields were for the most part barren. And because of this, Ida's mother, who was the lady of the place, was as much reduced to poverty as the other people of the island. Seeing then the young girl, of noble birth but poor, considering her state, he thought that abundance of money ought to be able to get him what he did not think he could have by other means.

He spoke one day to the mother and began to praise lavishly to her the beauty of her daughter, and, in praising her, he told her that he had seen just how far the encroachment of the sea had affected her and that it hurt him very much that her daughter would not have a dowry worthy of her, she who deserved not this little island rendered barren but a great kingdom where she could be the wife of a great king, such indeed as she was worthy of in view of her outstanding perfections of both mind and body.

The mother, who had in part known the desire of Astatio, understood the drift of his speech, and for that reason she replied to him that she had so much faith in the King of Heaven that she was sure that the injury received from Fortune would be so well amended and ameliorated by His goodness that when the time should come He would have her provided with all that she would need to be decently settled. He [Astatio] added, 'God does not help those who do not know how to seize time by the forelock, when good fortune presents itself—one of whom you will be now if you do not know how to act for your own profit and that of your daughter from what you have in your house. For if you will let me lie with your daughter, I will give her so much money that you can be assured that she will not remain unmarried for lack of a dowry.' At these words the lady turned pale and said to him, 'I marvel at you, Astatio, who judge that I would put my daughter's honour up for sale, and who think that the great sum of money earned dishonestly might better serve her in the making of a marriage than the prize of virtue which is more useful to a nobly born woman than all this world's goods. Be sure that I would kill her with my own hands before I would let her belong to any other than the one it will please God to give her to in marriage.'

At these words Astatio lost hope of being able to enjoy Ida if he could not find a way of marrying her. Because of this he took it into his head to have Arenopia put to death, which was the name of his most noble wife. So, having left Mona, he made his way to Scotland where he had intended to go before Fortune had assailed him, bearing still a very deep wound in his heart for the love of Ida. Now, having spent a few days in Scotland with his father-in-law, he went back to his kingdom, where his wife, burning with most chaste desire, came to meet him with a very joyful countenance, being glad that he had returned in good health; and how lovely she was and how the manifest joy of her heart and the loyal love she bore her husband shone in her face! However, Astatio saw her only as if she had been ugly and disloyal, so much had his little-controlled appetite stifled reason in his lascivious and inconstant mind. He, however, assuming as best he could a joyful countenance, tried to conceal his wicked will and plan, and yet behaved with his wife with no less uneasiness than if he had lived with a mortal enemy.

A few days later he summoned one of his captains, who was cruel and wicked, and told him he wanted him to kill Arenopia, but in such a way that her death would seem acceptable to the King of Scotland so that he would not take arms against him. The captain, who was one of those who, provided they do what is pleasing to their lords, do not consider whether it is just or unjust, honest or dishonest, promised to do all that he would command him. There and then Astatio said, 'I have decided to go hunting in three days' time and to stay out at least two days. When I have left you will look underneath the pillow of my bed and you will find there a letter of mine which will tell you what you have to do.' This done, Astatio then went off to his room and wrote in this way what he wanted the evening of the day he would depart: when Arenopia had gone off to bed and when the captain thought she was asleep, he should secretly enter the bedroom (of which he would give him the key) and should take with him one of his friends and should kill his wife and the chambermaid for fear of her revealing the fact, and afterwards that he should kill the friend who had gone with him; he should strip him and put him naked by the side of the dead queen; and he should circulate the rumour of having found her in adultery with this man, by reason of which, moved with zeal for the honour of his master, having found them together, he had also killed them together and similarly the chambermaid, who knowing all about it had brought the adulterer to Arenopia. Having written that on the day he wanted to leave, he left the statement under the pillow as he had said, so that the captain might execute what he had ordered.

But God, just defender of the innocent, willed it that, as soon as the king had left accompanied by the captain who was supposed to carry out the evil deed, a little boy in whom Astatio used to take pleasure entered the bedroom, as was his habit, and playing underneath the bed, as we often see children doing, he put his hand under the pillow and, having found the paper, he took it to Arenopia, who seeing the letter that her cruel husband had written regarding her death and dishonour remained so confused and grief-stricken that she thought she would fall down stone dead. And the poor queen, not knowing why her husband wanted to have her thus cruelly killed, turned over many things in her mind and did not know what to do to escape. For considering she had taken Astatio almost against the wishes of her father, she dared not go to him. She dared not either stay at the court, because she well saw that when the captain came back he would prepare to kill her that night according to Astatio's command or in any other way possible. She would have much liked to send the letter to her father, but she saw that that might cause her husband's death, the husband whom she loved more than she loved herself. She thought of tearing up the letter and burning it, but weighing up in her mind that Astatio would think she had it and had not let it come to the captain's hands, and that for this reason he would be all the more vexed and would not fail to make her die by another means, she restrained herself from doing this; besides which she was sure that Astatio had given this order by word of mouth to the captain in such a way that she could not fail to be still in danger.

Amid this diversity of thoughts the poor queen finally made up her mind to put the letter back in the place from which the child had taken it, so that the captain finding it would have no suspicion, and to go out secretly from the court and get herself taken to Scotland to her father, letting it be understood that she had gone there for another purpose. So Arenopia put back the letter and, having been taught in her father's house to manage and use arms in such a way as to be able to hold her own against any knight, she pretended to want to go with a page to a place near the town where she often used to go in order to test her skill at arms, and gave instructions that she should be expected back at the court in the evening.

When she had gone out, the captain came, for it was already late, and having entered Astatio's bedroom, he found the letter under the pillow and also the key to the secret passage; and being disposed to obey the king implicitly, he was notified, to his great pleasure, that Arenopia had gone to exercise herself in arms, thinking that on returning she would be so weary that when she was in bed she would be taken with such a deep sleep that he would accomplish his plan easily.

As soon as Arenopia arrived at the said place she armed herself with all her weapons, and having mounted her horse with her lance on her thigh, with her page she made towards the sea in order to go to Scotland. As it was already one o'clock at night, the captain, not seeing the queen, suspected that she had found out about the plan and that she had left the court to go to Scotland. And so he armed himself promptly and set off to where Arenopia had said she was going, and not finding her, he began to follow her.

In the morning, at the dawn of day, he caught sight of her and, having put his lance in rest, he spurred on his horse against her. The queen, hearing the horse's steps, turned round immediately and, seeing him alone, trusting in her innocence, she hurried to meet him, and the encounter was such that both of them bent right down as far as their horses' cruppers. Then, the lances being already broken, they went at each other with thrusting swords in their hands; but while she was guiding her hands, the queen's helmet opened and she was wounded on the head by a great blow. And being weak because of the abundance of blood which she was losing, she could no longer resist the captain's strength. But God gave her a timely remedy, for a knight came by unexpectedly, who had left Reba to go to Saint Patriel and who, seeing the queen in a bad way, delivered her from the hands of the captain. Nevertheless, he thought she was a knight and not a woman, because having been very ill a few days before it had been necessary to cut off all her hair, so that she looked like a young man of fifteen or eighteen years.

So the knight, having saved her and seeing her thus wounded, overcome with great compassion, went back to Reba and took her to his house and, having had the doctors summoned, he had her wound carefully dressed. But the queen would never have any but her page to serve her, who, instructed by her concerning all that he had to say, never said anything else but that the queen was a Scottish knight called Arenopio, who had come to Astatio's court and, having had a quarrel with this captain, had taken leave of the king; and that when he wished to withdraw to the sea in order to be taken to Scotland, the captain, who had many times refused to fight, had hidden in a wood and had attacked him with both superior arms and horse and had reduced him to the state in which he had been found; which tale was so vivid that everyone believed it to be true.

The captain returned to the court, and being ashamed to tell his lord that the queen had escaped from his hands, and being certain that she would die from the great blow which he had dealt her, he told him that he had caught up with her on the road fleeing and that he had killed her and left her a prey for birds and wild beasts. Astatio was very joyful at this news and thought that the death of Arenopia had thus come about well and opportunely for him so that he could have her reputed disloyal by everyone and even by her father; since being thus armed she had fled in the night. Thinking then that Arenopia was dead, he sent a rumour throughout the kingdom that his wife had been an adulteress and that she had fled on being discovered with the adulterer, fearing death, and that, caught fleeing by his captain, she had been killed by him as she deserved. He thought by this story that he would so placate the queen's father that it would seem to him a just vengeance had been taken on his daughter.

Now Astatio, thinking he was rid of the obstacle which was the cause of his not being able to enjoy Ida, went off to Mona to take her for his wife; but the mother, who had seen what danger her daughter had been in when Astatio was in the house, fearing some strange accident, had married her to a very noble young man of the island, preferring to give her to a private man with honour than to deliver her into the hands of a king with great dishonour. Astatio's vexation at finding Ida married could not be described. He felt himself driven mad by the whole affair and went back home filled with melancholy, and would often say to himself, 'Ah! how unworthily I caused my wife to die in order to have Ida, and now I am without both of them. Arenopia did not deserve such an end but eternal honour.' And having always this remorse and this worm which was gnawing him, he hated himself and used to think that Arenopia was always before him reproaching him with the outrageous death he believed her to have suffered.

However, the King of Scotland, who had known his daughter to be entirely attentive to honour and chastity according to the manner in which he had reared her, could not in any way persuade himself that she had changed so much that by a lascivious desire she had abandoned herself to another, especially having wanted, because of her love, to have Astatio for her husband rather than any other great king in the world. He did not fail to search out by every possible means the truth of this matter. And in so doing, having sent informed people to Astatio's court, he found that the common opinion was that the queen had been most chaste and that the accusation which Astatio was making against her was false, and that it was thought that he had done all that in order to be able to take Ida. The king, believing that, mustered a powerful army, and having put to sea with his fleet, he went to fight Astatio.

However, Arenopia was beginning to get well again, but not sufficiently to have the strength to leave the house, and because she was very gracious and pleasing, the wife of the knight liked her very much indeed, not lasciviously but because of the noble principles and rare qualities of the lady, who she thought was a knight and whom she loved as a brother. She was very painstaking and diligent in doing all she saw that would profit the queen. From this care there grew what is sometimes seen to happen through the faithlessness of other people without women being able to help it, when simply and with a pure heart they show themselves gracious towards some charming man. For the knight became so jealous that, thinking Arenopia was a man, he repented of having brought her into his house. Arenopia, having perceived this, took a good and honourable opportunity to go away and thanked him humbly for the pleasure he had given her and offered always to be most prompt in pleasing him; then, having rented a house in Reba, she left the place. In spite of this, the knight was still affected by jealousy and, no matter what his wife did to free him from it, she made no progress, so much had he this false opinion grafted on his mind, and he was several times on the point of killing his wife and accusing Arenopia of perfidy, and for this reason challenging her to combat.

Now, as the war continued between the Kings of Ireland and Scotland, Arenopia, who knew it was all working to her advantage, withdrew incognito to the camp of Astatio, awaiting the means of recovering her husband's grace and of making peace with him and reconciling him to her father. The jealous knight came also to the camp to do service to his king. In doing so, he proved himself valiant, still however bearing in his heart his ill-conceived jealousy. However, the wicked captain, who had armed himself to kill the queen, had been killed in a battle with a lance blow by a brother of Arenopia's, which distressed her because she wanted to have him captured and made to tell the circumstances of her flight.

Being thus in the camp dressed in black in the uniform of a knight, she made up her mind to send her page to the court to ascertain what Astatio's attitude was towards her, and to know from that how she was to bear herself. The page went there, and bowed to the king as soon as he saw him and, as the king had asked him what brought him to the court, he answered him wisely that the happy memory of the queen whom he was accustomed to serving had brought him there. At these words tears almost came to Astatio's eyes, as he was touched by a continual remorse, hearing of her whom he believed he had killed so wrongly; and he could not prevent himself saying, 'Ah! Arenopia, how gladly would I wish you to be able to come back to life even were it to cost me half my kingdom.'

The page, taking good hope from these words, withdrew blithely from the court and told it all to the queen, who, having heard her husband's desire, made up her mind to make herself known. And desiring to reward there and then the happiness received from the knight who had delivered her from the hands of the murderer, and to remove the jealousy which was causing him to live discontented, had him begged to do her the favour of coming to her in order to speak of a very important matter which would be to his gain. The knight came to her, and Arenopia took him graciously by the hand and said to him, 'Knight, I want you to know how most wrongly men often become jealous of their wives.' And in that place she made herself known as a woman, at which the knight was dumbfounded. But after they had discoursed together about past events, and had laughed a great deal about the knight's jealousy, Arenopia said to him, 'Knight, your courteousness to me demands that I reward you for it in the best way I possibly can, so that I can make you know that you have not entertained someone ungrateful, as you thought in your unfounded jealousy. And so, having known secretly that the King of Ireland was most desirous that his wife should be presented to him living and that he would give much to whoever should present her to him, I want, if it please you, that you should be the one to win this large reward; and so that it may be advantageous to you, as I have just lately revealed myself to you as a woman, I also want you to know me for our king's wife—I am Arenopia. Go to Astatio, get the reward for it, and present me, for I am certain he will reward you for such a piece of news.'

The knight, hearing this, struck suddenly with wonderment and reverence, fell on his knees before her and honoured her as queen; and begged her pardon for the bad opinion he had formed of her, and because he had not honoured her in his house as her majesty deserved. Afterwards he offered to do immediately all that she wished. The queen raised him from the ground, and they arranged between them what was to be done.

The next day the knight and the queen, having armed themselves (the queen, however, incognito), went to the town where Astatio was holding his court. And the knight, having left the queen in a house near to the court, had the king told that he was desirous of speaking to him about a very important matter. The king had him brought immediately, and the knight, giving him to understand that he wished to speak of the business of the war—now telling him one thing, now another—prompted Astatio to say that all this evil had come from the death of Arenopia, his wife, and that if she were alive, the wars would cease and he would rest content, which could no longer be even though he should be victorious in this war and ruler of all Scotland, since he would never be happy, having lost his wife. Whereupon the knight said, 'Sire, I want to deliver you from this vexation by bringing you at one and the same time the end of the war and your wife alive.'

At these words the king thought that this knight was out of his mind and said to him, 'Are you God to cause the dead to be resuscitated?' 'Sire,' replied the knight, 'I cannot resuscitate the dead, but I can easily save you from the mistake you are making in thinking that one who lives is dead. And so that you may see that what I have told you is true, I will arrange that the knight who entitles himself "The Unknown One" in your camp will give you such a token of it that you will be able to know that your wife lives.' At these words Astatio remained completely astonished and said to the knight, 'I would make you great if that were true,' and ordered him to have the unknown knight brought.

The knight told all this to Arenopia, who, burning with desire to see her husband at one with her again, thus armed and unknown went to Astatio. Seeing her, he said to her, 'Knight, what do you know about my wife?' And she replied, 'Sire, I know so much about her that, before I leave here, I want to have you see her.' This being said, having lifted her visor and composed her face to command compassion, she said, 'Here, Astatio, is your unlucky Arenopia; here is she whom, because of a mad passion, you wished to have killed by a wicked captain who cruelly gave her a death blow. Behold her before you cured and living and completely yours. See, Astatio, that the great injury, the death which was prepared for her, the wounds undeservedly received, and other kinds of plots, could not separate her from you and turn her from loving you alone and coming to your aid in a dangerous war. Consider, I beg you, husband, whether the love and fidelity of your wife merited that she should be cruelly killed by your command as an adulteress, or whether she was worthy of love and reciprocal loyalty.'

And at this point, weeping tenderly, she ran to embrace him and said, 'Astatio, how much I vexed my father, as you know, who wanted to give me to the King of England and not to you: the love which I bore you caused me to become yours, and the love of you which I have engraved on my heart will hold me bound to you for ever, until the last day of my life; and in this manner I beg you to love me as my faith and friendship deserve.' Astatio, seized with a sudden joy, threw his arms round her neck and said to her, 'Arenopia, I well know I have grievously offended you; were it not for your goodness, I well know that I would not deserve you ever to come to me as you have done, but that I would be worthy of your extreme hatred, which might wish me dead. But since the wrong I did you could not stop you from loving me, I thank God for your goodwill. On the contrary, wife, repenting the wrong I did you, I will always be a loyal and loving husband to you. And where a vain desire caused me to become demented, henceforth love and faith will make me follow your example so well that you will never have occasion to repent having come back to your husband.'

Having in this way recommenced kissing each other affectionately, they confirmed the love that had united them in the first place. And after they had remained joyfully together for a few days and she had recited to her husband all the story of her misfortunes and the courtesy used by the friendly knight towards her, and how he had thought she was a man, because of which he had become jealous of his wife, Astatio greatly praised the knight and gave him most costly gifts, counting him always among his most favoured, and several times did he and Arenopia laugh over his jealousy.

Thereafter Astatio wanted Arenopia to go off as ambassador to her father, who, as soon as he saw her, was seized with such great joy that he could not speak to her. But when he recovered his wits, embracing her lovingly, he said to her, 'Daughter, how is it that you live? What happy fortune makes me see you before me, having long wept over you as dead?' The father and the daughter wept with joy, and she related to her father all that had happened to her, how she was at one with her husband, and because of this she was asking him to end the war, since all had been resolved so fortunately and happily. The king was content to satisfy his daughter's desire and, having overcome the hate he bore his son-in-law, he entered the town with his daughter, where he was received by Astatio as a father. And the King of Scotland warmly thanked the knight who had defended and cured her, and also gave him great gifts.

Henceforth Astatio and Arenopia were in such accord that they lived the rest of their lives in entire peace. And the knight went back very joyfully to his house, and always considered his wife most chaste and most loving, as in truth she was, and as all who are married should be.

Index to Annotations

An asterisk indicates that the annotation referred to contains information to sense or usage not provided by the *Oxford English Dictionary*; where more than one reference is given for a word, the asterisk refers to the first reference, unless otherwise noted. When a gloss is repeated in the annotations, only the first occurrence is indexed.

Abject, II. ii. 49
abuse (*sb.*), I. i. 243
accept the time, I. i. 235
accompany, I. i. 147
accord (*vb*), V. iv. 69
accord, wily, IV. iii. 25
acquit of . . . doubt, V. i. 38
adamant . . . filed . . . by itself, II. ii. 153–4
advice, bad, IV. v. 96
advised, be, I. iii. 46
affects, I. i. 157
affection, II. i. 65
after-life, V. vi. 186
against, IV. iii. 107
age, time brought me to, Ind. 43
a-huff, cap, IV. iv. 13
aldertruest, V. vi. 192
ale and toast, II. i. 175–6
alone, Chor. II. 2
aloof, I. i. 0.4
a-low, II. i. 9
al's ene (Scot.), Ind. 4
altered, case is, V. vi. 51
amain, V. ii. 20
amend, young . . . and may, II. ii. 87–8
amorous cut, IV. iii. 43
an (*if*), Ind. 11
ancient name, I. ii. 102
and if, V. iv. 107
Andrew, Saint, I. iii. 7
angel, III. i. 55

annotations upon Machiavel, III. ii. 53
antic, Ind. 0.1
apart, cast, I. i. 230
Apollo, I. i. 137
appear in entrance of, I. i. 237
appoint, V. v. 37
approved truth, III. iii. 35
Aristotle, II. i. 179–80; IV. v. 41–2
art, man of, I. i. 187
arts, V. iv. 66
as (*so that*), IV. iii. 68
aspects, dire, I. i. 189
ass, I. ii. 90
assure . . . stay, II. i. 111
attaint, V. vi. 171
attempt (*vb*), I. i. 71
attend, I. i. 68
awarrant, Ind. 99
awl thrust through your ear, IV. iii. 75
axioms, I. i. 208
ay (Scot.), Ind. 1
ay's (Scot.), Ind. 5

Back parts, III. ii. 48–9
bagpiper, IV. iii. 110–12
ball, Fortune's, II. i. 11
bands, fancy's, I. i. 210
battlements of a custard, IV. iii. 39
battles, V. vi. 92
bear a little, I. ii. 54
beck, II. i. 27
be for, I. ii. 75–6

143

before, I. ii. 15
befret, IV. ii. 20
beguile, V. iv. 35
behold, I. i. 205-7
belly, III. ii. 128-9
bequest, II. ii. 36
beseem, IV. ii. 51
beset, fair, IV. ii. 27
beshrow, IV. iv. 36
best, gains the, V. iv. 33
be the mass, Ind. 19
betray the effect, Ind. 66
betrust, IV. iii. 86
bewray, Ind. 65
bills, I. ii. 0.1
blab (*sb.*), V. iv. 91
black-jack, II. i. 166-7
blemish (*sb.*), I. iii. 41
blend, IV. v. 44
blind my shame, III. iii. 11
blot (*vb*), II. i. 25
bloud (Scot.), Ind. 42
bode ... weal, V. vi. 26
body, become a loose, II. i. 188-9
Bohan, Ind. 45
bones, by my ten, III. ii. 115
bonny (Scot.), I. iii. 14
book, I. iii. 74
booted, I. iii. 0.1
brave, IV. iii. 37
bravely, V. vi. 63.1, 3
bread ay Gad (Scot.), Ind. 35
*break the neck of, Ind. 82
breast, V. iii. 23
bridle, chewing on the, I. ii. 100
briefs, III. iii. 60
bring ... forth, III. iii. 135
brisk, III. i. 16
brook of, I. i. 253
brother, I. i. 12
brutish, V. iii. 19
bum (*vb*), III. ii. 12
bushel, peck of grist in a, II. i. 91-2
busy with the mouth, I. ii. 99
but (*merely*), V. vi. 182
but (*nothing but*), III. ii. 59
by me, V. iii. 43

Calves' leather, IV. iii. 60

cambric, II. i. 26
cap a-huff, IV. iv. 13
cap and knee, I. i. 222
caper in a halter, IV. iii. 113
capon, I. ii. 22
care (*sb.*), II. ii. 49
care, husband's, V. i. 89
careless, III. iii. 22
carry, II. i. 35.1
case, II. i. 102
case is altered, V. vi. 51
case, weighty, V. i. 25
cast ... apart, I. i. 230
cat, lick a dish before a, I. ii. 15
catch, II. i. 12
catch thy grave, V. vi. 75
cat's abroad ... mice be still, V. i. 31
caudle, III. i. 37
cell, Chor. II. 16
change turns, I. ii. 6
chaos, first, II. i. 181
charge (*sb.*), Ind. 58
charge, take, V. i. 41
charm (*vb*), II. ii. 107
chars, Chor. VI. 10
chary, V. i. 87
chawing, III. i. 13
cheer (*sb.*), II. ii. 108
cheer, small, Ind. 61-2
cheer, take, V. i. 33
chewing on the bridle, I. ii. 100
chiefest parts, II. i. 65
choleric of complexion, III. ii. 66
Cicely of the Whighton, IV. iii. 95
circumstance, I. i. 63
clacks, Ind. 85
clauses, V. iv. 26
clerks ... not the wisest, greatest, III. ii. 63-4
cloak (*vb*), V. iv. 73
clocks on Shrove Tuesday, tongue ... like, IV. iii. 94-5
clout, I. i. 104
Clytia, V. i. 76
cog (*vb*), Ind. 53
cogs, II. i. 102
combust, I. i. 205-7
come to it, I. ii. 3
common, than, Ind. 101

INDEX TO ANNOTATIONS 145

common-pleas, V. iv. 37
commonweal, III. ii. 19
*compact (*composition*), II. i. 48
compact (*contract*), I. i. 16
compare, exceed, V. ii. 19
compass (*vb*), I. i. 233
compeers, V. vi. 200
complexion, choleric of, III. ii. 66
compromise (*sb.*), V. iii. 6
conceit (*fancies*), IV. v. 29
conceit (*idea*), V. i. 21
conceive, III. ii. 95
condescend, V. vi. 107
confirm, III. iii. 33
consequence, V. vi. 108
conserve, II. ii. 43
constable's staff, IV. iii. 89–90
constellation, I. i. 188
construe, I. i. 47
contain, III. iii. 69
contempt, IV. v. 10
control, V. i. 18
count, I. i. 112
countenance, I. i. 260
counterbuff, II. i. 187
country (*adj.*), II. i. 33
Coventry-blue, IV. iii. 40
coy, I. i. 49
cozening trade, I. ii. 20–1
crack (*vb*), IV. v. 93
craft, Ind. 57
crave, III. iii. 51
crocus, I. i. 263–4
crook, by hook or, IV. v. 82
cross (*sb.*), V. i. 59
cross (*vb*), III. iii. 29
cross-point, IV. iii. 107
crow, hopper, V. ii. 10–11
crowns, IV. iii. 88
curious, I. i. 115
curry (*vb*), Ind. 21
curtsies, Ind. 104.1
custard, battlements of a, IV. iii. 39
cut, amorous, IV. iii. 43
Cyrus, Chor. VII. 2.1–8

Dab (Scot.), Ind. 89
dagger, rapier and, IV. iii. 80
dainty, II. i. 189

dally, III. ii. 73
Damon, IV. iv. 23–4
dance in a hood, a fool may, III. ii. 64
dance within a net, IV. v. 80
daw (*vb*), V. i. 68
Daymonds (Scot.), Ind. 19
daze (*vb*), I. iii. 39
dead (*sure*), III. i. 45
dead, thou art but, III. ii. 59–60
deadly, V. vi. 101
debate, III. iii. 130
deceive, V. i. 58
deel (Scot.), Ind. 9
deem (*judge*), IV. ii. 50
deem (*ponder*), II. ii. 22
default (*vb*), II. ii. 68, IV. v. 39
denounce, II. i. 186
depaint out, V. iv. 82
depart, furnish..., III. iii. 122
depend upon, I. i. 69
despite (*contempt*), Chor. II. 3
despite, revenge, V. v. 39
despites (*injuries*), Chor. V. 8
detract, I. i. 193
devised for the nonce, Ind. 94.1
dictamnum, IV. ii. 54
digest, II. i. 193
dire aspects, I. i. 189
disbuse, III. i. 2
discontented, V. i. 99
discover, IV. iii. 28
discovery, V. iv. 79
dish before a cat, lick a, I. ii. 15
displace, II. ii. 186
disport (*sb.*), IV. iv. 29
disposition, at my, I. ii. 122
dissolve, I. i. 240
divide, V. vi. 77
divine (*vb*), V. v. 19
*docket, stiff, I. ii. 88
door at a whistle, keep the, I. ii. 78–9
doubles, IV. iii. 106
doubt, acquit of, V. i. 38
doubts, Chor. I. 10
draw, II. i. 20
draw out red into white, III. i. 12–13
draw... over to, I. iii. 4
draw... tables, I. ii. 94
dressed, IV. iii. 66–7

drift (*course*), I. i. 161
drift (*purport*), I. i. 182
drift (*scheme*), II. i. 203
dwarf, etymology of..., I. ii. 118

Eagle, II. ii. 117–18
ear, awl thrust through the, IV. iii. 75
earnest (*sb.*), III. i. 45
earnest penny, III. ii. 121
Edinburgh, I. ii. 133
eel, as skittish as an, IV. iii. 96
effect, betray the, Ind. 66
effect my love, I. i. 262
employ, I. i. 93
ene (Scot.), Ind. 89
ene, al's (Scot.), Ind. 4
enforce, V. v. 14
ensample, IV. iii. 11
entertain (*sb.*), II. i. 199
entertain out of his service, I. ii. 57–8
entrance of, appear in, I. i. 237
erect your state, II. i. 144
ergo, III. i. 8
ermine skin, so full of spots, V. iv. 4
err, man... born to, II. i. 139
essence, II. ii. 165
estate, II. ii. 79
estates, high, III. iii. 75
estimate (*sb.*), II. ii. 83
estrange, I. i. 173
etc., I. iii. 75
etymology of... dwarf, I. ii. 118
even the mark, I. i. 46
everywean (Scot.), Chor. VI. 5
*exceed, I. i. 14
exceed compare, V. ii. 19
except (*vb*), V. iv. 26
expect for, V. ii. 38
eyen, have thine, Chor. VI. 13

Face (*vb*), I. ii. 60
fain, Ind. 19
fair (*adj.*), IV. iii. 81
fair (*sb.*), II. i. 46
fair beset, IV. ii. 27
fall to, Chor. VI. 15
fancy (*sb.*), I. i. 215
fancy (*vb*), V. v. 52
fancy's bands, I. i. 210

farm, in, IV. ii. 9
fashion is stale, that, IV. iii. 44
fast, hold, II. i. 189
fat, II. ii. 63
father, I. i. 12
father's toil, gentlemen... lose...,
    V. iv. 101–2
faults without amending, see...
    others', V. iv. 53–4
favour (*sb.*), I. i. 67
feathers, gather, V. ii. 10–11
feign, V. v. 29
fellow, I. ii. 128
fellow, situation, II. i. 84–5
fiddlers, IV. iii. 111
field, V. iii. 25
fig for, III. ii. 24
filching trade, I. ii. 20
firmly, V. vi. 158
first, make at, V. vi. 13
first chaos, II. i. 181
fishing to the sea, no, I. ii. 40
fit (*adj.*), II. ii. 15
fit (*vb*), III. ii. 16
fit the humours, I. ii. 43
flap before, IV. iii. 43
flies, swallow, V. iv. 85
follow well, I. i. 215
fond, Chor. VI. 1
fondly, V. vi. 75
fool may dance in a hood, III. ii. 64
for (*as*), V. vi. 81
for (*as for*), I. i. 260
for that, I. i. 251
for thy life, Ind. 85
forage, V. iv. 48
forehead, broad, I. ii. 96
foreign, V. vi. 141
Fortune's ball, II. i. 11
forward, III. iii. 72
forward time, IV. v. 15
for who, III. i. 30
forwhy, V. i. 73
foster up, V. vi. 124
fox, I. ii. 89–90
frame (*vb*), II. i. 161
(*French translated*), III. ii. 30, 31–2,
    37, 38, 44, 45, 118; IV. iii. 3; iv.
    56; V. ii. 7, 22

INDEX TO ANNOTATIONS 147

*friend it, V. vi. 218
frolic (*adj.*), IV. ii. 29
frolic (*vb*), II. ii. 210
frolic it, V. vi. 234
from, I. i. 40
frump, II. ii. 76
full, skin, III. i. 53
furnish depart, III. iii. 122
fute, Gad's (Scot.), Ind. 28

Gad (Scot.), I. iii. 75
Gad, bread ay (Scot.), Ind. 35
Gad's fute (Scot.), Ind. 28
gain (*sb.*), V. ii. 40
gain the best, V. iv. 33
gainsay, V. iii. 22
gallery, Ind. 110
gang (Scot.), Ind. 4
gar (Scot.), Ind. 5
gather feathers, V. ii. 10–11
gay, V. iv. 36
*gay-built, Chor. V. 10
generation, IV. v. 47
gentle trade, I. ii. 33
gentlemen . . . lose . . . fathers' toil, V. iv. 101–2
gentles, V. iv. 104
ghosts, V. vi. 33
gif (Scot.), Ind. 73
give . . . place, I. iii. 65
glee (*sb.*), Chor. II. 15
glee (*vb*), Chor. IV. 5
gloss, partial, V. iv. 78
Gnatho, II. ii. 77
go, like a man you, V. v. 23
*goby, single, II. i. 172–3
good time, in, Ind. 68
goods, IV. ii. 39
Gos sayds (Scot.), Ind. 27
gossips, Ind. 65
grace, V. iii. 12
gratulate, Ind. 77
grave, catch thy, V. vi. 75
grave, live in, II. i. 143
greatest clerks are not the wisest, III. ii. 63–4
Greek to me, IV. ii. 14
greet (*sb.*), Chor. IV. 5
greet (*vb*), I. i. 66

grief, V. i. 5
grist in a bushel, peck of, II. i. 91–2
groats, IV. iii. 36
ground, V. iv. 22
ground, one turn above, IV. iii. 10
grounded, V. iv. 9
gudgeon, swallow a, II. i. 85
guid (Scot.), Ind. 3
guide (*sb.*), V. vi. 126
guidly (Scot.), Chor. V. 7
guise (*habit*), V. iv. 34
guise (*manner*), V. iv. 46

Hail, Chor. V. 7
halter, caper in a, IV. iii. 113
hamper (*vb*), IV. iii. 97
hand, III. iii. 24
hand, out of, II. ii. 5
hang . . . ill, I. iii. 61
happy, V. iii. 2
harbour, Chor. I. 14
hard of ward, I. ii. 97
hare, I. ii. 90
harp shilling, III. ii. 96
hart, IV. ii. 51
haud (Scot.), Ind. 85
haughty, V. vi. 122
head, raise her, IV. v. 54
health, in, I. i. 56
heavens are just, V. ii. 17–18
heaviness, IV. iv. 6
height, to his, I. ii. 4
high estates, III. iii. 75
highest, stand, I. ii. 1
hind, V. vi. 121
ho, Ind. 84
hold fast, II. i. 189
Homer, V. iv. 30
hood, fool may dance in a, III. ii. 64
hopper crow, V. ii. 10–11
horn (*vb*), IV. iii. 97
*hummer, Ind. 94
humours, Chor. II. 3
humours, fit the, I. ii. 43
hunt with the hound, run with the hare, IV. v. 85
husband's care, V. i. 89

Ill, hang, I. iii. 61

import, II. ii. 113
in her pride, I. i. 37
in one, V. vi. 218
incense (vb), IV. v. 33
include, II. ii. 168
inconvenient, I. i. 201
increase (sb.), V. vi. 173
indirection, by, I. ii. 49
infect, I. i. 127
install, I. i. 31.1
intend, II. ii. 111
intent, III. iii. 37
intent, for that, V. ii. 3
intentive, II. ii. 48
invade, III. iii. 112
invert, V. iv. 24
*invite, I. i. 2
Irish wars, III. iii. 121
issue, Chor. VII. 2.7
(*Italian translated*), III. ii. 29, 36, 44; IV. ii. 21, 22; iii. 3, 21; iv. 43

Jaques, II. ii. 201
jet, III. iii. 103
jig (*a dance*), Ind. 94.1
*jig (*a play*), Chor. II. 17

Keep, IV. iii. 102
keep the door at a whistle, I. ii. 78–9
keep . . . unto, in, V. vi. 123–5
ken (Scot.), Chor. V. 4
kill me, there you, I. ii. 82
kin, V. ii. 9
kind (sb.), V. v. 27
kind, work in, Chor. II. 1
king, little, Chor. I. 1
knave from a rat, smell a, I. ii. 14
knaves well met, two, III. ii. 94–5
knee, cap and, I. i. 222
*knot in a rush, seek a, III. ii. 24–5

Lack (vb), I. ii. 75
lack a servant, I. ii. 36
laddie, Chor. IV. 8
lads, V. v. 5
lambs' skins, IV. iii. 63
lament, shadow my, IV. ii. 35
land, neighbouring, I. i. 1
lantern, V. iv. 28

(*Latin translated*), I. i. 0.1; IV. v. 24–6; Chor. VII. 2.8
law, martial, V. vi. 214
law, your will is, I. i. 249
leaden shot, I. i. 125
lean, V. i. 78
leap upon, I. ii. 97
lease (sb.), I. i. 224
leather, neat calves', IV. iii. 60
leave (*abandon*), Ind. 39
leave (*allow*), Chor. V. 2
leave (*neglect*), I. i. 265
let (sb.), I. i. 244
let (vb), I. i. 255
let . . . alone, V. v. 30
letters-patents, II. i. 100
levy, Chor. VI. 8
lewd, V. vi. 200
lewely (Scot.), I. iii. 75
lick a dish before a cat, I. ii. 15
lick the pan, I. ii. 79
liefest liege, V. iii. 29
life, II. ii. 80
life, for, V. iv. 82
life, for thy, Ind. 85
lift a pot, III. i. 48
lifter, III. i. 46
light, set . . . , II. ii. 73
lion, I. ii. 87–9
lion, king of brutish race, V. iii. 19
list (vb), Ind. 44
listen, III. iii. 37
little, Chor. VII 2.5
little, bear a, I. iii. 54
little king, Chor. I. 1
little prove, I. i. 118
live in grave, II. i. 143
loath (sb.), Chor. V. 6
lockram, IV. iii. 41
loggerhead, Ind. 101
long (vb), I. i. 102
long journey, I. ii. 98
loose body, become a, II. i. 188–9
lope (Scot.), Ind. 26
lordings, II. ii. 101
lour, II. i. 30
love, effect my, I. i. 262
Love hath a little sting, I. i. 121
lovely, I. i. 13

INDEX TO ANNOTATIONS

lowest, stand, I. ii. 5
luck . . . on the left (hand), I. ii. 6–7
luck . . . on the right hand, I. ii. 6–7
luckless, Chor. II. 5
Lucretius, III. iii. 26–7

Machiavel, annotations upon, III. ii. 53
mad, IV. v. 74
magnificent, I. i. 229
maims, V. iv. 17
make (*sb.*), IV. iii. 56
make a marble weep, Chor. III. 3
make at first, V. vi. 13
make ends, Chor. V. 1
man (*vb*), III. iii. 129
man . . . born to err, II. i. 139
manor, I. i. 224
march (*vb*), I. i. 278
mark, even the, I. i. 46
marks, V. v. 13
marks, mother's, IV. iii. 71–2
martial law, V. vi. 214
mary mass, Ind. 6
Mas, V. iv. 7
mass, be the (Scot.), Ind. 19
mass, mary, Ind. 6
mate, II. i. 183
mates, shifting, II. i. 80
may (Scot.), Ind. 5
mean (*vb*), I. i. 194
mean . . . good, II. i. 37
means, IV. v. 86
means of, V. iv. 94
meet (*adj.*), IV. ii. 6
mend, V. i. 47
mend thyself, physician, V. iv. 87
mere, ne (Scot.), Chor. V. 7
mice be still, the cat's abroad . . . , V. i. 31
mickle, I. i. 119
mind, move her, II. ii. 171
miracle, II. i. 182
mirk (*dark*) (Scot.), I. iii. 10
mirk (*wicked*) (Scot.), Chor. VI. 4
mischief, V. i. 82
misconster, II. ii. 84
misdo, V. vi. 210
misled, youth hath, V. vi. 160

moly, I. i. 263–4
*money, III. i. 55
money, he for my, IV. iii. 112–13
moon, wat'ry, I. iii. 9
Moor . . . washed white, V. iv. 5
morglay, IV. iv. 51
motes, I. i. 244
mother's marks, IV. iii. 71–2
motions, Chor. III. 1
mould, II. ii. 62
mouth, busy with the, I. ii. 99
move (*anger*), II. ii. 188
move (*solicit*), II. i. 155
move her mind, II. ii. 171
moving, well, I. ii. 98
muse (*sb.*), II. ii. 3.1
muse (*vb*), V. v. 47
muttering, IV. v. 67

Name, ancient, I. ii. 102
name, by, I. ii. 134
Nano, Ind. 84.1
*napery, IV. iii. 47
near, I. i. 129
near, ne'er the, Ind. 62
nearly, V. iii. 3
neat calves' leather, IV. iii. 60
*neck of, break the, Ind. 82
need (*sb.*), II. i. 13
needs must, needs sall, Ind. 41
ne'er the near, Ind. 62
neighbouring land, I. i. 1
ne mere (Scot.), Chor. V. 7
nene (Scot.), Ind. 6
Nestor, II. ii. 14
net, dance within a, IV. v. 80
netherleather, IV. iii. 65
nightgown, I. ii. 103
nill me stay (Scot.), Chor. V. 3
Ninus, Chor. VI. 8
nip (*vb*), I. i. 153
nocent, V. vi. 99
nonce, devised for the, Ind. 94.1
northern (*sb.*), IV. iii. 36
nose of wax, V. iv. 8
nurture, III. ii. 74
nutbrown, V. iv. 103

Oberon, Ind. 0.1

occasion, I. ii. 10
of (for), V. i. 3
officious, I. i. 64
olive, Chor. VII. 2.1–2
on sudden, IV. v. 75
one, in, V. vi. 218
one, yoke in, V. ii. 26
open ... estate, V. i. 71
opposite, I. i. 200
oppositions, I. i. 189
order of, IV. v. 92
orient pearls, IV. v. 56
out of hand, II. ii. 5
outface, III. ii. 132
outrun, Ind. 51
overthrow (sb.), IV. v. 92
Ovid, II. ii. 104–5
oyster, V. vi. 49

Pack (vb), II. ii. 142
packet, IV. v. 76
paint (vb), Chor. VI. 2
pan, lick the, I. ii. 79
parasite, I. i. 226
(parasite's activities), I. ii. 43–6
part, III. ii. 94–5
parts, chiefest, II. i. 65
partake, II. ii. 42
partial, V. vi. 25
partial gloss, V. iv. 78
partner, II. ii. 134
parts, back, III. ii. 48–9
pass, Ind. 38
pass, wise, III. ii. 27
passing, Chor. IV. 2
patent sealed, I. i. 224
pearls, orient, IV. v. 56
peck of grist in a bushel, II. i. 91–2
penny, earnest, III. ii. 121
penthouse, IV. iii. 47–8
*pepper de watchet, II. i. 172–3
perfect, V. i. 30
peur (Scot.), Chor. VIII. 7
philautia, III. ii. 66
Phyllis, IV. iv. 23–4
physician, mend thyself, V. iv. 87
pickerel, II. i. 82
pill (vb), V. iv. 47
pilot, II. ii. 64–5

pinch, V. iv. 40
pitch (sb.), II. i. 85
place, give ... , I. iii. 65
plain harp shilling, III. ii. 96
pled (p. part.), II. ii. 96
*plough, V. iii. 7
policy, III. iii. 92
poll (vb), V. iv. 40
poor man ... rich man ... in law,
  V. iv. 32–3
portions, IV. ii. 8
pot, lift a, III. i. 48
pots, V. vi. 57.2
practice, III. iii. 34
practise, V. ii. 31
prank (vb), II. ii. 4
pranking, V. vi. 74
prate, Ind. 53
prayers, V. v. 8
precise, II. ii. 158
present (adj.), III. i. 33
pretend, II. i. 157
pretext of due proceeding, V. iv. 36
*pretty, Ind. 99
prevent, III. i. 34
prick upon, II. i. 71
pride, in her, I. i. 37
privy, IV. iv. 69
proceeding, pretext of due, V. iv. 36
proclaimed in the market-place,
  III. ii. 91–2
progress, in, III. ii. 140
promotion, IV. iii. 9
proof, put her to the, II. i. 97
proper, III. iii. 100
(properties of a horse), I. ii. 86–100
prosecute, Chor. VI. 16
prove, II. i. 174
prove, little, I. i. 118
provident, V. vi. 173
provisoes, V. iv. 35
publish, I. i. 273
puppits (Scot.), Ind. 13
purveyor, III. ii. 0.1
put to proof, II. i. 97

Quaint, III. iii. 106
*quarie, II. i. 172–3
*quincy, II. i. 172–3

quit, v. vi. 71

Raise her head, IV. v. 54
ransom, repay the, V. vi. 84
rapier and dagger, IV. iii. 80
rat, smell a knave from a, I. ii. 14
rate (*vb*), V. iv. 95
ravished in, I. i. 276
read, V. iv. 56
ready ... as an oyster for a ... tide, V. vi. 49
reasons, subtle, V. iv. 26
reck (Scot.), Ind. 3
reckon (Scot.), Ind. 5
record, I. ii. 44
recured, IV. iv. 68
recureless, II. ii. 105
red into white, drawing out, III. i. 12–13
Redesdale man, Ind. 0.4
refluence, IV. iii. 106
remission, IV. v. 10
rent (*sb.*), I. i. 259
repay the ransom, V. vi. 84
repent she was, Chor. III. 6
repine, I. i. 252
reputation, in such, Ind. 47
resign, III. iii. 61
resort, shun, II. i. 79
rest (*sb.*), III. iii. 126
revenge despite, V. v. 39
rich man ... poor man ... in law, V. iv. 32–3
rid (Scot.), Ind. 20
rifest, I. iii. 3
right Greek, IV. iii. 109
rip up, V. i. 15
rising sun doth call me (*Oberon*), Chor. V. 11
room for, III. i. 54
roseal, V. iii. 25
rot (*sb.*), IV. iii. 22
round (*sb.*), Chor. I. 0.2
royalty, in all, I. i. 73.2
run on wheels, world doth, I. ii. 48
run with the hare and hunt with the hound, IV. v. 85
*rush, seek a knot in a, III. ii. 24–5
ruth, I. i. 192

Sale (Scot.), I. iii. 7
sall (Scot.), Ind. 6
salute (*sb.*), II. i. 41
Samles, V. iii. 0.1
Saturn combust, I. i. 205–7
sayds, Gos (Scot.), Ind. 27
scorns, V. vi. 57.2
sealed, patent, I. i. 224
sect, V. iv. 19
see ... others' faults without amending, V. iv. 53–4
*seek a knot in a rush, III. ii. 24–5
seek not ... water from the sieve, II. ii. 71
semblance, III. iii. 98
sence (Scot.), Ind. 10
senseless, IV. ii. 53
serve, V. vi. 230–1
serves, time, I. ii. 20
service, V. ii. 0.2
service, entertain out of his, I. ii. 57–8
service, solemn, V. ii. 0.1
service to a king, nor, I. ii. 40
Sesostris, Chor. VIII. 5
sessions, end of a, III. ii. 59–60
set ... light, II. ii. 73
set out, I. i. 265
shadow my lament, IV. ii. 35
shadow out, V. iv. 81
shall, III. i. 23
shame (*vb*), V. vi. 18
shame, blind my, III. iii. 11
shapes, III. iii. 117
shift (*vb*), II. i. 91–2
shifting mates, II. i. 80
shilling, plain harp, III. ii. 96
shot, leaden, I. i. 125
show ... myself, V. v. 18
shroud (*vb*), Chor. I. 14
Shrove Tuesday, tongue is like clocks on, IV. iii. 94–5
shrow, IV. iv. 10
shun resort, II. i. 79
sickest, I. ii. 60
sieve, seek not ... water from the, II. ii. 71
sight, II. ii. 159
sights, I. iii. 61

sike (Scot.), Chor. VIII. 4
silly, II. ii. 65
simonies, V. iv. 72
single (*adv.*), III. iii. 115
*single goby, II. i. 172–3
sinister (*corrupt*), V. iv. 106
sinister (*erring*), V. vi. 141
situation fellow, II. i. 84–5
skin-coat, Ind. 46
skin full, III. i. 53
skins, lambs', IV. iii. 63
skipjack, Ind. 36
skittish as an eel, IV. iii. 96
Slipper, Ind. 84.1
slippery, I. i. 50
small cheer, Ind. 61.2
smart (*sb.*), IV. ii. 53
smell a knave from a rat, I. ii. 14
so that, II. ii. 204
solemn service, V. ii. 0.1
sooth, I. i. 203
sooth, in, I. i. 117
soothe, II. i. 153
soothing, II. ii. 78
sorrow it, V. i. 16
sort (*sb.*), V. vi. 46
so-so, I. iii. 22
sought . . . to, III. iii. 52
sound (*vb*), IV. v. 31
soundest, I. ii. 59
Spaniard, IV. iii. 66
speculation seen, in, V. v. 24
speed (*vb*), Ind. 53
spoil (*destroy*), V. vi. 66
spoil (*rob*), V. vi. 67
sports, V. vi. 57.2
spots, ermine skin full of, V. iv. 4
spread, III. iii. 95
spring (*sb.*), V. iv. 22
spy, I. i. 124
staff, constable's, IV. iii. 89–90
(*Stage-business*), Ind. 0.1, 0.2, 0.4, 13, 91–2, 110; I. i. 0.4, 31.1; iii. 75; Chor. I. 0.2; II. i. 175–6; ii. 1, 2, 3; III. ii. 88; iii. 115; IV. ii. 25–49, 51, 56–7; iii. 17; V. ii. 0.1–2; iii. 9.1, 33.1; vi. 63.1, 96.4, 167
stale (*past tense*), I. i. 84

stale, fashion is, IV. iii. 44
stales, I. i. 113
stamp, III. i. 18
stand (*sb.*), IV. i. 3
stand by, I. ii. 74
stand highest, I. ii. 1
stand lowest, I. ii. 5
stand with, V. vi. 230–1
state (*sb.*), I. i. 44
state, erect your, II. i. 144
stay (*sb.*), II. ii. 146
stay, assure your, II. i. 111
stay, . . . nill . . . me (Scot.), Chor. v. 3
steal, I. i. 84
*stiff docket, I. ii. 88
still, I. iii. 60
sting (*sb.*), II. i. 58
sting, Love hath a little, I. i. 121
stoical, Ind. 23
stoop, I. i. 28
stoop to a thistle, I. ii. 6
store (*sb.*), II. i. 7
*storre, IV. iii. 46
story, Chor. I. 10
strange, V. ii. 24
style, I. i. 7
subtle reasons, V. iv. 26
subtlety, IV. v. 88
sudden, on, IV. v. 75
suggestions, III. iii. 30
suit (*sb.*), II. i. 102
Sunday, IV. iii. 107
suppose, IV. ii. 40
surcease (*vb*), V. vi. 151
surprise, V. iv. 109
suspect (*sb.*), III. iii. 6
swains, Ind. 57
swallow a gudgeon, II. i. 85
swallow flies, V. iv. 85
swear upon your sword, V. vi. 112
sweet (*sb.*), I. i. 115
sweet (*vb*), Chor. II. 5
sword, swear upon your, V. vi. 112

Tables, draw . . . , I. ii. 94
taint, IV. v. 51
take charge, V. i. 41
take cheer, V. i. 33

INDEX TO ANNOTATIONS 153

take ... order, V. vi. 45
tanned, IV. iii. 66–7
tarbox, III. i. 8
ten bones, by my, III. ii. 115
tender (*vb*), III. ii. 135
Tereus, II. i. 64
term (*vb*), V. iv. 31
that (*so that*), II. ii. 184
that (*that which*), Ind. 97
thay (Scot.), Ind. 6
there am I, I. ii. 82
there you kill me, I. ii. 82
thickest throng, I. ii. 42
think (*devise*), V. vi. 80
think (*intend*), III. iii. 25
think (*think of*), Chor. II. 11
thistle, stoop to a, I. ii. 6
though, what, II. i. 147
thou's (Scot.), Ind. 31
threap (Scot.), Ind. 25
ticket, III. ii. 9
tide, V. vi. 49
time, accept the, I. i. 235
time, forward, IV. v. 15
time, in good, Ind. 68
time brought me to age, Ind. 43
time serves, I. ii. 20
tire (*sb.*), V. v. 18
tire (*attack*), V. vi. 153
tire (*dress*), V. vi. 122
to (*beside*), V. vi. 96.3
toast, ale and, II. i. 175–6
tomb, Ind. 0.2
tomb, dwell in his, I. ii. 118–19
tongue is like clocks on Shrove Tuesday, IV. iii. 94–5
track (*vb*), I. iii. 10
trade, cozening, I. ii. 20–1
trade, filching, I. ii. 20
trade, gentle, I. ii. 33
traffic, V. ii. 33
transport (*vb*), II. ii. 148
trash, III. i. 24
trattle (Scot.), Ind. 85
treading, III. i. 14
trillill, III. i. 17
trim, III. i. 55
triumph, V. ii. 0.2
troop (*vb*), V. vi. 61

Trophonius, I. i. 217
trow, Chor. II. 13
truth, I. i. 238
truth, approved, III. iii. 35
try, IV. ii. 24
turn (*sb.*), IV. iii. 109
turn above ground, one, IV. iii. 10
turn me to, I. ii. 82
turn ... upon, II. i. 162
turns, change, I. ii. 6
*twain, III. iii. 78
Tweed, V. v. 5
two knaves well met, III. ii. 94–5

(*Unification of Scotland and England*), V. vi. 103, 180–2
unkissed, I. ii. 22
unmeet, III. iii. 104
unpent, IV. iii. 100
unpicked, I. ii. 23
unserved, III. ii. 2
untoward, II. ii. 98
unwieldy, III. iii. 47
upright, V. iv. 67
*upsy-turvy, III. iii. 50
urge, II. ii. 80
usury, V. iv. 92–104

Vain (*sb.*), II. ii. 47
variance, V. iv. 70
veiled, V. vi. 96.4
Venus, I. i. 205–7
ver meum, Chor. VII. 2.8
Vesta, I. i. 114
vouchsafe, II. i. 42

Wait, V. i. 41
want (*vb*), II. ii. 14
wanton, I. i. 266
ward, hard of, I. ii. 97
warp, Chor. VIII. 1
wars, Ind. 60
wars, Irish, III. iii. 121
watch (*sb.*), II. i. 135
water from the sieve, seek not ... , II. ii. 71
wat'ry moon, I. iii. 9
wax, nose of, V. iv. 8
wax (*vb*), III. iii. 96

weal, v. vi. 7
weal, bode . . . , v. vi. 26
weapon, III. ii. 128–9
wear, v. i. 27
wed . . . well, II. i. 144
wee (*oui*), IV. iii. 105
weed, III. iii. 94
weel (Scot.), Ind. 11
weighty case, v. i. 25
well moving, I. ii. 98
wemb (Scot.), Ind. 90
werld (Scot.), Chor. I. 3
what though (*even if*), II. i. 147
what though (*what then*), III. iii. 27
whay (Scot.), Ind. 3
whayet (Scot.), Ind. 5
whayle (Scot.), Ind. 13
wheels, world doth run on, I. ii. 48
whereas, II. ii. 2
which (*that which*), Chor. VI. 3
Whighton, Cicely of the, IV. iii. 95
whilk (Scot.), Chor. VIII. 4
whinyard (Scot.), Ind. 25
whist, II. ii. 187
whistle, keep the door at a, I. ii. 78–9
whit (Scot.), Ind. 9
white, drawing out red into, III. i. 12–13
white, Moor . . . washed, V. iv. 5
who, for, III. i. 30
will (*sb.*), II. ii. 54
will is law, your, I. i. 249
will, wind at, I. iii. 42
will (*vb*), I. i. 66
wily accord, IV. iii. 25

wind at will, I. iii. 42
wink, II. i. 137
wise, I. i. 91
wise pass, III. ii. 27
wisest, greatest clerks . . . not the III. ii. 63–4
wit, II. ii. 14
witch, Ind. 28
withdraw, III. iii. 112
withdrawn, II. ii. 195
wits, II. ii. 120
witty, IV. v. 86
woman, I. ii. 90–100
wonder, III. iii. 65
wooned (Scot.), I. iii. 12
work (*sb.*), II. i. 0.2
work (*vb*), V. v. 67
work in kind, Chor. II. 1
working (*sb.*), V. iv. 57
world doth run on wheels, I. ii. 48
wot, Ind. 3
wrest, V. iv. 8
wrought, II. ii. 155

Ye, II. ii. 28
year whayle (Scot.), Ind. 13
yield, I. iii. 53
yielding ones, V. iii. 24
y-met, II. ii. 21
yoke in one, V. ii. 26
young and . . . may amend, II. ii. 87–8
you's (Scot.), Ind. 21
youth hath misled, V. vi. 160